Blue Ridge O...
Five Little Orphans and How They Grew

by Roy Owenby

Catch the Spirit of Appalachia, Inc.
WESTERN NORTH CAROLINA

Copyright © 2015 by Roy Owenby

All Rights Reserved. No part of this book may be reproduced or transmitted in any form or by any means, electronic or mechanical, including photocopying, recording or by any information storage or retrieval system, without permission in writing from the author or publisher.

First Edition 2015

Books by Roy Owenby
"The Owl Knows" (2013)
Blue Ridge Mountain Heritage (2014)

Layout, Editing & some Images by Amy Ammons Garza
Images by:
Jennifer Green (Roy's niece)
Mark Ray, NC Wildlife Officer
Leroy Simonson, (Navy buddy & longtime friend)

Editor/Typist: Nita Welch Owenby (Roy's wife)
Typist: Susan Waldorf

Publisher:
Catch the Spirit of Appalachia, Inc.—Imprint of:
Ammons Communications — SAN NO. 8 5 1 - 0 8 8 1
29 Regal Avenue • Sylva, North Carolina 28779 • Phone/fax: (828) 631-4587

For additional copies of these books, please go to CSAbooks.com

Library of Congress Control Number: 2015938041

ISBN No. 978-09908766-5-6

PRINTED IN THE UNITED STATES OF AMERICA

Dedication

— TO MY GRANDSONS —
Jeremy, Nathaniel, Tyeson, Graham, Collin,
Johnathon and Jared

FOR: Ian Cook

Roy Avery

Introduction

This book was written for older children, animal lovers and other readers who enjoy a good story. "Blue Ridge Mountain Bandits" is a work of fiction based on known facts gleaned from personal experience and extensive reading about the life of raccoons. People who know these beautiful animals will tell you they have boundless energy, creative ways of finding food other animals do not possess and antics that would lead one to believe they have a sense of humor. Also, they make wonderful pets if they are bottle-fed and raised by their owner.

Over the years, I have learned that most people have no idea what a rough and often terrible life animals in the wild endure. Scarcity of food and the constant danger of predators often reduce their lifespan significantly. Raccoons, like many other animals, are in the unenviable position of being both predator and prey. The savage sport of coon hunting leads me to believe people who abuse animals will abuse other people, and several scientific studies have shown this to be true. Farmers and gardeners often kill raccoons and other small animals when they raid their cornfields and gardens. Back when people had to survive on the food they raised, that's understandable. These days, it's easy enough to buy a cage, trap and then release them in a forest miles from home. Unfortunately, most people don't consider it worth the trouble.

Woven throughout the later chapters of the book is a love story between two humans. Their growing feelings for each other complement their love of animals and how they treat them. There are no sex scenes that might cause consternation of young or old, and there are no vulgar or curse words anywhere in the book. If you are a caring person, this book will make you laugh, and it will make you cry. It will also make you understand a little more about the world of wild animals and how they live. No chapter is dull, and the scenes are often fast moving. So, read and enjoy a wonderful tale about my raccoon children: Becky, Cindy, Mandy, Misty and Packy.

A note to parents . . .
This book depicts realistic scenes between predator and prey to provide the reader with an accurate description of how life really is in the wild. If you allow your child to watch National Geographic and/or Animal Planet, there's no reason the child shouldn't read this book. However, I suggest to parents of children younger than thirteen years of age, read this book first, and then decide if you consider it appropriate for your youngster.

Table of Contents

Chapter One	Night Stalker	09
Chapter Two	River Bounty	23
Chapter Three	Mother Knows Best	41
Chapter Four	View from the Barn	59
Chapter Five	Enemies in the Night	75
Chapter Six	Mother's Bane	93
Chapter Seven	Midnight Memorial	111
Chapter Eight	Payback	129
Chapter Nine	Dream Come True	147

Table of Contents

Chapter Ten	A Friend in Need	163
Chapter Eleven	Church Calamity	179
Chapter Twelve	Becky's Plight	197
Chapter Thirteen	A New Generation	213
Chapter Fourteen	For the Love of Mandy	231
Chapter Fifteen	Home away from Home	247
Epilogue		257
About the Author		260

Chapter 01

NIGHT STALKER

At midnight, inky blackness permeated every corner of the forest. Overhead, an impenetrable cloud cover concealed the brilliant light of a full moon. Heat lightening crisscrossed a turbulent sky in a dazzling display of celestial beauty. Against a backdrop of the mighty Appalachians, the Little Tennessee River sang its perpetual song as it weaved through ancient cliffs and highland meadows.

Without warning, a horrific lightening bolt shattered the darkness as it burned a vacuum through the moisture-laden atmosphere. Faster than a fiery meteor, it raced toward an ancient hemlock protruding above the forest canopy. Struck in the heart by an incredible force, the aging conifer split asunder, hurling cones and limbs in all directions. An ear shattering thunderclap announced the fires of heaven had claimed another victim. Flaming splinters, ignited by fierce heat, started fires in the surrounding leaf litter.

Startled birds flew in all directions, and frightened animals scurried deeper into the dense underbrush. Above the noise and confusion, angry clouds roiled and churned, and then gave birth to a torrent of chilling water. Rolling thunder reverberated against the mountains, followed by fierce winds roaring across the valley. The fires sputtered out, reduced to an ashy pulp by the driving rain.

Deep in the bowels of a gnarled oak tree, five raccoon young-

sters sat wide-eyed, terrified by the intensity of the raging storm. They longed for the comforting churrs of their mother and waited eagerly for her return. Unknown to them, she fished along the river bank, ignoring the chaotic weather. She ate ravenously, knowing instinctively that her body required nourishment to maintain her milk supply.

The rain tapered off and then stopped. Interrupted only by the roar of the rising river, the quiet of the forest returned. Night creatures came out of hiding and resumed their nocturnal routines. The wind died down to a whisper, and the moon played hide-and-seek with fickle clouds.

The raccoon kits sat quietly, still hopeful their mother would suddenly appear through the upward tunnel. Packy, the only male, recovered first and then set about to calm his sisters. Soon, they were frolicking and wrestling all around the den, their mother all but forgotten.

Mandy, the largest of the five, rolled too close to the edge and fell out. She landed with a thump at the bottom of the tree. Her siblings peered down the hole and watched as she tried to climb back up. The inexperienced kit would climb part way and then fall back down. Finally, she gave up and began to whimper.

Packy knew in his heart he must do something. Cautiously, he put his feet out and looked down at his sister. As his front claws gripped the wood tightly, he overcame his fear and started down. About half-way, he encountered a rotten place in the wood. He lost his grip and fell, landing on Mandy's head. Unhurt, they wriggled around until they sat side-by-side. As Packy looked out into the night, an old screech owl hooted from her perch atop a dead tulip tree. Instinctively frightened, Packy scrambled up the hole in the tree, arriving at the den in a matter of seconds.

At he sat on the ledge catching his breath, he suddenly realized he had climbed up with little effort. He looked back down at Mandy. She sat balled up, too frightened to try again. Somehow, Packy understood he should help her, but he didn't know how.

Ignoring his frustration, he climbed down again. Sitting beside her, he could feel her trembling. He nuzzled her with his nose, and when that didn't help, he began licking her fur. Finally, she stopped shivering and raised her head. He nipped her lightly, pressuring her to try again. He started back up, and when she didn't follow, he went back down, and then started up again. Irritated, he returned to the bottom and bit her on the shoulder. She squealed and started to climb.

Half-way up, Mandy stopped. As Packy climbed behind her, he could hear her labored breathing, and then she began to whimper. He started pushing her with his nose. She lost her grip, and they both ended up in a heap at the bottom again. They rested for a while. When Packy looked up, he saw Becky, Misty and Cindy looking down at them.

Without warning, Becky suddenly started down. Packy hissed at her, but she ignored him completely. She reached the bottom and started encouraging Mandy in her childlike raccoon language. Then, as quickly as she came down, Becky climbed back up. Mandy watched until her smallest sister reached the top. Summoning her courage, Mandy started up again. She reached the top and climbed over the ledge.

Packy sat at the bottom for a long time. Somewhere in the distance, he heard the owl hoot again. Sensing danger, he marshaled his strength and scurried up the hole. His sisters greeted him warmly, and then they all crawled into the nest and huddled together. None of them heard mother raccoon as she climbed up inside the tree. When she lay down beside them, Misty and Cindy began to nurse. The others continued to sleep.

A full moon bathed the forest floor with comforting light. Dew glistened on newly-formed leaves, casting rainbow colors that mocked the darkness. Outside their den, the kits sat and watched in wonder, seeing but not understanding. With a series of growls and churrs, Mother had told them not to go outside the den tree without her permission. They listened to strange noises, instinctively knowing those that represented danger, and those that did not. Even so, they were at risk, for they were too small to fight a predator, should one approach unnoticed. Breaking the rhythm of the night, a wildcat screeched on a hill above the den tree. The kits dashed up the tunnel and huddled together, each comforted by warmth from the others.

Just before daylight, Mother brought the kits a small fish. Their milk teeth, although small and undeveloped, could chew soft food. At first, the kits just played with the scaly creature and wondered at its strange smell. Packy, as usual, was first to try chewing on the slippery trout. Before long, a fight broke out. Mother scolded them, and then broke the fish into three pieces with her sharp teeth. Packy chewed on a smaller piece and even shared it with Becky. Misty, Cindy and Mandy wrestled with the largest piece. Finally Mandy severed the head and sat at the back of the den chewing her first solid food.

The next night, Packy ventured outside and sat on a root running above ground for several feet. At six weeks, he only weighed three pounds, but he was a precocious kit, full of curiosity and mischief. When he saw water dripping from a jack-in-the-pulpit, he decided to investigate. In true raccoon fashion, he walked along the root on the balls of his feet. Water had pooled in a hollow between two roots, and Packy sniffed at it. The fruity liquid tickled his nose and tempted his palate.

Cautiously, he stuck his tongue to the crystalline surface. Un-

like his mother's milk, it was cool to the taste. He backed away and sat for a moment, licking and wondering. He decided to drink some more, and his noisy lapping attracted his sisters. They followed Packy's trail down the root. One by one, they sampled their brother's newly discovered drink while the others watched. They gathered in a circle and lapped heartily, oblivious to the potential dangers around them. They emptied the little pool, and then sat up and looked around. Their bright eyes glowed in the moonlight as they surveyed their strange surroundings.

Mandy was first to walk back up the root to the shelter of their tree, followed closely by Cindy and Misty. Becky started back, and then sat down and looked around some more. She saw Packy walk off the end of the root and venture across leaf litter and broken twigs. She followed at a short distance, stopping every few feet to look back. She remembered Mother's admonition not to leave the den, but the temptation to follow Packy led her onward.

Packy walked with his head down, spellbound by the many exciting smells that appealed to his sensitive nostrils. When he came to a stump, he climbed on top so he could get a better view of his surroundings. The moon stood at its zenith, and the forest glowed with tantalizing sights. Becky crawled up and sat beside him, staring at the wonderful world of trees and plants. The owl hooted again, and Packy turned to stare in the direction of the sound. This was Becky's first time to hear the raptor's call. She froze, her heart pounding, while her every instinct signaled danger.

Packy stood up as high as he could and sniffed the air. He cocked his head, first to the left and then to the right. Through the tree limbs, he saw the owl gliding toward them. An alarm went off in his head, as he watched the feathery killer ride the downdrafts. The huge screech owl pulled her sharp talons down as she prepared to seize the helpless kits.

Terror clutched at Packy's brain, but he still had the presence of mind to push his sister off the stump. For a moment he appeared frozen, but he recovered quickly. Bunching the muscles in his hind legs, he leaped across Becky and landed in a patch of ladyslippers. The owl's sharp claws clutched empty air as she swooped across Packy's head. A thousand water droplets sprayed into the air as she landed on a horizontal limb of a nearby maple tree. She hooted her frustration into the night as she walked back and forth along the limb.

The two kits hugged the ground as they waited for the inevitable. Looking directly at his sister's bright orbs, he churred for her to be still. Without warning, he made a bold dash for freedom. The owl's sharp eyes saw movement before he had gone two feet. In a flash, she bolted from the limb and flew toward the courageous raccoon. Packy knew he must lead the vicious raptor away from his sister. He bounded across the forest floor, looking for a hiding place. Looking left and right, he could see nothing that would protect him from the owl.

Then, just ahead, he saw a hollow log. He only had moments, and he knew it. Fear pumped adrenaline into his blood, as his speed matched the racing of his heart. Razor-sharp talons swept toward him as he scurried into the hollow of the log. The owl missed his tail by inches as her claws clutched rotted wood. The disgruntled bird sailed back to her limb on the maple tree and waited for the next strike.

Packy crawled several feet into the log before stopping. The hollow cavity magnified the sound of his thumping heart. For several minutes, he lay supine, too terrified to move. Finally, his heart slowed down, and his breathing returned to normal. He tried to back up and found he couldn't. A knot, harder than the softer pulp of the log, projected down inside and snagged his rump. He crawled deeper into the log until he found a knothole large enough to stick his head through.

He peered into the night but could see nothing. He wondered what had happened to Becky, opened his mouth to call her, then changed

his mind. Instead, he looked toward the base of his den tree and saw a pair of eyes shining from the entrance. He felt better, but thoughts of the owl still terrified him. He stared up into the trees, trying to locate the hungry bird. Unaware that the big raptor could see the fire in his eyes, he turned his head from side to side until he saw the feathery lump perched close to the maple's trunk. She sat motionless, her mottled gray blending with bark and limb.

Now, Packy had a new problem. He knew his mother would be home soon. He had to decide whether to wait and face her wrath or make a run for it and risk becoming the owl's dinner. He turned around in the narrow confines of the log, squeezed under the knot, and crawled back to the entrance. Cautiously, he looked out into the night. He was fifty feet from the entrance to his den, a long way for a baby raccoon to run. Looking to his left, he saw a patch of flowering trillium that stretched uphill in a semi-circle. The other side almost reached the rhododendrons that formed a thicket around one side of his tree.

Summoning his courage, he dashed toward the flowering plants. As he ran, he heard the muted swish of owl's wings as she left her perch. Three pounds of frightened raccoon lunged into the plants as the raptor's wings passed over his head. Sharp talons dragged flowers and roots from the ground, and then dropped them across the forest floor as she sailed toward her next perch. Packy lost his nerve and stopped in the center of the trillium patch. Again, he heard the swoosh of wings, and then a thump as the owl landed in the middle of the flowers.

Packy panicked and ran back toward the hollow log. The owl spread her wings and launched her light weight into the air. To Packy's advantage, the hunter could not gain enough altitude to strike at her prey without flying out and then circling back. As the owl flew down the hill, she screeched her anger, and Packy made a tactical mistake. Thinking he had enough time, he ran toward his tree. The owl turned and headed back, confident dinner was an easy catch.

Packy increased his speed, but he knew he would not reach his den tree in time. The owl intended to sweep him up in her claws, fly to another tree, and devour him in two gulps. In his desperate rush to safety, Packy passed by the stump he had sat on a few minutes earlier. This time, the owl made a mistake. Her line of flight took her directly toward the stump. At the last moment, she had to turn aside to avoid disaster. Packy's luck held; he had bought more time.

He could see the entrance to his den directly ahead. In a flash, the owl made a u-turn and headed back. Packy marshaled his strength, and somehow, increased his speed, but the owl closed in, determined to capture her prey. Wiser this time, the owl flew at an angle to the oak tree so that she could snare Packy without slamming against it. Neither prey nor raptor saw mother raccoon crouched under the rhododendrons just outside the entrance to her den. Just as the owl's claws reached Packy, Mother sprang into the air and grabbed the owl's wing in her sharp teeth.

The owl screeched in surprise and pain and tried to gain altitude. She was bigger than mother raccoon but weighed less. Bird and animal landed in a clump of blueberry bushes and disappeared from sight. Meanwhile, Packy made the den entrance, where Becky sat waiting for him. He tried to climb up the tunnel but lacked the strength. He fell back on Becky and began to whimper. Becky started licking his face and ears and in a moment, he quieted down. Recovering from his panic, he remembered his mother's plight.

The kits heard screeches and growls from the blueberry thicket but could see nothing. Finally, the noises ceased, and the bushes stopped moving. They stared anxiously into the darkness, and wondered why their mother didn't come out. After what seemed an eternity to Packy, he could stand it no longer. He ventured forth, heading for his mother. Becky followed. As he reached the bushes, he detected the familiar smell of his mother and the foreign odor of the owl. He stopped and listened. He could hear his mother panting. He glanced back at Becky and then went into the dim interior.

Mother lay on her side, blood running from several gashes in her fur. The owl lay crumpled in a heap, her feathers scattered among the bushes. Packy sniffed at the owl but could sense no movement. His anger flared momentarily, and he bit down hard on the owl's leg. Still, the raptor did not respond. He bit the other leg, this time, grinding his teeth from side to side. Nothing happened. Satisfied that his enemy was dead, he turned his attention to his mother.

Responding to her instincts, Becky began licking Mother's wounds. Packy joined her and began pulling and pawing at Mother's face. Guided only by their inherited knowledge of raccoon medicine and their love for the mother who nursed them, they worked carefully

and methodically. Mother nature had provided them with the right tools and after a few minutes, their mother began to move. When she sat up on her haunches, Packy and Becky became ecstatic. In a few minutes, Packy saw three sets of eyes coming toward them from the den. All five kits snuggled against Mother, and when she began licking them, they each purred in turn. Finally, she stood up. The kits moved aside to give her room.

Slowly, she limped toward the tree. At the entrance, she made them go in first. She growled at them to climb up into the den. Packy hung back and watched his sisters go up. Mother growled again, but Packy refused to climb up. Mother's panting wasn't normal, and he knew it. He understood she had fought for him, so he couldn't bear to leave her alone.

Seeming to understand Packy's need, she lay down at the entrance. Fearful she might chastise him, he hung back for a few moments. Finally, he decided to risk it, and snuggled against her. Too tense to sleep, he listened to her labored breathing. Just before daylight, her breathing returned to normal. Packy relaxed and drifted off to sleep.

The little guardian awoke to a blaze of sunlight across his face. Mother had disappeared, and he panicked. He jumped up and looked out. He had never seen daylight before. The brightness hurt his eyes, but they soon adjusted. He ran down the root, leaped into the leaf litter and headed toward the river. His heart jumped in his throat when he saw Mother coming up the hill. Water dripped from her fur, and she walked much better. Packy greeted her with churrs and purrs. He stood outside the entrance and waited for her to enter. She growled for him to go up first, and he obeyed this time. He sat at the top and peered down, anxiously waiting for her to join him in the den. Mother climbed up with an effort, but she made it. Packy sat to the side and watched his sisters greet her. She lay down in the feeding position, and they all started nursing, except Packy. Hunger gnawed at his sides, but he waited. Mother turned her head, looked at Packy and churred for him to join in. Joyfully, he squeezed in between his sisters and nursed eagerly.

The others finished first and began to play and wrestle. When Packy finished, he crawled across Mother's side until he reached her face. A gash on her cheek oozed blood, and Packy licked it until the bleeding stopped. Satisfied that he had done everything he could, he snuggled between her front paws. He felt at peace, but his love for her made something hurt in his chest. Although his feelings were too primitive for him to understand on a human level, he knew his mother was the most important being in his life. She had come to his rescue with total disregard for her own safety.

* * * * * * * * * *

On the fourth night after Mother killed the owl, she decided to take her young outside for a short walk. Still sore from her battle, she climbed to the bottom and then churred for the kits to follow her. Packy went first, then sat at the bottom and watched his sisters climb down. Becky came next. Her small body rappelled down the tree like a mountain climber. Clearly, she was the quickest of the group. Cindy and Misty came next, one behind the other. Still cautious, Mandy came last. The others watched patiently, until she reached the bottom.

The moon had not yet risen, and darkness blanketed the forest. Because of their nocturnal eyes, the raccoon family could see as well as humans could on a cloudy day. Once outside, Mother growled and churred until the kits understood her instructions. Confidently, she padded along the big root with her kits following in single file. Stopping under a stand of Solomon's seal, she counted heads. Knowing

Packy's tendency to wander off, she put him in front, directly behind her. Every few seconds, she glanced back to make sure her kits were following instructions. Becky brought up the rear, glancing from side-to-side, fascinated by the sights and sounds of the forest.

Next, Mother stopped at a rotten log. As the kits watched, she dug for fat beetles living in the decaying wood. One by one, she dug them out, and then invited her kits to sample the delicate meat. Their milk teeth were fully mature and in a few weeks, sharp adult teeth would replace them. Until then, they would continue to nurse, although Mother would gradually force them to eat increasing amounts of soft food. Crunching noises filled the night, as Packy and Mandy competed for the title of beetle-eating champion.

Finally, Mother decided it was time to move on. She issued a series of grunting orders, and the kits fell in line like little soldiers. Crossing the rotten log, she started downhill toward the river. During previous trips, she had marked a trail she followed easily but was invisible to any human who happened to pass by. Across the valley, the moon rose above spruce-covered mountaintops. Six pairs of eyes glowed, as filtered light reflected off the river and into the trees.

Just short of the river, the group came across a mole digging a tunnel just under the forest soil. Using her acute sense of smell and hearing, Mother quickly located the dirt denizen. With her human-like hands, she removed enough soil to uncover the mole. With one quick bite, she broke its back and tossed it aside. Moving quickly, Packy grabbed it with his soft teeth and started toward his mother.

Critically wounded, but still alive, the mole bit Packy on the leg. His squeal jarred Mother's nerves, as she watched him drop the feisty rodent. In one swift movement, Mother bit the mole's head off. After making sure the creature was dead, she went to check on Packy. Like an injured child, he held his leg up for her to inspect. Instead of pampering him, she growled and cuffed him on the head with her paw. Satisfied he had learned his lesson, she churred for the kits to regroup.

Feeling properly chastised, Packy fell in behind his sisters. Deciding the kits had had enough excitement for one night; she turned away from the river and headed back toward the den.

A few yards from the tree, Mother suddenly began to hurry. The kits scrambled to keep up. She herded them inside the entrance and signaled for them to sit quietly. Turning her back in a protective stance, she sat facing out. Grunting noises echoed into the night as a family of wild hogs passed by the den tree. Mother raccoon growled, but the hogs ignored her as they continued down the hill. When they reached the rotten log, they began digging for beetles the raccoon family had overlooked. A large boar ripped into the log with his tusks while the sows and piglets reaped the benefits.

Finally, the hogs wandered off, and Mother relaxed her fighting position. Turning to the kits, she urged them up into the den. Still excited by their first hunt, Packy and his sisters romped and played until Mother churred to stop. Packy found a corner and began licking his injured leg. Mother made a sound in her throat, signaling that he should come to her. She licked his leg until his pain stopped, and then she positioned herself for nursing.

* * * * * * * * *

Outside the raccoon den, spring rain bubbled and gurgled along the bark of the ancient oak tree. Clear, sparkling water rushed down stairstep falls and formed alluvial sandbars in the river below. Partridgeberry and ground pine clung tenaciously to moss-covered stones. Wildflowers blossomed, and rhododendron burst into brilliant bloom. Robins, wrens and sparrows chirped and warbled in the treetops. Hawks and falcons rode the updrafts, as they soared above fields and ridges.

Across the river, an aging tractor sat silently in the rain, reminiscent of better times when well-tended fields and gardens grew and prospered. Mother raccoon slept peacefully and dreamed of tasty crayfish and fresh corn. The next generation slept beside her, waiting for the world to welcome them into the warm summer nights of the river valley.

Chapter 02

RIVER BOUNTY

Like actors basking in the limelight of a brilliant performance, a million stars sparkled across the breadth of an ebony sky. Constellations competed for attention, challenging the mind to create familiar images of birds and animals. An incandescent moon dominated the southern sky, refusing to yield the stage to lesser gods. In the valley below, moonlight filtered through newborn leaves, casting an eerie glow along the forest floor. Spring-fed streams babbled across moss-covered stones as they flowed through groves of oak, hickory and maple. Mother raccoon prowled along the riverbank, oblivious to the silent mist that rose to greet the dawn.

Staying in the shadows, a hungry bobcat crept quietly down the hillside. Two hours earlier, he had followed Mother's trail across the ridge, only to lose her scent in the forest. Like a fox, she had disguised her trail by doubling back or walking in streams. Now, the bobcat backtracked along her trail, having figured out her strategy. As he approached the ancient oak, Mother's scent caused his empty stomach to rumble. He drooled at the thought of tasty raccoon. Hopeful that his efforts might yield an overdue dinner, he slipped into the rhododendron thicket and waited quietly.

Mandy had tired of wrestling with the others and sat looking down the entrance tunnel. She had heard the clandestine movements of the bobcat, and her instinctual warning system triggered an alarm in her brain. She growled low in her throat, and the other kits quieted immediately. Down below, the anxious bobcat recognized the sound and dashed out of the rhododendrons. Squalling as he ran, he charged into the den entrance.

He squeezed through the opening without difficulty, only to find that the upward tunnel narrowed a short distance above ground level. Famished beyond reason, he pressed upward along the constricted space. About half-way up, the rotted wood refused to yield, trapping the determined cat in the tunnel. Realizing he couldn't crawl in either direction, he panicked. Squalling and screaming, he flailed and clawed at his woody prison. The noise reverberated throughout the tree, and the terrified kits huddled in the back of the den, fearing for their lives. Finally, the frustrated cat realized that by exhaling, he could wriggle his body downwards. Leaving with less hair and skin than when he entered, he dashed wildly into the underbrush.

The bobcat's high-pitched scream echoed into the night, and mother raccoon quickly deduced that the ruckus had occurred near her den. Without hesitation, she dropped the choice bullfrog she had caught for her kits and rushed homeward. Sprinting on the balls of her feet, she dashed along the riverbank. Breathing heavily, she leaped across logs and tangled underbrush, oblivious to personal danger. In less than five minutes, she reached the entrance to her den.

Despite his fear, Packy's curiosity had driven him to peer down the hole. His sisters remained in a huddle and scolded him in raccoon language for leaving them alone. At the same time, Mother rushed through the entrance and charged upward, her claws throwing chips down the hole behind her. Taken by surprise, Packy tried to move out of her way. Mother hit him head on as her momentum carried her over the top.

Fortunately, the only injury Packy suffered was to his pride. Mother examined him first and then his sisters. Quickly recognizing

their terror, she assembled them together in the back of the den. She licked each face in turn, until they began to calm down. Finally, she lay down on her side and allowed them to nurse. Too upset to eat, Mandy, Cindy and Misty gave up and huddled together again. Seeing that Packy and Becky continued, they returned and drank sparingly.

One at a time, the kits stopped feeding and tried to rest. Raccoon nightmares troubled their sleep as they wriggled and twitched. Finally, Mother laid down beside them and purred softly; the equivalent of a lullaby in raccoon language. In a few minutes they slept soundly, oblivious to the outside world.

An hour after dusk, Mother tried to wake them, but they were sleepy and grumpy. Deciding to let them rest, she slipped out into the night. Thirty minutes later, she sat in farmer Mason's garden, munching on fresh vegetables.

* * * * * * * * *

Two nights from full, the waxing moon rose in the sky. Mother understood instinctively that the days before and after full moon were ideal for fishing. Now eight weeks old, the kits were healthy and happy, so Mother decided to increase their learning activities. June had arrived, and heavy spring rains had abated to an occasional shower. The sandbar teemed with crustaceans, and fish were plentiful. Tonight, Mother intended to teach her young the art of fishing. They woke up hungry and tried to nurse. She refused, knowing that full stomachs would diminish their interest in learning.

As usual, she gathered them under the Solomon's seals and counted heads. Satisfied no one had lingered behind, she headed for the river. Knowing predators were an ever-present danger, she walked in the shadows. Spring plants were in full bloom, and they provided protective cover from owls lurking high in the trees. Mother stopped frequently and sniffed the air, and then glanced back to make sure none of her kits had fallen by the wayside.

This time, Packy brought up the rear. A whippoor-will scurried from under a huckleberry bush, and Misty broke ranks to chase it. Mother growled low in her throat, and the errant kit understood her message. Remembering the drubbing Packy had received for grabbing the mole, she rushed back into line.

Mother had learned by experience that many dangers lurked in the forest. This, combined with her instincts, had taught her strict discipline made for a safer family. She knew a small raccoon could not be left alone, even for a moment. Most predators did not have the courage to tackle a full-grown raccoon but would not hesitate to attack and devour a small kit.

The family arrived at the river without further incident. Effortlessly, Mother climbed down the ten-foot embankment and turned to watch her young. Accustomed to gripping wood instead of dirt, all five sat at the top, unsure how to proceed.

Finally, Packy took the initiative and started down. He made the sandbar with little effort. Becky came next but slipped on the mud and turned end over end. This time, her small size and agility had not been an asset. She sat up quickly, pretending nothing had happened. As usual, Misty and Cindy came down together. Mandy, always cautious, crept along; fearful each step might be her last.

Mother led them to a large, flat rock where rainwater had pooled in a natural depression. Sand and dirt had washed into the bottom, making a natural breeding ground for tadpoles. She walked into the pool and sat down. Water came up to the top of her rump. Using her dexterous front paws, she felt around under the water. The kits sat at attention and watched, their eyes glowing in the moonlight.

In a matter of seconds, Mother pulled a large tadpole to the surface. Although it had just come out of the water, she moved it back and forth in a washing motion. Having fulfilled her natural instincts, she ate it in one bite. Satisfied her kits had been paying attention; she churred for them to join her in the pool. Mandy waded in first and sat down in the soft sand and mud. The other three sisters followed, but Packy hung back. Sensing his distraction, Mother climbed out of the pool to investigate. In a matter of seconds, she understood his problem.

Packy sat motionless, a frog trapped between his front paws and the rock. His fear of disobeying Mother and subsequent punishment prevented him from acting. Mother seized the frog and carried it into the pool. She killed it, performing the same washing motions and then carried it back to the rock. Placing it in front of Packy, she churred for him to eat it. He chewed the bumpy amphibian with gusto but found the skin tough and unmanageable. Mother intervened and bit the frog into several pieces. Packy ate the tender parts, leaving the rest for Mother. She quickly swallowed the tougher pieces and returned to the pool.

Again, she churred for them to watch. She gave the next tadpole to Mandy. The clumsy kit grasped the slippery creature in her front paws. As she held it up in the moonlight for inspection, the tadpole slipped out of her paws and fell back into the pool. Mother lectured her sternly in strict raccoon language.

Too young to understand he had been deprived of a turn because he had eaten part of the frog, Packy sat at the edge of the pool and pouted. Mother ignored his behavior until she decided it was his turn again. When she handed him the next tadpole, he cheered up immediately. Imitating his mother, he placed his food in the water and moved it back and forth. To his surprise, the tadpole was softer than the frog, allowing him to eat it without difficulty.

Mother ate the next two, and then churred for the kits to try

their luck at catching the elusive amphibians. They spread out and started feeling around in the water. For several minutes, their efforts produced nothing but frustration. Finally, they got the hang of it, and their crunching noises filled the night.

They would catch one, stick it back in the water and move it about. They had inherited this ritual through a thousand generations, and it never occurred to them not to do it. Before long, they had exhausted the tadpole supply in the little pool. Even Mother was having difficulty finding the slippery frog babies. She waded out of the pool, sat on her haunches and watched her young at work. Lacking more prey, the kits began playing and splashing water on each other. Finally, Mother churred for them to come out.

At the last minute, Packy startled a crayfish out of the sand and mud. He made a grab for it, unaware of the crustacean's powerful pinchers. Before he knew it, the spunky crayfish gripped Packy on the outside of his paw. The surprised kit started slinging his front legs in wild abandon. The crayfish refused to yield. For a moment, Mother looked concerned and then decided not to get involved. Shrieking at the top of his lungs, Packy ran out of the water. He scrambled to a higher section of the rock. Like a carpenter driving nails, he slammed the hard-shelled creature onto solid stone. Finally, the defeated crayfish relaxed his pincers and turned loose of Packy's paw. He scurried for cover with Packy in hot pursuit.

Sensing the baby raccoon was going to beat him to the river, the crayfish turned and prepared to fight. Packy grabbed its tail in his teeth. He jerked backwards and swung his head in an arc. At the apex of the arc, Packy turned the crayfish loose. It landed just in front of Cindy. She shrank back in horror and watched as the addled creature tried to regain its composure. Deciding to join the ruckus, Misty grabbed the crayfish by its stomach.

Sufficiently recovered to defend itself, it pinched the feisty kit

on the ear. Misty squalled and ran toward the river. Mother decided to intervene and dashed after Misty, catching up with the terrified kit in two long bounds. In one quick bite, she crushed the crayfish in her powerful jaws. She swallowed the creature in one gulp and then attended to Misty's wounded ear. More frightened than hurt, the terrified kit sat whimpering in a depression of the rock. Mother licked her ear until the whining stopped.

Mother concluded the family needed a break. She churred the kits to her side and made them lie down for a time out. They obeyed and gathered around, lying in a circle around her. Out in the open, she maintained a vigilant watch as she listened to the sounds of the forest. Somewhere in the distance, a whippoor-will called to its mate. An opossum came down the bank for a drink. Half-way across the rock, she spied the raccoon family and stopped momentarily. Deciding she wasn't in any danger, she walked to the river's edge and drank her fill of the refreshing water. Ignoring Mother and her kits, she walked back by the pool and climbed the bank.

A cloud passed across the moon, temporarily reducing the fire in the raccoon's eyes. In the early morning hours, the air temperature dropped slowly, and mist began rising from the river. The steady cadence of the rushing water droned on, as it had centuries before. The kits rested peacefully but didn't sleep.

An hour passed, and mother stood up. She instructed her kits to stay put and then walked across the rock to the river's edge. She paced back and forth until satisfied she had found a good spot and then waded into the water. Sitting on the rocky bottom, she groped around with her hand-like front paws. Feeling under rocks and into crevices, her sensitive fingers felt for signs of movement. Finding no crayfish or lizards, she began to search for fish.

Working its way upstream, a rainbow trout passed too close to the waiting raccoon. Quick as a flash, her agile fingers seized the

unlucky fish. Bringing the trout to her mouth, Mother bit it behind the head, breaking its spine. The fish flopped once before dying in her grasp. Holding it in both paws, she dipped it in the water. Her ritual completed, she waded out of the water and laid the fish on the rock. The watchful kits sat still, waiting for Mother's permission to participate in the feast.

Knowing the kits could not eat the fish without help, she used her sharp canines to break the trout into several pieces. Deft as a surgeon, she removed the sharp bones and laid the small fillets before her young. She growled several sounds in her throat, and the kits pounced on the trout pieces. Packy moved quickly and snared the largest section before his sisters could reach the fish. Mandy brought up the rear, and she took two pieces; one hanging from each side of her mouth. Becky, Misty and Cindy carried their fillets back to the little pool. Wading in, they emulated Mother's washing motions in the murky water.

Mandy ate her food on the rock, but Packy carried his piece to the river. Thinking he was in the shallows, he waded in and quickly found himself neck deep in moving water. Using his front paws, he removed the piece from his mouth and attempted to mimic Mother's ritual. The strong current knocked Packy out of balance, and he tumbled over. The rushing water pulled the fish from his grasp, and he scrambled to retrieve it. Mother watched in amusement, but she made no attempt to intervene.

In a matter of seconds, the swirling eddies pulled him toward the middle of the river. Instinctively, he started to paddle. On his first try, Packy became an accomplished swimmer; an attribute passed down in his raccoon genes. Because of his small size, he had to work twice as hard as his mother to cover the same distance. Fifty yards downstream, he came to a fallen tree that extended into the river. Breathless and excited, he grabbed a limb with his front paws and tried to pull himself up on the log. The swift current pulled him loose, and he panicked. He grabbed at limb after limb, until the current lodged him between two branches that crossed each other. Exhausted, but safe, he dragged himself up onto the log.

As he worked his way through the slippery limbs, Packy saw his mother coming toward him with a piece of fish in her mouth. He sat down on the river bank as she dropped the fish at his feet. Understanding his mother intended for him to eat, he bit into the tasty morsel. She watched until he finished and then licked his face and ears. Mother could have dragged him out of the water at any time, but she had allowed him to learn from his mistake. He had passed the test, and she rewarded him with an expression of her love.

When Packy and Mother arrived back at the rock, they found his sisters sitting in a huddle, looking anxious and dejected. When Mother churred for them to gather around, they moved quickly, thrilled to be a family again. Somewhere in the distance, a rooster crowed, and Mother decided to end their first night of fishing. This time, they needed no signal. As she moved out, they assembled in line behind her. The mist had thickened, and water droplets formed on their fur. Two hundred yards above the river, they walked out of the mist.

The moon waned toward the horizon, and daylight seeped into the forest. Clinched fist-like, bugle flowers that had closed for the night began to open. Ferns bowed under the weight of morning dew, sparkled in the light. In the treetops, a vigilant squirrel barked at the passing family. At the top of the ridge, crows quarreled and cawed for reasons known only to them.

When Mother arrived at the patch of Solomon's seal, she stopped and sniffed the air. Satisfied that no predator lurked about, she headed for the comfort of her den. The edge of the sun popped over the mountaintop, but the raccoon family didn't see it. For the first time, Mother sat up for the kits to nurse. Too tired for their morning frolic, they stretched out and slept until evening.

* * * * * * * * * *

The next night, Mother went out alone. She left her kits in the den to rest up from their previous night's adventure. Their adult teeth would be coming in soon. Once their new teeth matured, the kits would be able to eat anything she could catch or find. Meanwhile, she had to bring them along slowly. By late fall, they must learn to find and catch their own food. As part of their passage into adulthood, she must wean them. If she didn't, Mother Nature would, because her milk would dry up before winter came. As she prepared to leave, she licked each of them affectionately. They understood they were not to leave the den until she returned.

She slipped out into the night. Instead of taking her usual

path toward the river, she went up the ridge behind her den. This route would take her to a different food source. She needed protein and other nutrients that would make her kits grow strong and healthy. At the top of the ridge, she sat on her haunches and looked down into the valley below. Directly below her, a large barn stood in a field at the edge of the woods. Beyond the barn, several large walnut trees grew along a brook, sheltering a farm house from the north winds. Outbuildings lay sprawled between the barn and the house, and a safety lamp cast its rays into the night.

Mother had reconnoitered the farm on several occasions. She knew, by now, a large brown dog slept in the house at night. By trial and error, she had learned if she got too close to the house, the dog would start barking, and the farmer would come out and turn on the porch light. She understood she should not fight the dog on his own turf, nor could she outrun him. Over time, she had figured out how close to the house she could get without arousing the dog.

Early one morning, she had sat high in a walnut tree and watched the farmer carry cat food to one of the outbuildings. On that same day, the dog chased her into the barn. She had climbed onto a rafter and sat quietly until the dog gave up and returned to the house. Now, her stomach grumbled because she hadn't eaten much the night before. The memory of cat food lay heavy on her brain, as she headed down the hillside. At the edge of the pasture, she crawled under a barbed-wire fence, taking great care not to touch the electric wire. One shock had taught her never to allow her tail to come in contact with the charged line. She knew from experience the cattle were no threat, but she steered clear of them anyway.

Keeping the outbuildings between her and the house, she looked for and found the four-inch hole the cats used to enter and exit the building. She squeezed through and went inside. A startled cat squalled its displeasure at the intruder and dashed out into the night. In the dark interior of the building, Mother could see three bowls scattered about on the wooden floor. The first bowl was empty, but the second and third had a small amount of food remaining. She ate the pellets quickly, savoring the meaty taste. Unfortunately, the food did not fill her empty stomach. She gave the third dish a final lick and then crawled out through the hole.

The next building was a hen house, but Mother knew not to go inside. The chickens would stir up a ruckus, and farmer Mason would come out to investigate. She went to the brook and searched for salamanders. Working downstream, she felt under rocks and logs until she found and consumed several of the delectable amphibians. She left the brook at the intersection of the river and turned back toward the barn. Avoiding the horses, she climbed into the barn loft. At the back of the loft behind a stack of baled hay, she found a hen sitting on her nest. Despite her best efforts, the terrified fowl eluded her grasp and flew out through an open door. Upon investigation, Mother found three warm eggs resting in the bottom of the nest. She sat on her haunches, broke open the eggs with her paws and ate the delicious contents. She tossed the shell pieces aside as she ate. After finishing, she looked around for other possibilities.

As she walked across the barn loft, she heard a whir of wings and looked up to see two barn owls light on the rafters. Not wanting to tackle both owls at the same time, she decided to search for their eggs at a later time. Her stomach felt full, and daylight seeped in through the loft door. She knew it wouldn't be long before farmer Mason let the big brown dog out for a run. She slipped down the side of the barn and crawled under the fence. Several cows grazed on the hillside, while a large bull stood guard. In ten minutes Mother had climbed back to the top of the hill. In the distance, she saw a truck coming up the river road toward the farm.

Tired but satisfied, she turned and headed down the hill to-

ward her den. The sun's rays punctured through a dense mist that blanketed plants and vines. Working her way downhill and to the left, she followed a small stream, checking the availability of crayfish and salamanders. About fifty yards from her den, she came across a low-hanging Muscatine vine. Young grapes were within her reach. She stood on her hind legs and sampled one. The green fruit tasted sour and bitter, and she spat it on the ground. Threading her way through the rhododendrons, she came out about ten feet from her tree. Four of her kits sat in the entrance, eagerly awaiting her return. Packy sat on the big root looking down toward the river. He sensed his mother's presence and turned to look in her direction. After joining his sisters in an enthusiastic greeting, they climbed the tunnel into their den.

* * * * * * * * *

As the brilliant summer moon stood directly overhead, Mother slipped out of the den with her kits in tow. About half-way down her path to the river, she turned right. Every few yards, she stopped and counted heads. In about five minutes, she came out onto an old logging road. The road ran away from the river and then picked it up again, as it came downhill toward an adjoining farm. Abandoned for years, the property provided an ideal hunting ground for nocturnal creatures. A slow-moving stream meandered across the untilled fields and emptied into the river.

The kits had not walked this far before. Mother knew she must challenge their endurance. At a curve in the road, she suddenly stopped and gathered the kits around her. In a few moments, the kits saw the reason. A large male raccoon stood in the middle of the road. As the male approached Mother, they both growled and churred and then upon meeting, they rubbed noses. The male turned, and without further ado, left the road and walked into the woods. The kits had just met their father, but they didn't know it. Even though her affection lingered, the memory of their mating had receded to some hidden place in her brain. She gave no thought to the connection between her mating and her offspring.

A few minutes later, the family reached the stream and climbed down the shallow bank. Mother led the group upstream until she came to a wide place in the creek. A myriad of crayfish holes opened onto a mud flat at the side of the stream. Mother selected a large hole and churred for the kits to gather around her. Digging furiously, she reached the bottom quickly and seized the frightened crustacean by the middle of its back. Its claws flailed uselessly, as it tried to pinch her head. She brought it to the kits, broke its back in one snap and laid it at their feet. Mother held Packy, Becky and Mandy back and churred for Cindy and Misty to examine the dead prey.

The two kits approached with trepidation. It only took them a few moments to turn the creature on its back. Misty grabbed a claw, and Cindy grasped a tail. They began to pull, and the crayfish broke into two pieces. Now it was a simple matter to eat the soft meat and avoid the hard shell. They finished eating and looked at their mother. Mother churred her satisfaction and moved to the next hole. Following the same process, she dug another crayfish out. This time, Becky and Mandy shared the entrée.

Packy looked on in anticipation, thinking he was to receive the next treat. Mother walked toward the next crayfish hole and then sat down about two feet from it. She churred for Packy to start digging. For a moment, he looked at her in total confusion. Finally, his eyes sparkled as he recognized her intent. Without hesitation, he attacked the hole with enthusiasm. When he reached the crayfish, he remembered the pinch he had taken before. As the crustacean tried to scramble up the side, Packy grabbed it behind the head. The wily creature slipped loose, and Packy caught it a second time. He squeezed as hard as he could with his soft milk teeth, and finally heard shell cracking, just before the crayfish went limp. He carried it out of the hole and dropped it in front of his mother.

For a moment, Mother looked perplexed, and then she understood. Accepting Packy's gift, she ate the crayfish in two bites, dropping the claws on the mud as she munched. Without being told, Packy attacked another hole. He took his next kill to Becky, and she accepted his offer. One after another, he fed his sisters until Mother intervened and made them dig their own. When the kits began to tire, Mother decided to give them a break. She led them to a grassy spot on the bank for a well-earned rest.

Before long, Mother's internal clock told her the night had almost passed, and she wanted to be home before daylight. At the last minute, she decided to detour across the field. She remembered an old barn stood on the abandoned property. On a previous trip, she had discovered several barn owl nests in the eaves of the barn. At the time of her discovery, the birds had not yet laid their eggs. She also knew that these birds were nocturnal and hunted at night. It had occurred to her this might be an excellent time to rob their nests.

Tired from digging, the kits lagged behind, and Mother had to stop more often. After three short breaks, they reached their destination. She churred for the kits to wait while she climbed the side of the barn. Once in the loft, she looked down and growled instructions. Packy started climbing. Close to the loft, he caught his right paw on a sharp nail. Startled, he pulled away and lost his grip. He landed in a pile of debris by the barn, shaken but not hurt. Not to be daunted, Packy scrambled off the pile and started up again. This time, he arrived at the loft without incident.

Usurping his mother's authority, he churred for his sisters to start up. Without hesitation, she slapped him across the head with her paw. Packy grunted at the sudden pain and moved out of her reach. The others started up, side by side. The agile Becky scrambled up like a squirrel. The others arrived in short order, breathing heavily by the time they sat down in the loft. Tired but elated, they sat attentively awaiting Mother's instructions. She churred for them to stay put. While they watched, she climbed a support post and reached the rafters in a matter of seconds.

She found no eggs in the first nest, but the next one contained five eggs. Carefully taking two in her mouth, she climbed down and placed them on the floor for her kits. She made two more trips. Now, each had an egg. With instructions from Mother, they broke the eggshells and ate the contents. Packy thought it was the best thing he had ever tasted. Mother climbed up to the rafters again. She found another nest with three eggs and wolfed them down quickly. She spotted another nest higher up and decided to investigate.

As she climbed a diagonal beam, she heard an angry screech and the whir of wings. Three owls flew into the barn loft at the same time. The barn owls were not large, but they were fierce and determined. Recognizing she was outnumbered and at a disadvantage in the barn loft, Mother retreated toward the floor. She scurried down the rafters, churring for her kits to hide. Packy and his sisters crawled under a pile of hay.

Before Mother could reach the floor, the largest of the owls launched herself directly at the retreating raccoon's back. Sharp claws dug into Mother's fur, and she lost her grip on the upright timber. She fell with a thump to the floor. Before she could recover, the other two owls attacked. Somewhat dazed from the fall, Mother was not yet able to fight back. For the second time, sharp claws pierced her skin. She grabbed at one, but it managed to escape. The third owl clung to her back and began pecking her head with its sharp beak. The first owl returned, attacking Mother furiously.

Disturbed by the noise, the kits crawled to the edge of the hay and looked out. As Packy watched, his memory of Mother defending him against the larger screech owl came to the forefront. His love for his mother overcame his fear, and he dashed across the barn floor to help. Covering twenty feet in a few seconds, he launched himself at the owl sitting on Mother's back. Seizing it by the leg, he bit down with all his strength. The owl screeched with pain and released its grip on Mother.

The owl tried to fly, and two of Packy's milk teeth pulled out. Loosened by the growth of his permanent teeth, they had little holding power. The injured owl flew to the rafters with a raccoon tooth stuck in its leg. One of the other owls attacked Packy, and Becky rushed to his defense. Her ferocious spirit overcame her size, and she bit and clawed at the feathery attacker.

The other two owls ganged up on Mother again, but this time they had to deal with Misty, Mandy and Cindy. The three acrobatic owls flew around in circles, dodging beams and rafters as they launched one attack after another. The largest of the owls came at Mother again, but this time she knocked it to the floor in a furious counterattack. Misty and Cindy grabbed the owl by leg and wing. The owl fought valiantly, but Mother moved in for the kill. One bite to the head, and the feathered warrior lay motionless.

The other owls gave up the fight and flew to the rafters. Mother gathered the kits around her and churred for them to sit silently. In a few minutes, the two remaining owls returned to their nests, and Mother knew the battle had ended. Ignoring the dead owl lying next to her, she led her kits out of the barn loft. The raccoons had a few scratches and bites, but there were no serious injuries. Three of the kits had lost teeth in the battle, but their adult teeth would be out in a few days.

Outside, Mother counted heads and started across the field.

Taking a different route, she climbed the hill east of the barn and cut diagonally across the ridge. They came to an old rail fence, and Mother followed it. The fence circled around a croissant shaped hill, and then made a ninety degree turn down toward the river. At a broken place between two rails, she crawled through the fence. Sitting on the other side, she watched her kits follow. When she was sure that they were all safe, she started down again.

Just below the fence, a small stream tumbled over time-worn rocks. A large pool had formed at the bottom, creating a perfect place for animals to drink. Mother had the kits wait while she checked for predators. Finding the little glen free of enemies, she gave the all clear to her young. Sitting back on her haunches, she stood guard while they drank their fill of the clear, sparkling water. Keeping to her schedule, she hustled them out of the glen and followed the stream back to the old logging road. Stopping frequently so the kits could rest, she arrived at her den just before daylight. Exhausted but content, they crawled into their nest for a long day's sleep.

Chapter 03

MOTHER KNOWS BEST

The first days of June brought glorious weather. Heavy rains in April and May had turned the forest into a paradise. The raccoon family thrived on the abundance of food Mother Nature had provided. Each day brought new adventures for the kits as they grew and learned. Their adult teeth grew through their gums, and the irritation caused them to chew everything in sight. Packy accidentally swallowed a milk tooth, and had a stomach ache for several hours. Mother didn't know how to help, but she cuddled him as a human mother would comfort a sick child. By dark, the pain had eased, and he went to sleep. For the first time, she left him alone, and took his sisters to the river for a night of fishing.

About midnight, he woke up, wondering where everyone had gone. He sat in the darkness for a few minutes, and then climbed down and went to look for his family. He followed their scent down the hidden path, stopping to investigate interesting and unusual sights and sounds.

    A stand of Indian pipe attracted his attention, and he wondered at the strange growth that glowed in the moonlight. The smell was sweetly pungent, so he licked one of the stalks. It burned his tongue, and he backed away while he choked and spat. As he sat recovering, he spied a trap-door spider sitting on a maple leaf. Packy gave chase, but the spider outran him. It dashed down its hole and closed the door from the inside. He dug the door loose, but the hole was too deep, and he lost interest quickly. Turning his attention back to his missing family, he continued toward the river.

    A few yards farther on, the young raccoon encountered a strange smell. Again, he left the trail to investigate. He found a mother skunk teaching her young how to dig worms out of the forest loam. In the subdued light, the skunk family looked like his mother and sisters, but they didn't smell right. He approached cautiously, allowing his curiosity to govern his emotions. One of the baby skunks stood directly in his path, so he stopped and churred a greeting. Mother skunk didn't like strange animals near her baby, so she turned toward Packy and raised her tail.

    The spray missed Packy by a few inches and hit a maple tree to his left. Some of the droplets ricocheted off the tree and splattered his shoulders and face. The awful stench gagged him immediately, and he ran off into the undergrowth. Completely baffled, Packy sat under the branches of a fallen tree and wondered what had happened. He tried licking the smell off his fur, but the taste made him gag and spit. He tried moving away from the terrible odor, but no matter what he did, it followed him. Finally, he gave up and headed toward the river.

    Confused by the smell, he had trouble locating the sandbar. Finally, he found his mother and sisters sitting in the pool by the rocks. Mandy was eating a crayfish while the others looked on. As

Packy approached, they started backing away. Totally confused again, he didn't understand their actions. After a few minutes of avoiding him, Mother grabbed him by the neck with her mouth and carried him into the pool. She dragged him back and forth in the water until he nearly drowned. A few minutes later, she turned him loose, and he waded out of the water and sat on a rock. The cool air felt good, and his fur began to dry.

For the next few days, the family treated Packy like a pariah. His sisters wouldn't play with him, and his mother backed away when he came close. The first day, Mother made him sleep at the bottom of the tree. Fearing a predator might devour him, she slept just outside the entrance. When they went hunting, Mother made him walk a few yards back from the family. She refused to allow him to nurse, but she was in the process of weaning all of them anyway. Eventually, the smell dissipated, and the family allowed him to come closer. By the sixth day, they stopped avoiding him, and he rejoiced in the fellowship.

Packy's strength and agility increased, and he now outweighed Mandy by two pounds. Becky was still the smallest, but she was a scrapper and had no compunctions about challenging Packy to a wrestling match. Misty and Cindy still looked like identical twins and spent most of their time together. Mother continued to teach them, using the river and the forest as her classroom. Packy was a good student, but he became bored easily. He would watch Mother intently for a while, then break away and chase his sisters. Sometimes he and Becky would fish as a team. One dark morning, they captured a catfish so large the entire family dined on it. Mother congratulated them in raccoon language, and they doted on the praise.

On the way back to the den, they came across a large rattlesnake lying in their path. Mother stopped the kits immediately and made them wait a few feet back. She approached the snake gingerly, careful to stay clear of its head. The snake coiled and rattled, but the cool morning temperature caused it to be sluggish. Mother had eaten her fill of catfish, and after a few minutes, she decided to leave the snake alone. Had she been hungry, there would have been a struggle between animal and serpent. She churred to the kits, and they followed her on a path around the snake. When the sun rose, they were sleeping contentedly in the comfort of their den. Sometime in the late hours of the afternoon, Packy dreamed about the snake. He woke up, shaking with fright. Mother pulled him to her and and churred her raccoon lullaby. Packy snuggled closer, and dropped off to sleep.

* * * * * * * * * *

On the tenth of June, heavy clouds rolled in from across the mountains. Their blackness increased hourly, and by noon, it was so dark birds thought night had fallen and went to roost. At dusk it began to rain. Lightening zigzagged across the sky, and thunder clapped and rolled across the river valley. The rising wind ripped shingles off houses and barns and slammed shallow-rooted trees to the earth. Frightening in its intensity, the storm continued throughout the night and into the next day.

By daylight, brooks and creeks overflowed their banks, and the river rose three feet. Many animals drowned in the rising waters. Others found high ground and huddled in their dens, brush piles or hollow logs. Birds avoided tree tops and open spaces, opting instead to stay close to large tree trunks and wait out the storm. The raccoon's favorite fishing spot disappeared in the rising floodwaters, and other sources of food were almost impossible to reach. Mother forbade the kits to leave their den tree, and then she dashed out in the raging storm to search for food.

She found several dead animals, but refused to eat anything she did not kill herself. She discovered a frightened baby rabbit under a brush pile, but took pity on it, and left it to wonder at its good fortune. In the farmer's pasture, she came up on a fallen apple tree. Sitting in the shelter of the trunk, she tried to eat one, but found it sour and distasteful. Next, she went to the barn but found nothing edible. She sat in the dry hay for a while, wishing she had time to sleep. She considered moving the kits here, but the danger was too great. If the farmer discovered them, he would either kill them or give them to the dog.

A few minutes later, she slipped through the hole in the outbuilding where the farmer left food for his cats. As usual, two of the bowls were empty, but a big yellow tomcat fed at the third. This time, Mother was in no mood to be kind. She rushed the cat with a ferocity borne of instinct and hunger. The cat stood its ground, refusing to relinquish the remaining pellets. As Mother closed in, the cat reacted with surprising speed and agility. Biting and scratching, it fought bravely, only giving ground to aid its defensive maneuvers. In the end, the cat was no match for Mother's strength and speed. When her sharp canines ripped off half of the cat's left ear, it gave up the fight and rushed out through the hole in the wall.

After the cat fled, Mother sat on her haunches for a few seconds and caught her breath. Again, she was in a dry place, and the temptation to sleep overwhelmed her. She nodded off briefly. A bolt of lightening split the sky, and a clap of thunder reverberated through the old shed. Mother came awake instantly. Resisting the urge to flee, she sat at the cat's bowl and ate the remaining food. Famished, she licked the dish until no cat food taste remained. Still hungry, she began a methodical search of the shed in hopes of finding more food. After a fruitless inspection, her thoughts returned to the henhouse. It occurred to her that in a raging storm, the farmer might not hear the hens squawking. And even if he did, he might not come out in the rain. Back out in the storm, she searched for a hole in the henhouse. Just under the roof, she found a loose section of wire. Using her dexterous paws, she pulled at the wire until it came loose. She folded the wire downward until she had a hole large enough to crawl through. She worked her way through the hole and crawled down the wire on the inside. As she crossed the floor, the chickens began to cackle and squawk. Paying them little mind, she began to search for eggs. In three nests, she found seven eggs and ate them all. Now that she was full, she turned her attention to gathering food for her kits.

She climbed up a support post to locate a chicken she could carry back to her den. The hens squawked louder and began flying about the henhouse. Selecting one small enough to carry, she made a dash for it. As the hen tried to go airborne, she grabbed it by the leg. The hen squawked and struggled until Mother broke its neck. Remembering that the farmer could appear any minute, Mother dragged the hen toward the hole she had made in the wire. As she climbed down on the outside, she heard a noise from the farmhouse, and then the dog began barking. When she reached the ground, she laid the chicken down and peered around the building.

The farmer and his dog stood on the porch, but had not yet decided to go out in the storm. Mother grabbed the chicken and ran toward the barn. When she found that the footbridge was under water, she turned right and ran up the hill toward the pasture. She heard the dog coming down the path toward the henhouse. Just as she reached the barbed wire fence, the dog turned the corner and rushed after her. Carrying the chicken slowed her down, but in any event, she could not outrun the dog. She squatted down low and crawled under the fence, pulling the chicken after her.

Barking loudly now, the dog rushed uphill toward her. When he reached the fence, he lowered his body and ran under the bottom wire. Rushing to catch his prey, his back touched the electric wire. The rain and wet ground worsened the shock, and the dog howled in pain. His momentum carried him on under the fence, and his tail touched the wire. Two jolts were more than the dog could stand, and he rushed across the pasture yelping and howling. Forgetting about Mother, he circled around and headed toward the house. Knowing the electric wire would shock him again, he jumped between the second and third strands of the barbed wire. As he passed through, he dragged his hind legs on the second wire, and the barbs ripped gashes in his flesh. His front legs crumpled as he hit the ground, and he tumbled end over end. Summoning his last measure of energy, he ran back to the house to seek comfort from his master.

Mother rushed up the hill dragging the hen as she ran. She made it through the second fence without incident and continued on into the woods. Every so often, she would stop, lay the hen down and rest. The rain continued without letup. As she worked her way downhill toward the den tree, she encountered heavy fog. Even for a raccoon, the going was tough. In dry weather, she could follow her own scent home, but the heavy rain had eradicated the smell of everything.

Now, she had to depend on her sense of direction.

She overshot her trail and ended up at the stream at the fence rail. She had walked too far south, but now, she knew the way. As she followed the brook downhill through the fog and rain, the roar of the river sounded louder. When the noise began to frighten her, she turned back east, keeping the river on her right. When she missed the den tree again, she sat down and rested. Turning south again, she walked uphill farther away from the river. She sensed her kits before she smelled them. They all sat at the bottom of the tree, anxiously awaiting her return. Mother put the hen down, and they all greeted with licks and nuzzles. After a brief rest, Mother ripped the chicken open with her canines, using her deft fingers to remove feathers. She watched in silence as the kits sat in the pouring rain dining in regal splendor.

* * * * * * * * *

By morning of the next day, the old farm tractor across the river stood in four feet of muddy water with only the smokestack and the aging tires protruding above the surface. Many animals had abandoned their dens and nests in an effort to find higher ground and dryer living quarters.

As thunder and lightening increased, Mother became restless and paced back and forth in the den. The kits became even more apprehensive as she churred for them to stay and then climbed down the tunnel and disappeared into the night.

An instinctual urge told Mother to move her family to different quarters, and she mounted a search to that end. Although she didn't understand her feelings, she knew she must act on them and do it in a hurry. About fifty yards uphill from her den tree, a hollow log lay horizontally on the hillside. Both ends were open, but the center was still dry. Realizing this was the best she could do in a pouring storm, she returned to the den.

She nudged the reluctant kits to the tunnel's edge and made them climb down. When she reached the bottom, she found them sitting in an inch of water, waiting for instructions. She licked and nuzzled each of them in turn, trying to comfort them for their short journey out into the storm. Using her teeth, she picked Becky up by her neck and went outside. She carried her uphill to the hollow log and went inside. Depositing Becky in the middle and instructing her to stay put, she returned to the den tree. She carried each of them in turn up the hill, leaving Packy for last.

As he sat alone in the bottom of the tree, he felt lonely and afraid. Mother was always there when he needed her, but now it seemed she had abandoned him. He was too young to understand he would eventually prefer solitude. Mother suddenly appeared out of the darkness, and his heart leaped for joy. Although he greeted her warmly, she seemed cold and distant. He remained still while she picked him up in her jaws. He was the largest and hardest to carry, but she managed it. None of them had thought to question why she had not allowed them to walk, they just knew. If they got lost in the rain and darkness, Mother might never find them. In a few minutes, they arrived at the log and went inside. Moving around inside the log wasn't as easy as their den, but they managed it.

As the family drifted off to sleep, the storm increased in intensity. Lightening flashes mingled with the dawn, giving the forest an eerie appearance. Thunderclaps bounced between the mountains, sounding like a thousand broken calliopes. Strong winds created driving rains that pelted plants and leaves into green strands of useless vegetation. The river crashed and roared, sucking the unwary into a maelstrom of fury. A tremendous blast startled the raccoons awake as fire and splinters leaped from their den tree. A monstrous bolt of lightening blew their den tree asunder, and in the wink of an eye, the raccoons' home ceased to exist. Pieces of bark and wood flew in all directions, and several large sections continued to burn, even in the heavy rain. A piece of the trunk landed in the forks of a maple tree, and the fire lit up the surrounding forest for several hundred yards. Mother sat quietly, refusing to panic. Somehow, she knew remaining calm was important, although she certainly didn't feel like it. Her kits were her life, and she must protect them at all costs. Misty and Cindy shook with fear. The ever-curious Packy decided to look outside, but Mother changed his mind with a warning hiss. He slinked back to the huddle and lay down by his sisters. Mother could only see in a straight line through the hollow log, but somehow, she knew her home had disappeared in the fire and smoke. A feeling of sadness came over her, but she drew comfort from the warm bodies of her youngsters as they lay huddled against her. The hollow tree had been a perfect place to raise her young. The hollow log had no permanency, because predators could easily enter while she was away searching for food. In a few minutes, the heavy rains put out the fires. The family lay quietly, too tense and distraught to sleep.

  The storm continued for two more days. Mother allowed the kits to nurse, but her milk soon dried up because she wasn't eating. Hunger pains drove her out in the rain, but concern for her kits kept her from going far from the hollow log. She dug beetles out of a rotted stump, and ate some acorns she found piled between some tree roots. She found a partridge sitting in its nest and captured it before it had time to fly away. Starved as she was, she ate the meat slowly, relishing every moment. She passed by the log several times to check on her kits, but she forbade them to come out in the rain. By daylight, her digestive system was working again, and her milk glands began to function. Her milk didn't satisfy their hunger, but it was enough to keep them alive.

* * * * * * * * *

At noon on the fifth day, the rain stopped. The river, now six feet above normal, roared and churned, swallowing everything in its path. The winds stopped, but the skies remained dark. Mother decided the subdued light was an excellent time to den hunt. With the kits lined up behind her, she worked her way through the wet forest. Everywhere she went; broken limbs and branches mingled with fallen plants and damaged vegetation.

After a few hours, the need for a permanent home became obvious. The kits were not yet mature enough to keep up with her. She had to wait every few minutes for them to catch up. She must find a place secure enough to leave her kits alone while she hunted. At midday, she found a groundhog den with an entrance between some rocks. The surprised woodchuck tried to defend his home, but he was no match for Mother's fierce attack. He ran off down the hill, grunting his displeasure at being evicted.

She led the kits inside the earthen den. The hole was damp and cold and did not contain soft rotted wood that added to their comfort in the dry den tree. She sniffed around until she found a spot to her liking, then scratched dirt into a bowl–like depression. Using her front paws, she pushed and moved the rocks outside the entrance until the opening was about four inches in diameter. Large predators did not normally have enough dexterity or intelligence to move the rocks, although a bobcat might paw and try to dig his way in. In any event, the kits were much safer in the groundhog den than they would be in the hollow log. In her absence, the kits were old enough to go outside and play. They were more alert now, and if a predator approached, they could dash into the den for safety. It was unlikely the groundhog would return, but even if he did, he posed no threat to the kits. He was too big and fat to get into the smaller hole Mother had made.

    Mother knew that she must find food for her hungry kits. They would try to nurse every time she came close. She thought about another chicken, but she knew the farmer and his dog would be more vigilant than ever. The river was too high and dangerous to attempt a fishing expedition. The roar and thunder of the waters sounded a warning to all animals to stay away. Deciding to leave the kits at home, she set out for the abandoned farm a few minutes before sunset. When she reached the top of the ridge, she looked down toward the den. Packy sat on top of the rocks, looking uphill in her direction. She had given them a stern warning to stay home, and she hoped that he wasn't foolish enough to go off by himself.

    As Packy watched Mother disappear behind the hill, his stomach rumbled, and hunger gnawed at his brain. His sisters usually followed him outside, but this time they had decided to stay in the den. Remembering Mother's warning, he sat for a while and stared at the mountains. He had never seen the sun set before, and he marveled at the strange display of light and shadow. He continued to sit in the gloaming while his battle between food and safety raged inside him. The desire for food won out, and he jumped down from the rockpile onto the leaf-littered forest floor.

    Picking his way through brush and broken limbs, he walked downhill toward the river. In his own mind, he only intended to go a little way and then return. He found a broken gooseberry bush and decided to sample the green fruit. The berries tasted sour and bitter, and he gave up after the third try. Mother's warning had receded in his brain, and he continued to explore the mysteries of the night. After a day of sunshine, the forest smells had returned to normal.

    Mountain laurel and rhododendron were in full bloom. Flaming azalea had opened to the sun, permeating the forest with its tantalizing smell. Ground plants such as trillium and lady slipper had stopped flowering, but their green fruit emitted pungent odors of their own. Packy was now only a few feet from the river, and the noise and rush of raging water both frightened and attracted him. Lured by the thought of tasty fish, he came to the water's edge. Keeping a safe distance, he walked downriver, hoping to find a sandbar. Not realizing the rushing water had washed it away, he continued to look. He came to a swampy area at the convergence of a creek and the river. A bullfrog croaked from a grassy hummock, and he waded into the water to search for it. Part swimming and part crawling, he made his way into the swamp. He found a good location and began to feel around the water as his mother had taught him.

A salamander came too close, and he grabbed it. Holding it tightly in his front paws, he moved it back and forth a few times. Satisfied with his instinctual movements, he ate the wriggly creature in two bites. Before long, he had consumed a half-dozen, and his hunger began to abate. He waded deeper into the swamp, and for the moment, forgot his own safety. He startled a water moccasin, but it slithered away, and the danger passed. Fortunately, nothing else lived in the swamp that was big enough to harm the young raccoon. As the half-moon waxed in the sky, he continued to search and eat. His luck held, and a hapless bullfrog came too close to his nimble paws. Packy grabbed a leg and held it tightly. The frog kicked and squirmed, trying to break free. Finally, he bit it behind the head, and the frog went limp.

Ironically, Packy had food in his paws, but he was no longer hungry. His sense of safety returned, and he remembered his mother's warning. He also thought about his sisters alone in the den. Deciding to take the frog to them, he began to look for a passage out of the swamp. Holding the amphibian in his mouth, he crawled and swam to solid ground. Following his own smell back along the river, he soon came to the place where the old den tree had stood. Temporarily confused about the location of his den, he put the frog down and prowled around through the debris of the old oak.

After a while, he picked up his own smell again. He retrieved the frog and started up the hill. In a few minutes, he saw his sisters sitting among the rocks of their new den. They greeted him with churrs and chattering, and Becky rushed down the hill to meet him. He deposited his gift by the rocks and watched as they ripped the frog into small pieces. In a short time, the frog disappeared. Soon, they were frolicking and playing among the rocks.

At sunrise, Mother returned, carrying a rabbit in her mouth. She ripped it open in her usual fashion and laid it out for the kits to eat. Mandy, always hungry, ate heartily. Becky, Misty, and Cindy ate sparingly. Packy didn't eat at all until his mother growled at him. He pulled off a piece of the rabbit, sat next to his sisters and ate slowly. With some effort, he finished the piece of meat. He felt full and bloated. He lay down next to a rock and went to sleep. In a short time, Mother nuzzled him awake. She knew Packy was acting strangely, but she didn't understand why. They all crawled into the groundhog's den and curled up for a long day's sleep.

* * * * * * * * *

Once the rain stopped, it didn't rain again for six weeks. The river receded slowly until it returned to its normal level. Scattered along the river's edge, huge tree trunks and stumps had lodged on rocks and stuck into banks and curves. Sandbars had washed away, and new ones had formed at different locations. Mother's favorite fishing spot no longer existed. The kits continued to act strangely when she brought them food. Eventually, Mother became suspicious, and one dark night, she followed Packy to his swamp. After a strong scolding and a smack on the head, she churred for him to stay put. She returned to the den and brought the others with her.

The swamp had a plentiful supply of food, including frogs, crayfish, waterdogs, and other aquatic creatures. One bright night, the family encountered a large water moccasin. Mother churred for the kits to remain quiet. Completely unafraid, the snake swam directly toward Packy. The snake opened its jaws, and four fangs glistened in the moonlight. Just as it passed Mother, she grabbed it with both paws, one at its midriff and one behind its head. The snake jerked and twitched, and tried to reach her with its fangs. One bite was sure death, and Mother knew it.

Holding on for dear life, she sank her teeth into the snake's back and stomach. Biting down hard, she ground her teeth together. Not easy to kill, the snake thrashed and bit at the air. As life ebbed out of the moccasin, its thrashing slowly stopped. Not taking any chances, Mother held on for a long time after all movement ceased. Finally, she swam away from her kits and dropped the serpent in the swamp.

Completely exhausted, Mother rested for a while, and then returned to her kits. They surrounded her immediately, and began to churr and touch. Soon, they resumed their search for food, the snake forgotten. The rest of the night was uneventful, and they all returned to their den with full bellies.

Mother took them to the swamp for several nights in a row, and then one night she churred for them to stay in the den. She wanted to check out the farm, but she was not yet ready to expose her kits to additional risk. She sat at the top of the hill and watched the farm for a long time. Finally satisfied that the danger was minimal, she crossed the pasture by a different route and circled around the barn. At the foot bridge, she sat and watched again. There was no sign of the farmer or his dog, so she started out again. This time, she had a different destination.

Last year and the year before, she found many tasty delights in the farmer's garden. She turned right at the footpath, and in a few seconds, she sat between a row of tomatoes. She selected a large red one and began to eat. After finishing the third, she worked her way down to the cucumber patch. They were still small and succulent, and she ate several of those. Continuing downhill, she crossed into the corn rows. This was her favorite, and she hoped the delicious ears were ripe.

She pulled down a stalk and sampled the ears. Finding they were too small to eat, she tried three more. Soon, she realized she must wait several more days. From the corn rows, she crossed into the watermelon and cantaloupe patches. Again, no luck. The watermelons were still green, and the cantaloupes were tiny balls of sour fruit. Disappointed these would also require several days to ripen, she sat in the patch and pondered her next move.

She left the garden and walked toward the creek. Crawling through the wild roses, she climbed down the bank and searched for crayfish. Her luck held, and she caught and ate several. She foraged until daylight began to lighten the sky. Satisfied, she climbed up the creek bank and followed the stream until she came to another fence. Sensing that she had left her territory, she cut through a stand of white pines and came out above the pasture. Careful to avoid the spines, she climbed a black locust tree.

She sat on a limb and looked out across the valley. She needed to find a better den for her kits, but she didn't know where to start. Her inherited sense of orderliness dictated she balance comfort and safety. Anything less left her with a sense of uneasiness. The groundhog's den didn't satisfy either to a great degree, but it was certainly better than a hollow log. She gave little thought to the den tree. That was in the past, but in her mind's eye, she needed to find something similar. Tomorrow, she would mount a new search. She climbed down the tree, being careful to keep the sun out of her eyes. Damp as it was, she looked forward to the comfort of her hole. She would sleep the day away, and then tonight, she would take the kits on a new adventure.

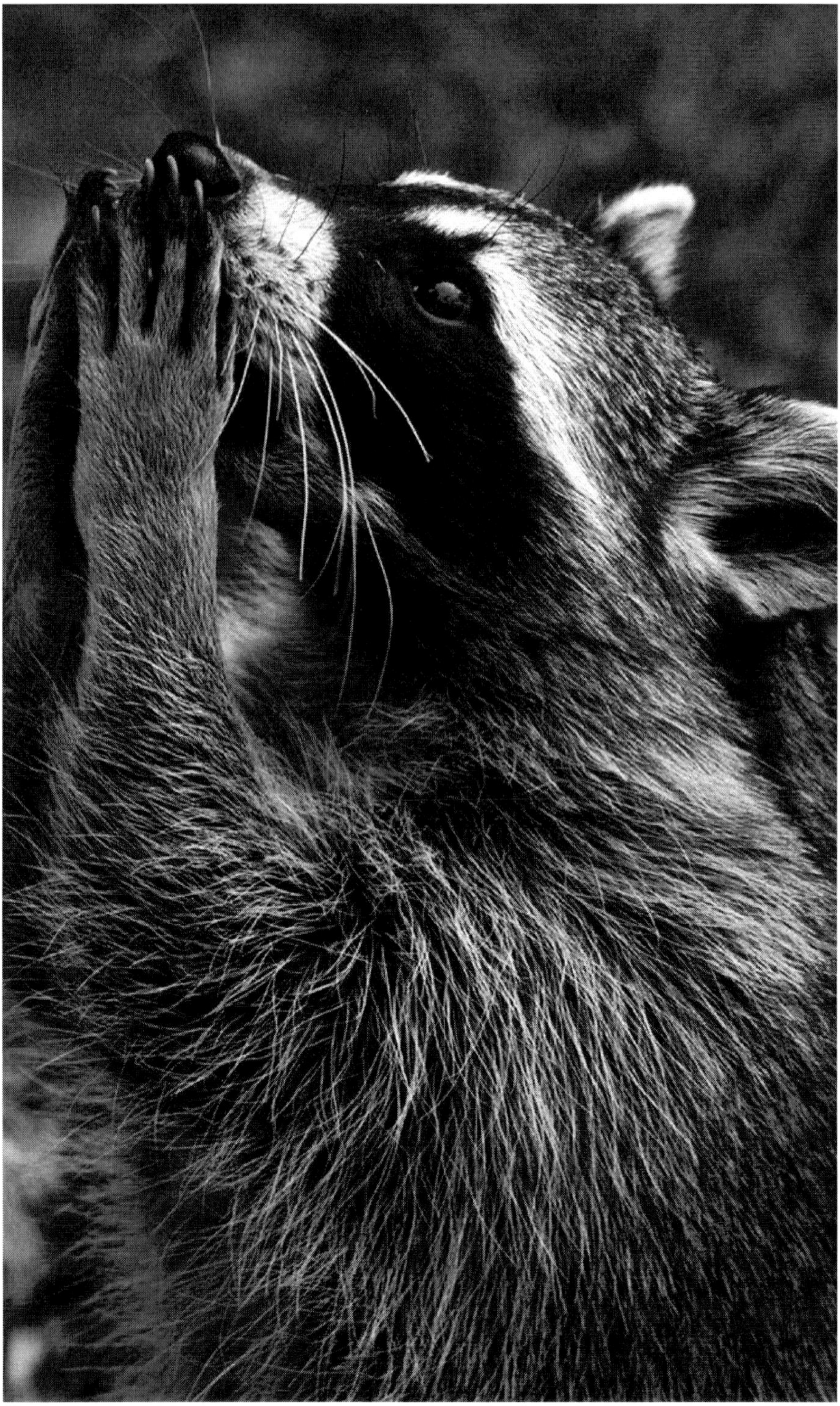

Chapter 04

VIEW FROM THE BARN

Day after day, July's summer sun burned down through a cloudless sky. By noon on any given day, oppressive temperatures drove animals and birds into or under the nearest shade tree. The cool of the groundhog's den turned into a blessing for Mother and her kits. Drought had replaced the flood, and crops and gardens withered in the stifling heat. Worms and beetles dug deeper into the ground in search of moisture, leaving many small creatures without their usual food supply. June's raging river had turned into a shallow stream, and many of the larger fish went downriver in search of deeper waters. Forest and meadow cried out for rain, but the sun showed no mercy as it blazed down on hills and valleys. Despite the warm night air, nocturnal animals ventured out as soon as the sun dropped behind the mountains.

Mother taught her kits from experience and instinct, never wavering in her determination to mold them into capable hunters. They were still youngsters, of course, but their confidence increased, and their clumsiness diminished. The raccoon family did not suffer in the drought as many animals did. They simply expanded their hunting range and worked harder at finding food. When the night air cooled to a reasonable degree, Mother collected the kits and took them into the forest for their nightly hunting lessons.

The extended range necessitated longer walks, and daylight

often found them en route to their den.

Despite the added hardship, Mother managed well, and her kits rarely suffered from hunger. They could keep up with her for longer periods, but their stamina still did not match hers. Packy came close, but even he required an occasional break. Both his survival skills and his judgment had improved significantly. He became more patient with his siblings and soon fell deeper into the 'big brother' role. He would either stop and wait with Mother or take short side trips, which she now allowed. Like all raccoons, his curiosity knew no bounds, but he recognized danger more readily and backed away from it on his own. Mother's warning hisses became less frequent, and he was quick to alert his sisters when he thought they were getting into dangerous situations.

Packy's swamp became their favorite hunting place, even though the water level had dropped considerably. Finding crayfish now required digging them out of their holes, whereas before, they had caught them on the surface. Flies and gnats increased, but for Packy's family, they were more of an inconvenience than a serious discomfort. They were at their worst after daylight when Mother and her kits threaded their way back through the forest toward their den. Mother would detour along the river so they could sit in the cool water and relax before turning in for the day.

Late in July, Mother turned to the abandoned farm as an alternate source of food. It was a long walk for the kits, but there were no humans, so they could hunt in relative safety. Many smaller animals had moved into the uninhabited buildings, and crayfish and frogs were still plentiful along the stream that meandered through the farm. The old farmhouse had two stories with a basement that teemed with mice. Mother taught the kits how to sit by a mouse hole and wait patiently until one came out. The wait was usually short because the nocturnal rodents came out frequently to search for nuts and insects.

Mother considered moving her family into the farmhouse, but on occasion, she detected human scent, causing her to fear for the safety of her kits. Although the visits were infrequent, one smell was always the same. The other scents varied, often never returning, and they were always daytime visits. Mother's experiences with humans had not been good ones, and early in her life, she had learned to avoid them. Still, the smells did not stop her from foraging around the farm for food, but she maintained a cautious vigil just the same.

One night, Packy found several jars of shelled walnuts in a pantry off the kitchen. Mother recognized his find immediately, and she salivated at the thought of tasting the scrumptious nuts. She pushed a jar off the top shelf, hoping it would break. The jars were of good quality, and the impact only dented the lid. She sat the jar upright, held it against her stomach and tried to twist off the lid. When this failed, she showed Packy how to hold the jar with his front paws while she twisted, but still, the lid would not break free.

Desperate needs required desperate action. She brought Cindy and Mandy into the act. They held the jar tightly from two sides while Mother and Packy twisted the lid. Packy felt the lid turning and churred triumphantly. In a few minutes, they had removed the lid, and Mother turned the jar over to empty the contents. In one sitting, the raccoon family ate a quart of walnuts. After that, they were too full to look for anything else. The kits played and chased each other around the farmhouse while Mother watched. After a while, she made them stop and rest in preparation for their long walk back to the den.

The next night found them back in the pantry again. This time, the nut-cracking team had no trouble getting another jar open. Again, the family consumed walnuts for the better part of an hour. After opening a fourth jar on the same number of nights, the taste of nuts began to grow stale. Mother and kits decided to investigate the second shelf. Despite their best efforts, two jars would not yield their contents. The third jar turned out to be peaches, and the sweet syrupy taste delighted all of them. Becky and Mandy came down with diarrhea, and Mother had to wait on them several times on the way home.

On the sixth night, they were back opening jars again. After opening a can of green beans, they decided to leave the vegetables on the floor and search for another flavor. This was Mother's lucky night. Having taught the kits how to open jars, she sat back and watched. When they opened a can of corn, she joined the feast with much enthusiasm. This was the first night they ate two cans, and it was Mother's turn to have diarrhea. She churred for them to stay put and then went off by herself. After a short absence, she returned and gathered them in a huddle for the return trip home.

By early August, the food in the pantry had played out. The raccoons had either eaten the contents, or the cans wouldn't open. Now, only one jar remained on the top shelf. It had leaked, and sugar had caused it to stick to the wood. Packy and Becky pushed and pulled together. The jar came loose suddenly, and both kits fell with it. It landed dead-center on another jar they hadn't been able to open. There was a loud popping noise, and glass flew all about the pantry. Becky cut her mouth on a loose piece of glass, and Packy cut his foot. Mother intervened quickly and led them outside. This was the last time she allowed any of them to enter the pantry.

For the next three days, Mother left the kits at home while she foraged for food on her own. She wanted Packy and Becky to recuperate from their injuries. Packy limped when he walked, and Becky bled when she tried to eat. Mother licked the injuries daily until the cuts healed over. Her saliva contained a natural antibiotic Mother Nature had provided. Mother didn't know how it worked, or why, she simply reacted to her instincts and her love for her offspring.

* * * * * * * * *

Mother liked the abandoned farm, but she didn't enjoy the long walk to get there. She had made up her mind to move closer; but in the meantime, she kept a close eye on farmer Mason's garden. The empty Dills farmhouse stood about a mile from the Mason farmhouse. Mother had no idea why one of the farms had no people living on it, but she liked it that way. The elderly Dills couple had died, leaving no will. The state had taken possession of the property, but the bureaucratic wheels turned slowly, allowing the farm to lapse into disrepair. Except for an occasional trespasser, ninety acres stood unused by people, and that suited the animals just fine. The occasional smell Mother encountered was a state-appointed representative who had been hired to locate a relative of the deceased couple.

Finally, the agent located a niece, Juanita Dills, who fortunately had retained her maiden name, living near Atlanta, Georgia. Recently widowed by the death of her husband, a veterinarian, she saw the inheritance as an opportunity to restart her life. Once she learned about her family history, she decided to move there right away. Her great-grandfather had bought 600 acres just after the Civil War, and the Dills farm was all remaining of the original purchase.

A widow before her fortieth birthday, Juanita had also inherited her husband's successful business. She knew nothing about farming, but she was tenacious and a quick study. She figured it would take about three months to get her affairs in order. Meanwhile, she located a cousin who owned a construction business near the Dills farm, and he agreed to renovate the farmhouse for her. She wanted the house restored to its original architecture, and this would take several months.

Juanita had a secret she had not yet shared with anyone. She had decided to do something with her money that would be useful to others. This meant visitors would be traveling in and out of the farm on a regular basis. She quickly realized the old farm road was not suitable for daily traffic. The heavy dust would discourage many hoped-for visitors from venturing onto the road. Despite the considerable expense, she had her cousin find a paving contractor who agreed to start right away.

* * * * * * * * *

The time had come to wean the kits, and they weren't taking it lightly. True to her instincts, Mother had made her decision, and there was no turning back. She did wean them gradually, allowing them to nurse occasionally. Later on, she cut back in both nursing time and amount of her milk she allowed. At first, she would refuse kindly, gently pushing them away until they gave up. Later on, she would growl ferociously or swat them with her paw. Eventually, they acquiesced and stopped trying. At least they all did, except Packy.

More aggressive than his sisters, he didn't concede easily. At one point, he made a serious error in judgment. He attempted to tackle Mother and hold her down. She relaxed for a moment, and when he reached for a nipple, she moved with rapid speed. After biting him hard on the rump, she cuffed him across the head and face several times. Escaping from her wrath, he bolted for the safety of a laurel thicket. Mother chased him hard, and to her surprise, he outran her. Taken aback at his speed, she gave up the chase. At his age, he should not have been able to outrun her, but he did. Even though he had escaped successfully, his attitude improved significantly, and that was the last time he ever tried to nurse.

In mid-summer, Mandy came down with an illness of unknown origin. She became lethargic, and refused to leave the den. Mother and Packy brought her tidbits of food when they returned home. At one point, she became too ill to eat, but she recovered and began to improve. Packy caught a trout, gutted it, and then brought it to her. She ate ravenously, and the next night, she went outside and walked around. Her health never fully recovered, but by the next full moon, she went on hunting trips and did her part in their search for food.

The crushing summer heat continued, and one morning, the raccoon family returned to find their home had become infested. The coolness of the groundhog den had attracted insects, and they bit the raccoons in their sleep. That night, Mother went off by herself to search for a better den. After rejecting several possibilities, she found a huge elm tree in the meadow behind the barn on the abandoned farm. The first row of limbs were twenty feet up, too high for most animals to climb, and the trunk was four feet in diameter and thirteen feet in girth. The ravages of time had made several raccoon-sized holes in the trunk and a few in some of the larger limbs.

Just under the third layer of limbs, Mother located the largest hole in the tree. Directly above the hole, two limbs had grown together, providing a natural roof. Her sensitive nostrils told her raccoons had denned there sometime in the past. The faint but distinct smell gave her a feeling of security, and she decided to move in immediately. The hole was large enough for all of them to get inside and move about freely. Even though there was nothing to pack, the kits knew their mother was preparing to move out of the groundhog's den.

They would leave the insect infestation behind and hope the elm tree provided more comfortable quarters. This time, Mother made no attempt to carry them; they were old enough to walk on their own. Despite the heat, there was no danger they might get lost in a raging storm. Also, they were old enough now that she didn't require them to walk in single file. Packy often walked ahead of the group, sniffing out possible food sources to share with his family. Invariably, Becky followed Packy, while Misty, Cindy and Mandy fanned out to the side or just lagged slightly behind. They did not yet go off on their own, but roamed the perimeter of Mother's trail.

Even though the family had left the groundhog den, they still needed to rid themselves of the fleas they carried on their skin. At the edge of the abandoned farm, a small clear stream came down from the mountaintop. Mother found a small pool deep enough for the raccoon family to submerge their bodies. After a few growls and churrs, the kits understood. Even in summer, the water was biting cold, and fleas didn't like it. The raccoons sat in the water so long they began to shiver. One by one, the fleas either jumped off or died. The method wasn't perfect, but it provided relief, and repeat applications kept them down.

Ticks were another matter. The cold water didn't move them. Once they buried their heads in the raccoon's skin, they were there to suck blood until they died. Mother inspected the kits on a regular basis. When she found one, she would bite it off. The kits would return the favor for Mother. They weren't as skilled as she, but they learned.

As it turned out, the elm tree provided a perfect home for Mother and her kits. Immediately after moving in, they started perfecting their climbing skills. The height of the elm tree alone gave them cause to practice. Due to the large diameter of the tree trunk, not even Mother could wrap her legs around it. They all had to rely on the strength and agility of their paws and claws. The kits learned how to back down as rapidly as they could climb down in the head first position. They could walk on the large lower limbs as easily as a human taking a Sunday stroll in the park. At ninety-five feet in height, the elm had hundreds of limbs, and the kits never tired of climbing on them.

They would chase each other out to the end of a limb, and then drop down to the next one. They fell out of the tree on several occasions, but they would get up, shake themselves off and climb up again. On one occasion, Misty climbed to the very top branches. The wind started blowing, and she lost her nerve. She began to squall, and refused to climb down.

Mother went up after her. After several minutes of useless churring, Mother's patience ran out. She seized the branch in her front paws and began shaking it. Finally, Misty fell, grabbing at other limbs as she descended through branches and leaves. She landed on the ground with a thump and lay there as if stunned. By the time Mother reached her, she had recovered. With some gentle licking for encouragement, she climbed back up the trunk. Soon, she was chasing Cindy and Becky through the branches again.

* * * * * * * * *

The next afternoon, Packy woke up earlier than the rest of his family. He lay in the den for a while, listening to the gentle breathing of his siblings and the heavier, deeper breathing of his mother. Boredom and hunger pains motivated him to slip out into the hot afternoon. He climbed down the lower level of limbs and sat for awhile, looking out over the farm. Offset at an angle behind the barn, the elm tree stood almost a quarter-mile from the farmhouse. Packy could see people moving back and forth around the house. At that distance, people didn't worry him, but his instincts told him to stay away from humans. Being young and curious, he decided to investigate anyway.

Climbing down from the tree, he scurried across the meadow to the shelter of the old barn. He climbed up the side and entered the loft. He crossed the floor and sat in the door on the other side. He watched for a few moments, until he decided he couldn't see as well as he liked. Forgetting for the moment that several barn owls slept in the rafters, he climbed up a support beam and out onto the hay lift. He sat on the beam of the lift and watched the activity around the farmhouse. Three men went in and out of the house on several occasions. Packy could seen them carrying things in, but they seldom brought anything back out. He didn't know what to make of it, but he hoped these people hadn't come to stay.

On the north side of the farmhouse, a road ran along the river and disappeared around a curve. Mother had never taken her kits to that side of the farm. Always curious, Packy wondered about the world down the road. Some kind of machine was moving toward the farmhouse, and it stirred up a lot of dust. He had never seen a bulldozer before, and he marveled at all the noise it made. At sixteen weeks of age, Mother had already taught him not to trust people, but still, he wanted to know more about these strange creatures. Perhaps it wouldn't hurt to get a little closer. After all, there were so many things to learn.

As he turned to go back inside, one of the owls spotted him and raised a ruckus. The others soon joined in. Their buzzing and biting forced him to crawl back out onto the hay lift. The birds soon gave up their chase, but they watched Packy intently. As soon as he tried to go back inside, they would start up again. Two of the men stopped what they were doing and looked toward the barn. They couldn't see Packy from where they stood, so they soon went back to work.

In an effort to get away from the irate birds, Packy climbed up on the barn roof. As soon as he was outside, the owls stopped harassing him and flew back to their nests. On the sunny side, the old wooden shingles were hot, and they hurt his feet. He quickly crossed the top of the roof and climbed down on the cooler side. He sat down and looked out across the farm. The panoramic view stirred something in the young kit he didn't understand. He could see the curve in the river and many of the mountains he had never seen before.

He turned his attention back to the men and watched them for a while. Their quitting time arrived, and they began packing their tools in a truck parked just outside the farmhouse. The man driving the machine turned it off and walked toward the house. He joined up with one of the other men, and they started walking toward the barn. An alarm went off in Packy's head, causing him to start looking for a place to climb down off the barn roof. It only took a matter of seconds for Packy to realize the only exit was back at the hay lift where the owls sat waiting for him. As he scurried back and forth on the roof, one of the men spotted him.

"Hey! Look, Charlie, there's a raccoon up there on the roof."

The other man looked where his companion was pointing. "You're right, Calvin, there is. I wonder how it got up there."

"The question I have, is how it's going to get down?"

"Let's have some fun," Calvin said, and picked up a stone from the ground.

He threw it at Packy. The stone missed by several feet and rolled off the barn roof onto the ground. Packy ran to the other side of the roof. That side was still hot, although it had cooled down some. Packy stayed out of their view, and hoped they would go away. In a few seconds, the men appeared around the other side of the barn. This time, both men had a stone in their hands, and they tried to hit Packy again.

The frightened raccoon ran across the roof top and down on the other side. The men continued to play their game and came around the other side of the barn again. Luckily, for Packy, they decided it was more fun to make him run than to hit him. They continued their stone tossing, and Packy was getting tired. After a few minutes, a third man came toward the barn.

"Calvin, what are you guys doing?"

"We're throwing rocks at a coon that got hisself stranded on the barn roof."

"We have better things to do than hassle a raccoon," Luther said. "You guys need to pack your tools so we can leave."

"Let's go Charlie. It sounds like Luther's in a hurry to go nowhere."

Without further discussion, Calvin and Charlie turned, walked past the truck and onto the porch. Packy sat frozen on the cooler side of the barn roof.

"Idiot rednecks," Luther said, as he watched them go.

He turned and walked back toward the truck. He opened his lunch box and removed a leftover bologna sandwich. He walked back to the barn, stood just below the roof and tossed the sandwich up and onto the wooden shingles. It landed about five feet from Packy. Luther walked back from the barn until he had a clear view.

"Maybe this will make up for some of the torment those two idiots caused you, little feller."

He spoke to Packy as if he expected an answer. He stood quietly, trying not to make any sudden moves.

"How long have you been up there, ol' boy?"

He continued talking to the young raccoon in soothing tones. The kind words made Packy feel better, and he churred down to the sympathetic man.

"Well, at least I know you're still alive."

Suddenly, the man disappeared from Packy's view. He walked into the barn and poked around for a while. In about two minutes, he reappeared with a long pole in his hands. He put one end of the pole on the ground and the other end on the edge of the roof.

"Okay, ol' boy, you can get down now without having to jump off the roof. You take care and live a long life."

He turned to leave, and as an afterthought, he turned back and looked up at Packy.

"Oh, and by the way, stay out of the barn loft. Those owls are vicious little devils."

Luther turned and walked back toward the house. In a few minutes, the truck drove away. Packy sat still for a long time. Soon, the smell of food overcame him, and he approached the sandwich cautiously. The human smell worried him, but he was too hungry to care. He pulled the top piece of bread off the sandwich and tossed it aside. He picked up the bologna and fingered it carefully. He thought the smell was wonderful. He began to eat, savoring the delicious taste. Still hungry, he picked up a slice of bread and ate it. It didn't taste as good as the meat, but the smell added to the taste. Finally, he picked up the other piece of bread. It had mayonnaise on it. The taste was strange, but he liked it.

Finished with his meal, Packy walked down the sloping roof until he came to the pole. He put his paws on it and pushed. The pole didn't move. He climbed down onto it, and began working his way to the ground. Soon, he was standing in the tall grass near the barn. Deciding he had experienced enough adventures for one day, he headed toward the elm tree.

* * * * * * * * * *

The raccoon family's first encounter with hunting dogs came on a warm, sultry summer night. As soon as the moon rose, they slipped quietly down the elm tree, and made their way across the meadow. Mother had decided the kits were old enough to swim the river, and she wanted to explore the other side. She had crossed a couple of nights before on one of her lone forages. She had selected the perfect place for the kits to cross. The water was deep and swift enough to make them struggle, but not so fast they would get washed away.

She demonstrated with a short swim out and back to the bank. She sat on her haunches and conferred with them in raccoon language. She made sure they understood what to do and how to do it. She directed all of them to get into the water at the same time and swim side by side. She had them wait while she walked downriver for about fifty feet. She took up her position, and like a good swim coach, she signaled for them to start out. If one of them got into trouble, she could get to the kit before a serious problem developed.

They all waded into the water at the same time. Packy was in the center with two sisters on each side. By the middle of the river, they had formed an inverted vee with Packy in the lead. Still downriver from them, Mother kept pace, neither ahead or behind. As it turned out, her precautions were not necessary, because they all reached the other side without difficulty. Even so, she had been wise to take the position she did.

She allowed a short break, and then started them out. The field was part of the abandoned farm, and no one had tilled it for several years. Despite the neglect, a few persistent stalks of corn still grew along the edges. At this time of year, corn was in its milky stage, not too small and not too hard. Mother had eaten corn before, and she salivated at the thought of the tasty kernels. The kits had yet to sample the delicious grain, and she knew a special treat awaited them.

After arriving at the first stalk, she had them sit quietly while she sniffed the air and surveyed the surrounding scene. Deciding no predators were in the vicinity, she climbed the stalk until it fell down. There were two ears all covered in shucks with silk hanging out the top ends. Mother stripped the shucks away from the first ear, exposing the golden kernels. She stepped back and churred for the kits to eat. Becky and Mandy started at one end, while Misty and Cindy attacked the other. Packy hung back for a few moments, and then started in the middle.

The food was delicious and all of them ate ravenously. In his haste to remove the kernels, Packy ate halfway through the cob. It only took them a few moments, working together, to turn the cob over, so they could get at the other half. They chewed all the milk out of the cob, and then sat back with self-satisfied smirks. If Mother had been human, she would have laughed, because all five of them had wet, milky faces.

The next stalk was only a few feet away, and they attacked it with the same enthusiasm. At the third stalk, Mother joined in, and before long, they had consumed at least a dozen ears. After the sixth stalk, they ran out of corn, and Mother had them sit quietly again, while she searched for more of the delicious food. After fifteen minutes of intensive exploration, she found a small patch containing five stalks. Nine ears later, they had all gorged themselves on fresh corn.

Even though they were all full, Mother made another search. Again, the kits waited quietly while she scoured the other side of the field. One lone stalk stood just above the riverbank, and three full ears stood at attention along the sides. This time, Mother allowed the kits to tear down the stalk. They divided two ears, and Mother ate one. Now, all of them felt bloated, a price all creatures pay for delicious food. As soon as they finished, she led them into a patch of doghobble for a well-deserved rest. The matted plants provided safety from predators, giving the family time to recover from overeating.

As the raccoon family rested, they heard the sound of dogs baying in the distance. Mother came to attention immediately. She knew she must get her kits across the river before the dogs discovered their presence.

Chapter 05

ENEMIES IN THE NIGHT

At the first sound of baying dogs, Mother didn't panic; she just stood and listened intently. In a matter of seconds, the change in pitch told her the dogs would arrive shortly. She knew if she and her kits stayed in the matted tangle of vegetation, the hounds would not be able to reach them. When they arrived, they would bark and yowl until they tired from the effort. Still, she had learned that when a pack of hounds ran through the night, humans usually followed close behind. Hunting dogs had killed two of her siblings, and she didn't intend to see her kits mauled before her eyes.

She growled low in her throat, a harsh warning the kits understood. As she worked her way through and out of the doghobble, they followed closely, understanding a crisis ensued. They quickly arrived at the river, only to learn they were farther upstream than when they came across the first time. Suddenly, a different danger faced the family. The water ran swiftly here, forcing Mother to look for a better place to cross. She made a quick decision to follow the river upstream. The baying sounded closer, and she realized little time remained. Instead of her usual churring, she growled at the kits to move faster. Misty stopped to look back, and Mother bit her hard on the rump. The chastised kit squealed once as she turned and ran toward the others.

Landing on the balls of their feet like humans do, the raccoons ran as fast as they could, with Packy out in front. He clearly understood Mother's intentions, and he wanted to help. As adrenaline pumped into his bloodstream, he surged ahead, hoping to assist Mother in their river crossing. He had a fifty-yard lead when he slowed suddenly and dashed down the riverbank. Looking across, he saw slow-moving shallows and knew immediately he had found their crossing point. He dashed back up the bank to tell Mother about his discovery.

As soon as she came down the bank to look, Packy backtracked until his sisters came into view. Mandy ran in last place, and Packy intended to help her in some way. He turned and ran beside her, churring for her to hurry. When they reached Mother, Packy knew she had accepted his choice of crossing point. She herded them down the bank to the water's edge. Using a variety of churrs to make her intentions known, she instructed Packy to lead his sisters across the river. Meanwhile, she would trick the dogs into following her north along the river.

Packy didn't like the idea, but he accepted his mother's wisdom. He churred for his sisters to line up behind him. When they were ready, they started out. As he swam out into the river, he feared for his mother. As he forced himself to concentrate on the task at hand, he realized he was too far ahead. He slowed his pace and waited for his sisters to catch up. Becoming impatient with their progress, he turned around and swam to the rear. He chattered like a chipmunk, hoping to spur them on to greater speed. He stopped swimming momentarily and looked upriver along the bank, hoping to catch a glimpse of his mother. He saw nothing, and his concern increased. He considered going off on his own to look for her, but he remembered his responsibility and began swimming toward his sisters.

* * * * * * * * *

Mother watched her kits swim out into the river. She could see Packy had followed her instructions, giving her one less problem to worry about. She ran back along their trail for a hundred yards or so, and then crossed into the field. She hoped the dogs would smell her scent, thus leaving her kits to cross the river safely. She ran parallel with the river in the upstream direction. Soon, she would be in unfamiliar territory, increasing the risk of being caught by the hounds. In less than five minutes, the dogs crossed out of the woods and started running up the road.

Facing the wind, they picked up Mother's scent and turned toward the untilled cornfield. When she felt sure the dogs were following her trail, she turned right and headed for the river. There would be no time to choose a crossing point; she would have to jump into the water as soon as she reached the bank. She knew she couldn't outrun the hounds, and there were too many to fight. She could best one dog in a fight, and maybe two, but not six. She had a fifty yard lead on the dogs when she reached the river. She plunged in and began to swim.

The dogs reached the river a few seconds later. As they ran back and forth along the bank, the tone of their baying changed.

Walking up the road a quarter-mile behind the dogs, their owners knew immediately their hounds had located a raccoon. They had hunted all night with nothing to show for their efforts. Irritable and tired, they hastened their pace, eager to see what their dogs had found. They left the road and hiked across the field, listening intently for the dog's exact location. Arriving at the riverbank, they subdued the hounds while they looked for the source of the racket. One of the men shined a flashlight up and down the river, hoping to locate their quarry.

"Look, Charlie," he said, as he pointed toward the middle of the river. He held the flashlight steadily on Mother as she swam toward the opposite bank.

"If we don't do something, that coon is going to get away."

"Not on your life," Calvin said and began driving the dogs into the water.

Two of the dogs started whining and refused to swim. Four of the hounds jumped into the water, but in a few seconds, two of them turned around and started back.

"You yellow-livered cowards," Calvin yelled from the bank. "Turn around and get that coon."

His words fell on deaf ears as the dogs continued to swim toward the men. When the first one reached the bank, Calvin kicked him hard, and the hound ran into the field, yelping and barking. The other dog turned away from the bank but went downstream instead of trying to go back across. Two of the dogs continued after Mother, but one lagged far behind the other.

The lead dog slowly closed the distance between him and the fleeing raccoon. When he reached her, he tried to get a grip on the back of her neck with his teeth. Mother turned suddenly, stuck her head under water and grabbed the dog by his throat with her sharp canines. She bit down hard and punctured the hound's trachea. The dog swallowed water and started gasping for breath.

Now he had a life-threatening wound, and he had no choice but to concentrate his energies on survival. Mother released him and continued swimming toward the bank. Now, the dog lacked strength to swim, and the current began carrying him downstream. The other dog, a slower swimmer, was still thirty feet away.

Mother knew she would reach the bank before the hound did.

As she swam, she could hear the men yelling on the other side of the river. Calvin cursed and shouted obscenities at the fleeing raccoon.

"That no-good, low-down, skunk of a coon has killed my best dog. Hand me my gun and hold the light steady."

Charlie hesitated, and Calvin jerked the gun out of his hand. Mother heard the 30-06 bark, and water splashed close to her head. She was almost to the bank, but now the current carried her downstream. Just as Calvin zeroed in on her, she passed a log lodged in the river. The angry shooter fired the rifle, and the next three bullets hit the log with dull thuds.

In a matter of seconds, the current carried the swimming raccoon downstream below the log. Again, Calvin had a clear shot. He sighted carefully and pulled the trigger. The gun didn't fire, and he heard nothing but a sharp click. He had emptied the rifle and had no time to reload.

In a fit of rage, the angry hunter threw the rifle into the river. Just as it splashed into the water, Mother reached the opposite side. Tired and wet, she climbed the bank and raced into the field.

* * * * * * * * *

As the kits swam across the river, Packy looked back constantly to make sure his charges stayed together. In his haste to reach the other side, he had gotten ahead of them again. He slowed his pace and allowed them to close the gap. For the first time in his life, he felt the weight of responsibility on his shoulders. It was a new experience for him, and he wasn't sure he liked it.

They reached the shallows and climbed the bank without incident. Packy churred for them to stay together. His instructions from Mother had been clear. He understood he should lead the family back to the elm tree, but he had a problem. They had crossed the river north of the farmhouse, landing them into strange territory. This, combined with concern for his mother, left him in a quandary. Should he wait for her, or go on. He understood his duty, but images of dogs pursuing his mother created a strange feeling in his stomach.

He gathered his sisters around him and churred for them to stay put while he investigated their situation. Disobeying Mother's orders, he walked upstream along the river. He hoped to find her after she came across. As he walked, the baying of the hounds got louder.

At the sound of gunshots, Packy stopped to listen. He had no experience with guns, but he knew the noise had something to do with her trying to lead the dogs away. At this point, he remembered his responsibility, realizing he must return to his sisters.

Reluctantly, and with a heavy heart, he turned back. Before he reached the others, he met Becky coming toward him. He growled at her for disobeying the same orders he had disobeyed. Becky followed him back, and they found Mandy, Misty and Cindy still sitting in the same place where he had left them. They exchanged greetings, and he felt a little better. He told them in raccoon language he was going to lead them home.

Feeling unsure about the proper direction, he started across the field. In a few minutes, they walked out onto the farmhouse road. He remembered seeing the road from the barn, and this reassured him he was on the right track. Making sure none of his sisters had gotten lost; he turned right and headed down the road. As they walked, he listened for any noises that might tell him something about his mother. He could still hear the baying of one dog in the distance.

Finally, they came around a curve in the road, and Packy could see the farmhouse. Dawn began to break, and he picked up the pace. A few yards from the house, he stopped and sniffed the air. He wanted to be sure humans had not returned. Thinking of the pantry and its contents tempted him to go inside. After a moment, he reconsidered. Things had changed, and humans had prowled about. Looking toward the barn, he could see the elm tree off to his left.

By the time they reached the barn, the sun had risen over the mountain. They walked around the side, and Packy saw the pole leaning against the roof. It occurred to him that he might be able to see Mother from the top of the barn roof. He churred for his sisters to wait while he climbed up. By the time he reached the top, Becky was half-way up. The others followed. They worried about their mother also, leaving Packy no choice but to include them.

Climbing to the ridge of the roof, they all sat on their haunches and looked off in the distance. The baying of the hounds had stopped. They looked upriver and along the road, but they could see no sign of Mother. The sun continued to rise, but the workmen still had not driven down the road. The kits had no way of knowing it was Saturday, and the men wouldn't return until Monday, nor did they know that two of them were upriver with a pack of dogs. Tired and sleepy but still upset, they climbed down the pole and struck off across the field toward the elm tree.

* * * * * * * * *

The second hound reached the riverbank about two minutes behind Mother. Tired from swimming and fighting the current, he sat down on the bank to catch his breath. His owner screamed at him from across the river. The dog stood up immediately, feigning interest in looking for the raccoon. He began roaming around in a small area, trying to pinpoint the direction Mother had gone.

Calvin screamed at him again, and he crossed the field hoping to satisfy his master. As he came out onto the farmhouse road, he picked up raccoon scent. He started baying and the hunters immediately recognized the pitch. The sky had gotten lighter, and the men could see without their flashlights. They walked downstream until they found a shallow place in the river. About midway, Calvin slipped on a rock and fell into the water. Wet and bedraggled, his anger at the fugitive raccoon rose again. He began yelling at Charlie to hurry.

Tired from a full night of activity, Mother's pace had slowed. Sensing a kill, the dog increased his speed. With every passing minute, the baying sounded closer, so she turned back toward the river. There wasn't a tree to climb, so she ran into a copse of elder bushes. She looked for and found a tight place between several small trees. Close enough to the river to jump in if it became necessary, she sat quietly and waited. She dreaded a fight with another dog, but she knew trying to run would be a disaster. Her breathing slowed, and some of her fatigue began to dissipate. She could tell from the baying sound the dog was closing in. She tensed her muscles and prepared to meet the hound straight on.

Long, lean and muscular, the dog ached for a fight. It was full daylight now, and he charged into the elder bushes without hesitation. Mother knew he would quickly find her. She wedged herself in tighter and waited. She knew he could only come at her from one direction. When the dog was five feet away, Mother growled fiercely. Momentarily nonplused, he growled back, trying to sound ferocious. He inched forward, thinking Mother would turn and run. He didn't know she couldn't flee. Deliberately placing herself in this position prevented an attack from the rear. The dog knew he needed to spook her into running, but he couldn't figure out how to do it. Summoning all her courage, Mother forced herself to wait.

The dog went around to the side, but he couldn't get through the bushes. The only way to get to Mother was to go straight into her face. He returned to his original spot, and after snarling and barking, he made his move. He leaped straight at her. As he charged, she lowered her head. Thinking she had given up, he jumped on top of her, exposing his underside.

As the dog tried to get a grip on her spine, Mother bit hard into his stomach. The dog screamed from pain and tried to back away. Moving backward by sheer strength, he dragged her with him. Somehow, he managed to get a grip on her and tried to break her backbone. She released her grip on his stomach and locked her jaws into his hind leg. As her canines ripped through bone and muscle, she dealt him a crippling injury. The dog released his grip and started writhing on the ground. Resisting the temptation to go in for the kill, she ran out of the bushes. Thinking the other dogs might be close behind; she headed straight for the river.

Too tired to swim, she waded in and allowed the current to carry her downstream. The cold water revived her, and she began looking for a good place to leave the river. About a quarter-mile downstream, she came to the creek where she and the kits had dug for crayfish. She knew that she had reached the abandoned farm. Fearing the other dogs would find her scent, she waded the creek until she reached the barn. She climbed the bank, and then climbed the side of the barn. Once in the loft, she worked her way back under the hay. She would not return to the elm tree until she was sure she had lost the dogs.

* * * * * * * * *

As Calvin and Charlie walked down the farmhouse road, they quarreled about trespassing on the Dills farm. Charlie thought they should get permission before hunting on the property, but Calvin disagreed.

"Possession is nine points of the law. The boss's cousin inherited the place. What does she care if we chase a few coons? Anyway, she lives in another state."

"I know that, but she still owns the property. We should get the boss to ask her. Chances are she would say yes."

"To heck with all that. My family has been coon hunting in these mountains for over a hundred years. These outsiders ain't got no right to come in here and tell us what to do."

"Well, they have a legal right. Anyway, old man Dills and his wife told us to stay off the property, and they weren't outsiders."

"Yeah, I know, but they're dead and gone. It's a whole new ballgame."

"Well, I don't want any trouble," Charlie said. "I've already paid a fine once for trespassing, and the judge told me the next violation would be thirty days in jail."

"Worry, worry. If anybody says anything, I'll tell them it's my fault. Besides, my brother is a deputy sheriff. If we have any problems, he'll get us out of it."

"The problem with you, Calvin is that you think your brother is a lawyer. Actually, he's just a deputy sheriff. He may have a little pull, but not much."

"Listen," Calvin said suddenly. "Ol' razor has that coon treed. Let's get a move on."

"How can he have it treed? He's on this side of the river."

"Then it's probably climbed an elder bush. This should be an easy kill. I'm going to shoot him right between the eyes for killing my dog."

"Where do you suppose the other dogs went?"

"Who cares? The lazy things probably went home. A couple days without food'l teach'em."

They crossed back into the field and walked toward the river. They wondered why the dog had stopped baying. As they approached the stand of elders, they heard a dog whining.

"Now what!" Calvin said.

"Sounds like he's hurt."

The hunters worked their way into the bushes. They found the dog lying on his side, whimpering and moaning.

"What's the matter, boy?" Calvin asked.

He reached down, petted the dog and then turned him on his back. Broken and bleeding, the right hind leg hung at an odd angle.

"God Almighty! That coon has killed my best dog and ruined another one."

Without further comment, he stood up, grabbed the gun from

Charlie's hand and shot the dog.

"Too bad, he was a good'un."

"Maybe a vet could have fixed his leg."

"Are you kidding? I ain't gonna spend a buncha money on a dog. Anyway, my uncle says he's got three he'll give me. You just wait, we're gonna hunt this farm out. It's got to be a she-coon with a bunch of babies. I'll bet the one we saw on the barn roof is part of the litter. There ain't been nobody around here in a couple of years. They're probably denned up in the barn loft."

* * * * * * * * *

The kits slept fitfully or not at all. Packy had nightmares about dogs chasing him in the night. It was a hot August day, and the air was still. Even the cool of the elm tree wasn't sufficient to keep down the heat. He awoke with a start, and thoughts of his mother filled his head. Careful not to wake his sisters, he crept out of the den and climbed high into the elm. He sat in the topmost fork of the tree for a while, but he couldn't see out. The dense foliage blocked his view.

Almost as a reflex, he started climbing down. He passed the den where his sisters slept, and at the bottom row of limbs, he climbed out as far as he dared. He could see a little, but not much, and only in one direction. Still frustrated, he climbed down to the ground and headed for the barn. He went back up the pole and onto the barn roof. Ignoring the heat, he sat on the ridgetop and looked in all directions. He could see no sign of his mother anywhere. Finally, the heat became unbearable, and he decided to leave.

As he started across the roof, he saw a car coming up the farm road. Fascinated, he sat down and watched. The car stopped in front of the farmhouse, and a woman got out. Holding her hand over her eyes to block the sunlight, she looked in all directions. Satisfied with her viewing, she walked onto the porch and sat in a lone rocker that stood by the door. She began to rock and sing. Packy could hear the clear pitch of her voice all the way to the barn. The sound was soothing, and it reminded him of the man who had put the pole against the barn roof.

After a while, the woman stopped singing, got up from the rocker and went inside. With nothing to entertain him, Packy suddenly realized he was still hot. He walked down the roof to the pole and climbed down. When he reached the ground, he saw his sisters walking toward him, with Becky in the lead. She churred an angry message to Packy that he had upset her by leaving them alone in the den. As if to apologize, Packy licked her face, and then did the same to each of the others in turn.

Tired, discouraged and hungry, they still resolved to find their mother. Daylight and intense heat worked against them as they struggled toward the stream behind the barn. As they came around the other side of the barn, Packy smelled his mother's scent. In a matter of moments, they all smelled her and began to churr to each other. They walked in one direction and then the other, but as soon as they walked away, the scent disappeared. Finally, Packy figured out that she had climbed up the side of the barn. Fearing for his sister's safety, he churred for them to wait until he investigated. When he reached the loft, he stared into the subdued light.

He smelled the barn owls immediately, but the smell of his mother was stronger. He looked down and churred for his sisters to come up. By the time they reached the loft, Packy heard a noise and looked around. Mother was walking toward him. Too happy to move, he sat and stared. Becky passed him in a flash with the others close behind. They gathered around Mother, and churred happy sounds. Finally, Packy came to his senses and joined the reunion. Mother finally got them calmed down, and they headed for the elm tree. In a few minutes, they were all asleep in the den.

* * * * * * * * *

Juanita Dills stood in the living room of the ninety-year-old farmhouse. The restoration had not been completed, but she could see results of her cousin's expertise. The furniture was a perfect complement to the house, but it, too, would need the services of a master craftsman. The restored staircase exuded beauty from every section as she ran her hand along the polished rail. She felt a kinship she couldn't explain, and she understood she had found a home. As she wandered through the downstairs, she pictured in her mind how the house would look upon completion.

She decided to climb the stairs to the second floor. As she walked up, she marveled that she heard no squeaking sound. The upper story would take more work, but she had known that at the outset. She hadn't quite figured out how she wanted the décor, but plans were forming in her mind. In another month, she would move in, even if her cousin had to work around her.

Juanita had decided the farm would be a half-way home for wounded and abandoned animals. She had counted nine outbuildings between the house and the barn, and they would provide a beginning. She would start out slow, and convert the buildings according to animal groupings she would house in them. She would hire two employees early on, then enlist volunteers as the enterprise grew. She would charge a small adoption fee for the animals after she treated their ills and injuries and prepared them to go back into the world.

Later, she would add a website. She would maintain an on-line list of her animals with their histories and the fee for adoption. She would solicit contributions and set up a system to make them tax deductible for the donors. Juanita also knew many elderly and low-income people could not afford her fee. To those people, she would allow adoption on an ability-to-pay basis. She would require that every person who adopted an animal to sign a contract promising to care for it. At any point, if the person no longer wanted the animal or couldn't care for it, she would take it back, no questions asked.

Central to her website, an education program would teach the proper care of animals. She knew many people who bought animals did not or could not care for them properly. Parents who bought pets for children, typically left their care to the child. More often than not, the well-meaning child left the animal to suffer or die. Part of her plan would be a mechanism to adopt these unwanted pets when the children grew up and no longer wanted or cared for them.

Juanita knew her plans were ambitious, but she was a capable woman and had confidence in herself. Fate had handed her an opportunity she couldn't afford to waste. She stepped out onto the back porch of the second floor and gazed across the fields. A hawk rode the downdrafts as he looked for a meal. Birds whistled and warbled in the trees, and a crow signaled a warning from the top of a tall maple. Across the river, the mountains stood tall and majestic, and as she watched, several small clouds drifted into view. She saw five raccoons on top of her barn and wondered what they were doing there on a hot afternoon. She knew they were normally nocturnal, and she was smart enough to know that something unusual had happened to upset their routine.

"Dear God," she said aloud, "thank you for this wonderful place."

* * * * * * * * *

The heat had finally broken, and the air had cooled to a comfortable temperature. For three consecutive afternoons, a thunderstorm had blessed the Dills farm with a rain shower. A few green spots had returned to grassy areas, and the streams had risen above their normal levels. Crayfish, frogs and other small creatures had come out from hiding to gather moisture from plants and grass. Summer wildflowers had sprung back to life, and a variety of bees resumed storing honey for the coming winter. Off in the east, dark clouds were forming a network of thunderheads, and a three-quarter moon stood high in the sky. Mother and her kits dug for crayfish in the mudflat behind the barn.

The sound of a pickup truck disturbed the night, and headlights came out of the curve north of the house. Mother knew immediately that something was wrong, and she churred for the kits to drop their food and run for the elm tree. As they climbed the stream bank, they saw the lights pass the house and head for the barn. Just as the raccoon family reached the tree, the truck stopped, and two men jumped out. The sound of barking dogs reverberated through the silence of the night.

Calvin and Charlie walked to the rear of the truck and let down the tailgate. The barking changed to howling, and Charlie banged on the side of the cage.

"Shut up, you idiots; you'll scare off every coon in ten miles of the place."

"Let them howl." Calvin said. "This is just practice. I want to see if my new dogs have enough sense to run a coon."

He opened the gate to the cage, and the hounds poured out. In their enthusiasm to get to the ground, they fell over each other as they leaped from the truck. Calvin whistled, and the dogs milled around, waiting for the signal to go.

"I wish I hadn't fed them last night," Calvin said, "but I didn't decide to go hunting until this morning. They'll only be half-interested, but they can still work their muscles."

"That suites me fine," Charlie said. "I don't like to starve dogs anyway."

"Will you get off it. Dogs are property, nothing else. When you start likin'em, all they want to do is lay around and eat. They lose their purpose."

"I suppose, but I was raised by poor parents. Sometimes we didn't have enough to eat. I know how it is to go hungry."

Calvin gave Charlie a strange look but said no more. He didn't have much sympathy for soft people. He had a deep, dark secret he had never told anyone. He enjoyed beating and killing animals. It gave him a sense of power and masculinity. Shaking his head, he gave a piercing whistle and the dogs raced off. They sat on the tailgate of the truck and watched the hounds race into the fields.

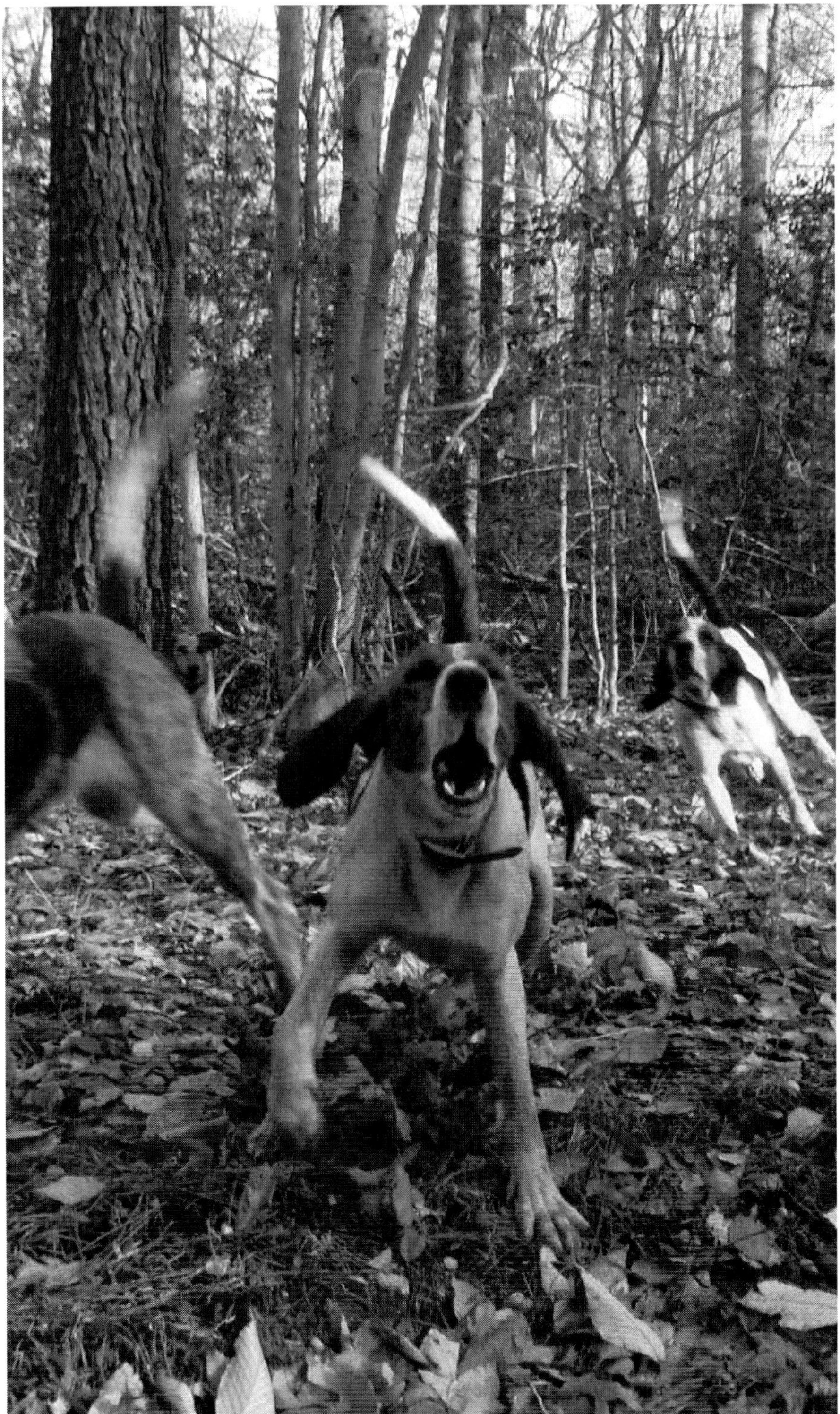

Chapter 06

MOTHER'S BANE

Calvin's hounds had little difficulty finding raccoon scent. They did have a problem sorting out old scent from the new because Mother and her kits had roamed all over the Dills Farm at one time or another. This led to several false starts. Calvin and Charlie watched as the dogs ran back and forth, hither and yon. Calvin, an experienced hunter, soon understood the dog's dilemma. He walked to his truck cab, removed four cans of beer and two sandwiches, and then came back and sat on the tailgate.

"Here, Charlie, we might as well eat while we wait. It's going to take a while."

"Is there anything we can do to help the dogs?" Charlie asked.

"Not a thing; we just have to give them time to sort it out."

After they finished their meal, the two men found two trees close together, sat down and leaned against them. Charlie talked about fishing, and Calvin talked about his love of the hunt. Neither man had any interest in what the other had to say, but it helped them while away the time. Abruptly, one of the dogs began to bay.

"That's ol' Stumpy," Calvin said. "My uncle said he was the best of the bunch, and it sounds like he was right."

They retrieved their flashlights from the truck and walked in the direction of the baying. The rim of a new moon hung low in the sky, giving no light. They shone their lights first one way and then another. Mist had settled around the farm, creating an eerie look in the flashlight beams. As they walked beside the barn, Calvin's head struck the pole that Luther had placed there for Packy. After voicing a string of curses, he kicked it loose from the ground. It landed with a thud in the grass.

As they rounded the barn, the din of baying dogs became louder. Their flashlight beams only penetrated a little way into the fog. As they approached the elm tree, they could see nine hounds milled around, falling over each other trying to climb up. Stumpy stood on his hind legs with his front feet against the tree, his cut off tail visible in the light. His high pitched baying reverberated across the farm. The two men walked up to the elm.

"God Almighty, look at the size of that tree," Charlie said.

"It's a big one, all right," Calvin replied.

"How we gonna get a coon up in there?"

Calvin stepped back and looked up. "I got a chain saw in the truck."

"Are you kidding? That thing is four feet thick. You ain't gonna cut that with an eighteen inch chain saw. Besides, it's bound to be over a hundred feet tall. If you fall it on the barn, the Dills woman will sue us both, not to mention all the racket you're gonna make. No telling who might show up to check out the noise."

"Well, I ain't leaving 'til I get me a coon," Calvin said.

"Think of something else. Maybe there's a ladder in the old barn."

"The boss left his long ladder behind the house. The one he brought to work on the roof with. You go get it. I'll stay here with the dogs and make sure the coons don't get away."

Charlie walked out into the fog, and the darkness swallowed him. Fifteen minutes passed, and Calving became impatient. Just when he had decided to go see what had happened to his companion, Charlie walked out of the gloom.

"What took you so long?" Calvin asked crossly.

"Are you kidding? This thing's too long for one man to carry. I had to drag it. Anyway, it wasn't where you said it would be."

"Never mind, let's get it against this tree so I can climb up and catch me a coon. I'll toss'm down to the dogs. That'll be their reward for a night's work."

The two men pulled the sections apart, snapped the clips into place, and stood the ladder against the tree. It was just long enough to reach the bottom row of limbs.

"Make sure you hold this thing steady, Charlie. The last thing I want to do is fall off and break a leg or something."

"Not to worry. If you fall off, it won't be my fault."

Calvin climbed up two steps and stopped. Charlie reached around him to steady the ladder. He placed his feet on each side and braced himself. Calvin resumed climbing. Every three or four rungs, he stopped, shone his light up into the tree, and then resumed climbing. When he reached the bottom row of limbs, he pulled himself up until he could stand and hold on to the next row. Again, he splayed the light around in the tree limbs. He could see no sign of any raccoon.

Charlie called from down below. "See anything?"
"Just a bunch of limbs and leaves, but they're up here somewhere. The dogs know it, and I know it."

As Calvin continued climbing, he felt around both sides of the trunk as he went. Finally, he located the hole where Mother and the kits sat huddled together. Holding on to the limbs above him, he worked his way around to the same side near the hole. Holding the flashlight steady, he peered around inside.

Six pairs of coal-fire eyes peered back at him.

"I found the little devils," he yelled down to Charlie.

"Can you get to them?"

"Of course I can. Just hang on. I'm gonna toss them down to the dogs like I promised. You're in for a treat but don't get too close. You might get bitten during the fracas."

Calvin reached around to his back pocket and removed a pair of heavy leather gloves. Leaning against the tree to steady himself, he put them on. He squatted down on a pair of limbs and held on to the tree trunk with his left hand. He laid the flashlight between two limbs so that the hole was clearly visible. He moved suddenly, reached in and grabbed a handful of fur. As he pulled his arm back, several sets of teeth locked into his forearm above the glove.

Calvin gave a loud scream and jerked back. He let go of the trunk and reached for the offending raccoons that had bitten into his arm. In the same motion, he tried to stand up, and his feet slipped off the limbs. He grabbed for another limb, but it was too late. As he fell, the raccoons turned loose and jumped. Their agility and sharp claws prevented them from falling, and the limbs easily held their small weight.

Knowing that the ground was fifty feet away, Calvin grabbed for anything and everything. As he turned upside down, his right arm slammed against the tree trunk. Bones snapped and he screamed.

As he fell twenty more feet, his left leg caught between two large limbs that crossed each other. He shrieked again as friction stripped away skin from his leg. His boot lodged in the limbs, and he stopped abruptly. Calvin hung upside down, thirty feet above the ground. He had a broken right arm, and bone protruded through the skin. He screamed for Charlie to help and then passed out.

* * * * * * * * * *

As Calvin fell, Packy, Becky and Mandy turned loose of his arm. They jumped onto limbs and crawled away. When the hand had reached into the hole, each had retreated as far back in the den as possible. Mother had placed herself in a protective stance in front of her kits. As the gloved hand gripped Mother by her fur, the kits had been in perfect position to bite Calvin's arm, and they never hesitated.

As soon as Mother determined the danger had passed, she churred for the kits to follow her. She climbed higher into the tree until she found another suitable hole. They all managed to squeeze in. They huddled together and wondered at the commotion below. The kits shivered from fright, and Mother tried to comfort them. They knew the humans below had them cornered in the tree as long as they and their dogs remained on the ground below.

Mother began churring a quiet noise in her throat, the equivalent of a human mother singing a lullaby. The kits began to relax, snuggling closer to their mother. After a while, she stopped churring and began licking their faces. Eventually, she stopped, but none of them slept. In about an hour, they heard the noise of a motor vehicle below. Mother hoped they weren't trying to climb the tree again.

* * * * * * * * *

Daylight penetrated the mist as a rainbow trout jumped in the river's rapids. The barn owls returned to their nests in the barn rafters. A woodchuck sat on a pile of stones and sniffed the air for predators. Parked next to the barn, an ambulance and a police car glistened in the morning sun. Several people watched as a fire truck backed up to the elm tree.

Calvin had regained consciousness, and a deputy sheriff tried to keep him calm as he talked from the ground. Finally satisfied with the truck's position, the fire marshal signaled for the driver to stop.

Leaving the engine running, the driver got out and went around to the side. He watched as two EMT personnel climbed into the bucket. Satisfied they had buckled in safely, he climbed into a chair behind the cab. He move levers until one of the people, a woman, told him to hold his position and lock it in.

They began the tedious process of removing Calvin from the tree. The man gripped Calvin's torso while the woman sawed on a limb. Shortly, the limb broke away, and they lowered him into the bucket.

"Stop cursing," the woman said to Calvin. "You're lucky to be alive. You could've fallen to the ground and broken your neck."

"You ain't the one that's hurt. The pain is killing me."

"Stop whining. We'll have you down shortly, and then we can give you some medication for the pain. You'll need it for the ride to the hospital."

"Yeah, yeah," Calvin said. "Get on with it."

"I gotta tell you, though," the man said, "you're the first coon hunter I ever pulled out of a tree."

"Yeah," the woman said as she winked at her partner, "It was really good of you to give the raccoon a sporting chance."

****

Defying raccoon instinct, Mother didn't move the den location after the attack by the hunters and their dogs. By the day after Calvin's accident, life returned to normal for the raccoon family. Except for continuing work on the house, the Dills farm was quiet. The workmen came on weekdays, did their jobs and went home. At night, the farm belonged to the nocturnal animals while the day creatures slept in their burrows and dens. Mother and her kits came and went without interruption, and life was good.

On the third Monday of August, Juanita Dills drove to Atlanta and stayed for three days. On the way back, she stopped at the library and borrowed several books on the habits of animals in the wild. Determined to learn as much as possible, she used her spare time to study the flora and fauna indigenous to the area. If possible, she intended to achieve a balance between her domestic animals and those already inhabiting the farm. She didn't want to save one group of animals at the expense of another.

While her cousin, Bob, worked on the house, she went for walks around the farm. The fresh air and open spaces breathed new life into her psyche. Until the death of her husband, she had worked long hours for fifteen years. She badly needed to exercise her body and refresh her spirit. Her husband, a veterinarian, had taught her much about animal diseases. Together, they had built a thriving business caring for pampered dogs and cats. Now, she would use her experience to help less fortunate animals.

Juanita learned quickly that more animals roamed about during the night than in the daytime. She had stopped at a military supply store and bought a good pair of binoculars and an expensive night-vision device. In the early morning and late evening, she sat on her second-story porch and enjoyed the surrounding scene. She watched fox, deer, wild turkey, hawks, herons, ducks and buzzards. She was also lucky enough to see a wild hog with piglets, a wildcat and a few geese.

As it turned out, she couldn't see much at night. After watching an opossum and catching a glimpse of a raccoon, she decided the house wasn't the best location for viewing. On her last night, she moved her operation to the barn. She took a thermos of coffee and a plastic chair to the barn loft. She soon learned nocturnal animals didn't move around much until well after dark. By midnight, she had watched a plethora of creatures.

The barn owls adjusted to her presence and began moving about freely. In a dead tree near the barn, a barred owl sat poised to strike at his prey. She watched him scoop up meadow mice in his deadly claws, then fly back to the tree and eat them in one or two bites. A hapless young rabbit made the mistake of crossing the meadow in plain view of the owl. A few minutes later, he filled the stomach of the hungry predator.

She watched a mother opossum and her young tear off sections of an old stump and devour the beetles they dug out of the rotten wood. A skunk family trotted out from behind a rise in the field and began to scavenge for food. A wildcat slinked toward the skunks looking for an easy kill. Thinking he could surprise them by staying downwind, he inched toward the busy family. The skunk mother spotted him and raised her tail. Moving swiftly, he tried to run out of range before the spray hit him. He didn't make it, and now he would smell terrible for several days. He skulked away to look for an easier meal.

At 2:00 a.m., Juanita moved her chair to the other end of the barn loft. She turned her night-vision scope toward the stream running by the barn and across the field to the river. Excitedly, she watched six raccoons dig for crayfish in the mudflat. They seemed to work as a team and would often bring food to each other. In a short time, she figured out that the larger one was the mother and the others were her young. Sometimes they would take their crayfish and dunk it into the water, then move it back and forth in a washing motion. Other times, they would just dig the crustacean out of its hole, rip off its claws and eat it.

She became so fascinated with watching the raccoons that time slipped away from her. Just as daylight crept across the mountains, mother and her kits stopped their feeding and climbed into the field. They disappeared from her view, and she quickly moved to the other end of the barn. She sat quietly and waited. Soon they came back into view and headed for the elm tree. When they reached the base of the tree, they huddled in a group for a couple of minutes, and then the mother stood up on her haunches and sniffed the air. Satisfied that her family was safe, she gave the okay to climb the tree. Soon they disappeared from sight. Now, she knew where they lived. She realized the tree hadn't been just a refuge from hunters; it was their home.

****

Toward the end of August, late-planted corn had reached its final stage of ripening. The season had arrived when raccoons increase their feeding, and Mother had not forgotten the garden on the Mason farm. By Thanksgiving, she and her kits must increase their weight by thirty percent to prevent starvation through the winter months. One hot afternoon, Mother dreamed she sat in a field devouring ears of fresh corn.

Just after dark, she churred for the kits to stay home. She walked south along the river, ears of scrumptious corn still prominent on her mind. She continued south until she came to Rose Creek. She turned left and followed the stream until she could see the front of the Mason house. She left the stream and made her way to the barn. She climbed up the side until she came to a hole at the edge of the roof. Climbing up on top, she walked to the other end where she had a perfect view of the house, outbuildings and garden. She sat there for a long time watching the farmhouse. She finally decided farmer Mason and his dog were asleep, so she climbed down and headed for the garden.

Ripe for picking, six rows of corn grew on the lower side. Mother walked into the middle of the patch and climbed a cornstalk. Halfway up, it broke with her weight and she landed in the soft dirt. Three golden ears lay on the ground in front of her. She ripped off the shucks, pulled back the silk and tasted the delicate flavor. She ate ravenously. When she had finished the three ears, she moved to the next stalk. Halfway down the row, she became sated and quit. Happily, she had a full stomach, and she headed for home.

When she reached the elm, she found an empty den. She knew Packy had led them off somewhere to feed. She realized they were old enough to go off on their own, but it still made her uncomfortable. With each passing day, they required less from her. Also, her sense of responsibility had diminished as they matured. Even so, she could not go to sleep until she located them. She followed their scent and found them in one of the outbuildings. Packy had discovered another source of food.

Unknown to the raccoons at the time, Juanita Dills had left an ample supply of dog food. She had selected that particular building because if had a small entrance hole on the side. She knew a raccoon could get through but a bobcat or a dog could not. The ever-curious Packy had found it in less than twenty-four hours. Instinctively alert, they smelled and sensed Mother's presence before she came into the shed. They greeted her happily, and then went back to eating. Full of corn, Mother sat on a wooden table and watched them feed. She knew no words, of course, but her chest filled with pride, knowing her months of training had produced results. They were all healthy and happy, and no mother could ask for more.

****

The next night, a summer storm kept the raccoons holed up in their den. Just before dawn, they went to the mudflat and dug for crayfish. The storm had driven the crustaceans deep into their holes, and the family had little to eat. Daylight caught them still looking for a meal. Saturday had arrived again, and the construction crew working on the Dills farmhouse had stayed home. Mother and her kits searched the other sheds for more dog food, but found none. At mid-morning, they returned to their den, hungry and grouchy. They finally dropped off to sleep, and didn't wake up until well after dark.

When they came out of their den, the night air had cooled, and they had an easy climb down to the field. Mother led them downriver to Packy's swamp. There, they split up and searched for frogs and salamanders. Still recovering from the storm, many of the nocturnal creatures remained in their holes. Two hours before daylight, Mother made a decision to take the family to Mason's garden. She followed the same route she had taken the last time. The kits sat by the barn while she went up on the roof to observe the farm for potential danger.

Upon arriving at the garden, they found that the farmer had

picked most of the corn. Still, there was plenty left to fill the family's stomachs one more time. They worked their way through the rows, breaking down stalks that appealed to them. Darkness began to slip away, and still they continued to feed on the corn. Like a herd of starving swine, they couldn't get enough of the sweet delicacy. Losing all track of time, they didn't hear farmer Mason come out onto the porch.

The barking of the big brown dog startled them out of their reverie. When Mother churred her emergency growl, the kits became alert immediately. It was now full daylight, and the farmer could easily see downhill into the garden. The ringed tails stood out between the corn stalks, and his anger rose immediately.

"Sic'em Buster," he said to the big brown dog.

The dog leaped off the porch and headed downhill across the yard. He ran across the gravel road, down the bank and into the garden. His big feet threw dirt in all directions as he dashed through the potato and squash plants. Farmer Mason ran across the yard where he could get a better view, yelling at the dog as he went.

Packy immediately decided to divert the dog away from his family. He ran toward Buster, and then veered left toward the barn. The dog was too big and clumsy to check his speed quickly enough to follow Packy. He tried to turn, but when he realized he had miscalculated, he increased his speed again and headed toward Mother and the other kits. Becky and Misty ran toward Rose Creek, hoping to reach the willow trees before the dog overtook them. Cindy and Mandy ran diagonally across the garden, heedless of their destination.

Temporarily startled by Packy's bold attempt to lure the dog away, Mother finally sprang into action. She ran directly into the dog's path. The dog crashed into her sideways, and they both tumbled end over end. Mother recovered quickly, but ran slowly so the dog would follow. Mindless of the damage to the garden, the dog raced after her. She glanced back, saw the kits had left the garden, and headed toward the farmhouse. At the driveway, she turned right and ran toward the well house. She circled the building with the dog in hot pursuit. Finding no hole to get inside, she dashed around the back of the house. She turned the corner and ran into the front yard, intending to run into the pasture.

She could feel the dog's hot breath as she reached the edge of the yard. She made a quick right turn and headed for the largest of the walnut trees. As her sharp claws dug into the wood, the dog bit at her tail but missed. Racing up the trunk, she climbed until she reached the third row of limbs. Panting heavily, she crawled out onto a limb and lay down, hugging it tightly. The dog barked loudly and attempted to climb the tree. He managed to go about three feet, and then fell back.

Mother's panting had subsided somewhat, and she looked down to check for danger. The farmer had disappeared, but his wife stood on the porch. The dog backed away from the tree, sat on his haunches and barked at Mother. The farmer reappeared on the porch with a rifle in his hand. His wife pointed toward the raccoon lying on the limb. Farmer Mason raised the gun and sighted down the barrel. Mother heard a loud noise, and felt a sudden pain in her side. She tried to crawl back toward the tree trunk. Everything went black, and she lost her grip on the limb.

    Darkness consumed her brain, and she fell into a bottomless abyss. She felt nothing when her body landed with a thump in the yard. The dog rushed over and began to sniff and paw at the lifeless form. Farmer Mason handed the gun to his wife and walked down the steps into the grass. He turned Mother over with his foot. Seeing she was dead, he picked her up by the tail and carried her toward the garden. He laid Mother on the ground next to the potatoes and walked to the tool shed. In a few moments, he returned with a shovel and began to dig.

                                            ****

    Packy made it safely to the barn. He ran inside, climbed up the side of a horse stall until he reached the loft. Thinking about his family, he sat in the opening and looked toward the farmhouse. He could see the farmer standing on the porch with something in his hand. Packy saw the puff of smoke and heard the noise. He watched as the farmer walked into the yard and disappeared from view behind the chicken house. His heart sank as he saw the farmer walk toward the garden carrying Mother by the tail. The dog followed, barking and yapping.

    Packy didn't know what had happened, but he understood something was terribly wrong. He knew his mother should not be in the farmer's hands. He wondered where his sisters had gone. He felt pain in his stomach, and his chest ached. From where he sat, he couldn't see what the farmer was doing; another building stood between them. He climbed back down by the horse stall and ran toward the garden. About half-way, he climbed a hickory tree. When he could see the farmer, he moved back into the foliage until he was out of sight. Mother's body lay on the ground a few feet away. Packy couldn't understand why she didn't get up and run away. This caused him great anxiety and confusion.

The man finished digging, and then removed his hat and wiped his brow. For a short time, he stood and looked at the hole as if in deep thought. Finally, he walked over to Mother's body and picked it up by the tail. It hung at an odd angle as he walked toward the grave. Placing the other hand under the back, he lowered it into the hole. Picking up the shovel again, he began to fill the hole with dirt. About every four shovelfuls, he would stop and use one foot to tamp down the dirt. When he had finished, he jumped up and down with both feet until the mound was level with the garden soil. As he started to walk away, the dog went over to the grave and started digging.

"Get away from there, Buster," farmer Mason said.

The dog continued to dig. Packy heard the shovel clang, and then the dog yelped in pain and ran across the yard and under the porch. Farmer Brown went back and repaired the hole the dog had dug. When he had finished a second time, he placed the shovel handle across his shoulder and walked toward the house, whistling as he walked.

****

Packy sat in the hickory tree all day. When he became uncomfortable, he would shift positions or move to another limb. Sometime in the afternoon, the dog came out from under the porch. He walked over to a container of food on the porch and ate until he had cleaned the pan. He walked around the yard, found a shady spot and lay down. Several cows came down to the lower side of the pasture and began grazing along the fence. The dog got up and watched for a while but made no attempt to bother them. Bored with the cattle, he walked down the road and disappeared around a curve.

A groundhog came out from under one of the buildings and climbed up on a pile of wood. He tested the air for scent. Satisfied the dog had left, climbed down from his perch and ran toward the barn. Two squirrels chased each other around the yard and into the walnut trees. Three crows flew into the garden and began pecking at something in the dirt.

Just before dark, the dog returned, and the farmer called him into the house. At the corner of the yard, a security light came on, illuminating the surrounding buildings. Somewhere down by the river, a loon called to its mate. A gray and white cat sat hunkered over a mole hill, listening for underground movement that signaled an easy catch. Finally, tiring of the wait, he ran across the yard and crawled through a hole in one of the outbuildings. At twilight, a red fox dashed across the pasture and disappeared into the trees behind the barn. Darkness blanketed the farm, and mist began rising from the river. One-by-one, lights went out in the farmhouse. Patches of clouds floated across the sky, white at first, but soon followed by darker ones that changed to black as the night progressed. Heat lightening flashed from cloud-to-cloud, illuminating the sky around towering cumulus masses.

The wind began to rise, and leaves and limbs began to move and shake with its force. By midnight, black clouds consumed the sky, and great jagged streaks of lightening raced to the earth in less time than a heartbeat. Thunder boomed across the valley and echoed against the mountains. Suddenly, the sky opened up and rain came down in great droplets, giving birth to a massive thunderstorm. In the upper pasture, an aging apple tree crashed to the ground, felled by violent turbulence. Down the road from the Mason farm, lightening struck a transformer, and the security light went dark. Water ran in rivulets down across the pastures, creating temporary streams that poured into the river. The clouds raced across the sky, and the storm ended as suddenly as it began. Still, Packy sat in the hickory tree, frozen in time and space.

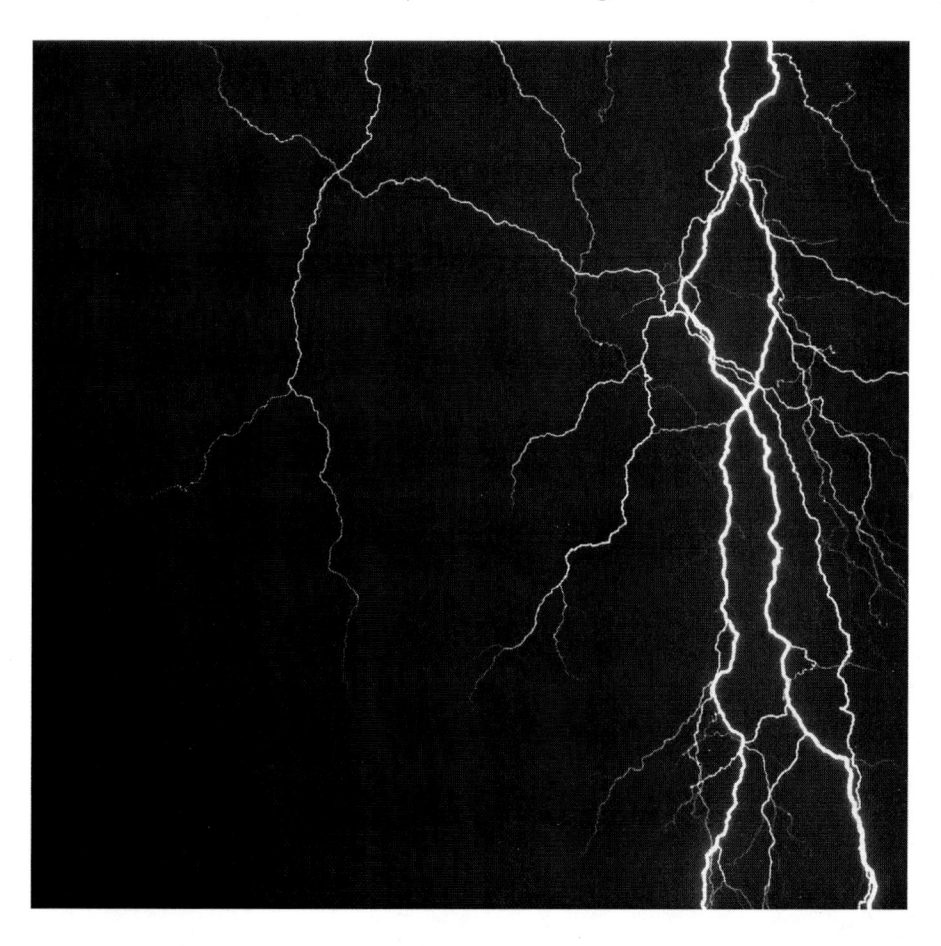

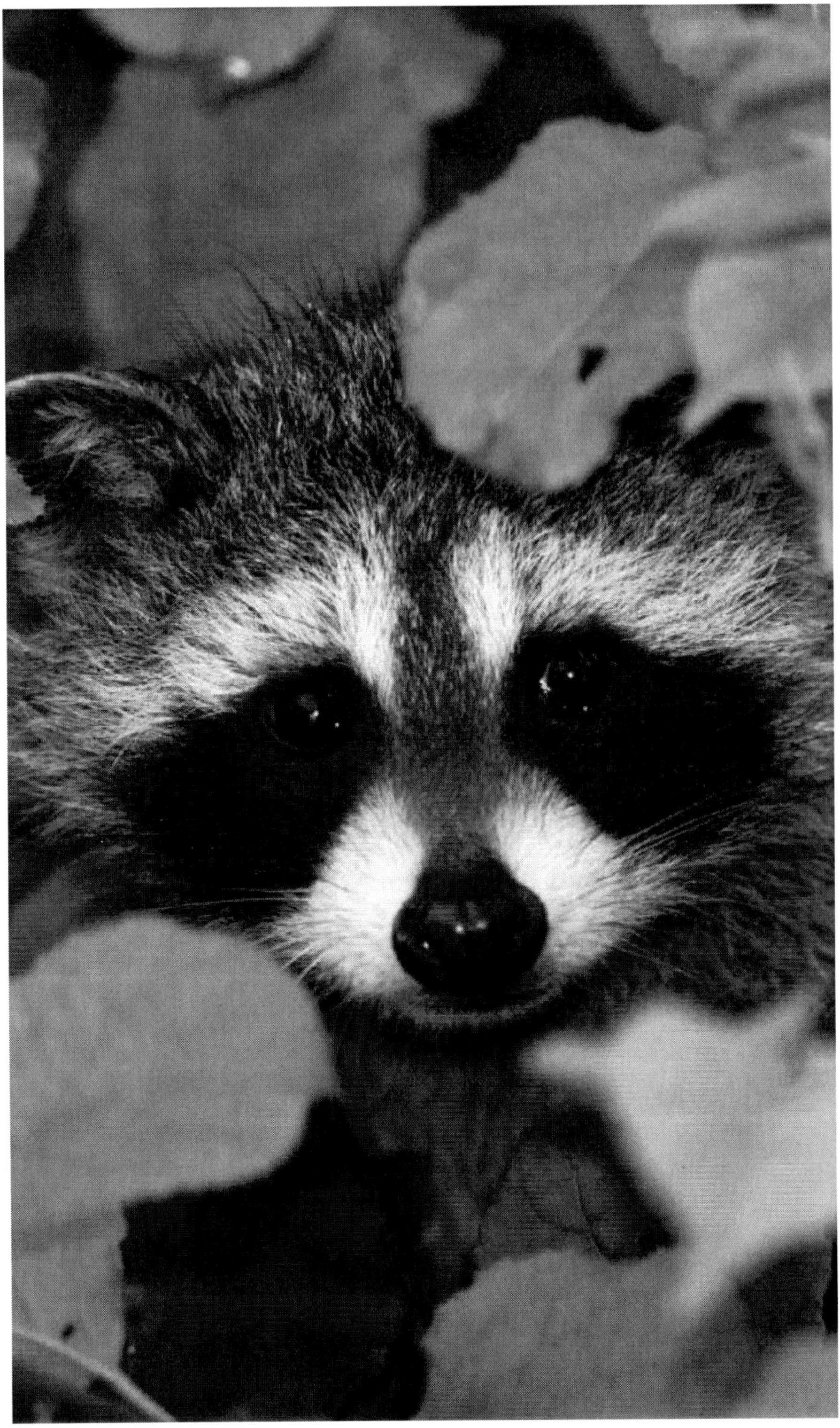

Chapter 07

MIDNIGHT MEMORIAL

The storm passed, and a brilliant, full moon shone down on the Mason Farm. Packy recovered from his stupor and gazed out over the surrounding landscape. He had no knowledge of how much time had passed, and hunger pangs gnawed at his stomach. Zombie-like, he climbed down the hickory tree and headed for the garden. Giving little thought to farmer Mason or his dog, he crossed the stream and walked downhill past the yard. A cat fight erupted near the well house, but Packy didn't hear it. As he turned the corner past the garage, heartache consumed him, and a strange ringing filled his ears.

    He stopped momentarily, unsure of his purpose or direction. Finally, he forced himself to continue, and he walked through black dirt between the grass and the upper potato row. Although he had only observed farmer Mason from a distance, he knew exactly where to find his mother's grave. He walked around and sniffed for her scent, but the storm had eradicated it. Still, he knew she was there in the ground.

    As he dug into the wet earth, Mother's scent increased with each scoop of dirt that he removed. Finally, his paw scratched across her fur, and he stopped digging immediately. The sight of her body enervated him like a will-of-the-wisp, and his remaining energy dissipated like fog in a hot sun. For a while, he sat motionless, too weak to continue. His mouth felt terribly dry and thirst consumed him. From somewhere in the depth of his heart, he summoned enough strength to walk back to the stream and drink from the icy brook. The cold water stopped his shakes, but not his dread, and he returned to the garden, still apprehensive and discomforted.

Shaking Mother's body with his paw, he growled for her to rise from the earth. He sat silently and waited, hopeful at any moment, the sweet melody of her churring would greet him. In his misery, he fantasized that she was licking and nuzzling his face. In a dream-like trance, he sat for a long time, unaware of the moon's passing across the sky. Although death is not a concept in raccoon language, Packy fully understood his beloved mother would never walk again. A cry emanated from his throat, long and mournful. After a while, his throat began to hurt, and he lay down in the hole he had dug.

The uncovered part of Mother's body felt cold, but for the moment, he could touch her, and this gave him an abnormal sense of comfort. There was nothing he could do to bring her back, and he sensed it to the bottom of his raccoon heart. As the night mist rose in the garden, droplets of water formed on his face and fur. His stomach hurt from lack of food, but he ignored the pain, oblivious to the world surrounding him. When daylight began to lighten the sky, he climbed out of the hole and stared at the mountains, seeing only his mother in his mind's eye.

Without conscious thought, he started piling dirt on his mother's body. Each scoop of dark earth wrenched at his heart and drained his life-force, but he pushed himself to continue. After he had finished, he stretched out on the grave like a protective blanket on a sleeping child. In his anguish, he didn't hear farmer Mason open the door and turn out the dog. The big brown dog might not have discovered Packy, had he not gone to his usual place to relive himself.

As he finished, he looked toward the garden and saw the black and white animal lying on the ground. With a ferocious growl, he raced toward Packy, mindless of the consequences. Despite his mental agony, Packy's instinctual alarm system prodded him into action. He had no time to run, so he turned quickly and prepared to fight. The dog's speed and weight knocked Packy over into the potato vines. The dog finally stopped in the third row. Ripping plants from the ground as he turned, he rushed back to assault the raccoon.

As the attacker reached him, Packy suddenly dropped on his back and grabbed for the dog's throat. He missed and sank his canines into the dog's chest. With sheer effort and his superior weight, Buster managed to shake Packy loose. Refusing to run, Packy stood his ground. The dog knocked him over again and tried to get a grip on Packy's stomach with his huge teeth. Buster knew he had the advantage, but in his inexperience, he didn't know how to use it. Packy wriggled out from his grip, but the dog attacked again. This time, he sank his teeth into Packy's side.

As Packy groaned with pain, another set of teeth attacked Buster from the rear. Becky had him by the tail, and she bit down hard. A few seconds passed, and three more sets of teeth bit at the dog from all angles. Mandy, Cindy and Misty threw themselves into the fight. Surprised momentarily, Buster lost his grip on Packy.

The dog fought with all his strength, but the kits showed no mercy. Frustration at heir mother's death made them ferocious fighters. Even though the dog outweighed them all by thirty pounds, winning eluded him. They bit, clawed and fought until the dog released Packy and sought to escape. Breaking loose from his adversaries, he ran for the house.

Realizing they had won, the kits regrouped in the garden. Ecstatic at seeing his sisters, Packy temporarily forgot the pain of losing his mother.

Relieved the farmer had not killed their brother also, the girls crowded around Packy in a show of their love and affection.

After calming down, they sat in a circle around Mother's grave. If a human had heard them, he would have thought they were talking. They churred, chirped and growled over the whole range of raccoon language to express their grief and sorrow. Packy knew his sisters had spent the night near the garden, even though they had no way of telling him. For the moment, they felt the closeness that any family feels during the grievous loss of a loved one.

Mandy, who sat facing the farmhouse, saw farmer Mason come out on the porch. She churred a warning, and they all ran toward the willow trees along the bank of Rose Creek. Once undercover, they regrouped, and Packy counted heads. His sisters sat expectantly, waiting for him to lead them home. Ignoring his exhausted condition, he accepted the lead and started out. Working his way north, Packy stopped at the swamp for a daylight feeding. The crayfish had buried deep in their holes, so the kits searched for salamander and frogs. None of them had eaten for two days, and they gorged themselves on anything they could find. When they left the swamp, they had not satisfied their hunger, but at least the pains had died down to an acceptable level.

By the time they reached their elm tree, the noon hour had arrived. They climbed into the den and made themselves comfortable. They missed Mother's warm body and her gentle caresses. None of them slept because their heartaches were too great. They didn't understand the loss of their mother, but they knew she had gone forever. It was a time of great confusion and the first major tragedy in their lives. For an animal living in the wild, every day is a struggle to survive, but some days are harder than others. Now, the kits had to fend for themselves. Mother's loving guidance no longer existed, but she had instilled ability and courage for survival in each of them. They snuggled closer together, grateful they were not alone.

****

  A huge moving van followed Juanita Dills' car up the road. Once at the farmhouse, the men started unloading furniture and household goods. An organized woman by nature, Juanita knew where to place each item. The men quickly assembled beds and unpacked dishes. Two hours later, the truck pulled away from the porch, leaving Juanita to complete her arrangements. Relieved to find her purchased items matched her inherited furnishings, she could now relax and begin her animal adoption business. First the dream, then the planning, and finally, reality had arrived. She made a mental note to call her cousin, Bob, and ask him to recommend someone to become her first employee.

  She walked out on the porch and stared into the distance. Daytime temperatures had started to drop, and early autumn smells permeated the air. She had a lot of work to do before winter came. She looked up at the porch ceiling and wondered how to remove the spider webs. She walked down the steps and stood in the yard. One of Bob's men had mowed the grass, and the smell of wild mint made her think of her childhood visits to the farm. Nostalgia consumed her momentarily, and she wondered where the years had gone. In her minds eye, she could see the farm in all its glory, well-tended and productive. Now, it had fallen into disrepair, aging and useless. But not for long, she promised herself. In the coming months, she would restore everything as part of achieving her goals. The farm would hum with activity, giving purpose to her plans and dreams. She missed her husband terribly, but she had resolved not to wallow in self-pity.

  She walked around the house, making mental notes and thinking aloud. Every few yards she would stop and write on her pad. She left the pad on the porch and walked toward the outbuildings. Now that she had committed her ideas to paper and placed the land deed in her safety deposit box, she felt better. She had been so lost in her thoughts she almost walked into the nearest outbuilding, one of three chicken houses. Long and narrow, they stood silently, waiting for their next owner. As she walked through, she realized she had planned well, but she must expand her limited knowledge. Next week, she would drive to Ohio and visit Ann Cowell, her new-found friend, who operated a successful animal adoption business.

She intended for her cousin, Bob, to remodel the buildings to house her new animal tenants. He had reluctantly agreed to go to Ohio with her, so he would have first-hand knowledge of the necessary renovations. This was not his usual line of work, but she had pressured him until he caved in. She had learned quickly that he took pride in his workmanship; just the type of builder she needed. He had some difficulty understanding why anyone would spend so much time and money on abandoned and unwanted animals. She remembered from childhood experiences how he cared about animals, and she reminded him of the time he had swam into the river to rescue his dog. He might be rough around the edges, but hidden beneath his male ego lived a caring person.

****

Farmer Mason took great pride in his garden, and he visited it daily. He and his wife picked beans, gathered okra and squash, pulled the remaining corn, and finally dug the potatoes. The third morning after he buried the raccoon he had shot out of the walnut tree, he found a dead crayfish on top of the grave. He scratched his head and wondered why the crustacean had crawled all the way from the creek to the garden. He picked it up and examined it, wondering how such a healthy-looking specimen had died. Somewhat perplexed, but not concerned, he laid it back where he found it.

On the fourth morning, he found another one. It lay about four inches from the first and appeared to be in fine condition, except it was dead. He asked his wife to come to the garden, so he could share the mystery. They could figure no practical reason for it, except someone or something had placed it there. When, on the fifth day, he found a third one, his curiosity reached a fever pitch. Maybe one of his friends was playing a practical joke on him, he thought. That night, he found a convenient hiding place and prepared to sit and watch until he discovered the prankster. At 3:00 a.m., tired and sleepy, he went to bed. The next morning, the number of crayfish had not increased. He put the problem aside, and gathered the last of his melons.

The next day, another crayfish appeared, and the grizzled old farmer decided to get at the root of the matter. His rustic carport stood only thirty feet from the garden. He cleaned out the overhead storage space and cut a large hole in the back. Just before dark, he pushed up an old mattress and pillow and made himself comfortable. He placed a bottle of water and a flashlight by his bed and prepared for a long night. He dozed off several times and finally decided his sleepiness had cost him the opportunity to solve the mystery of the multiplying crayfish.

Finally, in the light of the full moon, he saw a young raccoon cross the garden from the Rose Creek side. He watched intently, wondering what vegetable the thief was after, since he had already gathered all the corn. He scarcely dared to breathe, knowing the slightest noise would scare the raccoon away. As he continued to watch, the animal approached the grave, and he could see that it had a crayfish in its mouth. He concentrated so hard on the one raccoon he failed to see the other four until they began crossing the open potato mounds.

They all sat by the grave in total silence for a long time. Finally, the raccoon with the crayfish placed it on the ground next to the remains of the other dead crustaceans. The farmer could stand it no longer, so he pointed his flashlight through the hole and turned on the beam. Five pairs of coal-fired eyes gleamed in the night. Like startled deer, they sat mesmerized in the yellow light. Although he had not brought his gun, it occurred to him that he could easily shoot all five of them. Judging by their smaller size, he figured they were the offspring of the female he had killed in the walnut tree. He turned off the flashlight, and continued to lay silently.

He pressed the illuminate button on his watch to check the time. When he looked back, the raccoons had disappeared. Stiff and tired, he climbed down from his perch and walked to the garden in the moonlight. He shined his light all around the area by the grave. He counted the crayfish, although he already knew there would be five. Something tugged at his heart, and for the first time in his life, the old farmer felt sympathy for a wild animal. He wondered if he had found something unusual, but he had no way of knowing. He turned off the flashlight, and walked back toward the house. "Ain't nobody gonna believe this," he muttered, as he climbed the steps onto the porch.

****

Life was hard without Mother, but the kits adjusted and survived. Packy was the undisputed leader, not because he was male, but because he had leadership abilities and the other kits deferred that role to him. In this respect, animals are no different than people. Some are leaders, but most are followers. Despite her small size, Becky became second in commend. She was fearless in tight situations, and she was not afraid to challenge Packy should the need arise.

Despite all this, she had great affection for Packy, and she was always the first to snuggle up close to him at sleep time. They had always been a close family, but now they were closer. They had to fend for themselves without adult guidance, and they knew it.

On their nightly hunting trips, they stayed close together, often churring their position to the others. Although they were at the age where raccoon kits wander off by themselves, they seldom did. The lingering depression over their mother's death increased their loneliness, and the desire for each other's company manifested itself in everything they did. On one occasion, Packy led them across the river to search for new food supplies. They found some corn in the field where they had first encountered the dogs, but the kernels had hardened and the taste was bland.

They crossed the road and went into the woods. Just when they were about to turn back, Cindy and Misty smelled a pleasing scent in the air. They began to search for the source. Mandy, always hungry, scurried up a sourwood tree. A lightening strike had split the tree open and honey bees had made it their home. Honeycomb ran the length of the split, and sourwood honey filled the combs. Like a group of teenagers who had broken into an ice cream parlor, the kits gorged themselves on the rich-tasting nectar.

In the pitch black of night, the bees could not see as well as the raccoons. They fought in vain as the hungry predators consumed their winter's stores. By now, the raccoon's coats were thickening in preparation for approaching winter weather. For the most part, the bees stung in vain, although Packy and Mandy suffered facial stings. Even so, they ignored it and continue to eat. By the time they climbed down the tree, Packy had a lump on his jaw, and Mandy had a swollen eye. Every other day or so, the kits revisited the tree until they consumed all of the honey. Finally, the bees abandoned the tree and went elsewhere to restart their lives.

Many hazards Mother would have known to avoid, the kits had to learn anew, and sometimes the hard way. The leadership role matured Packy rapidly, causing him to cease most of his adolescent foolishness. Still, he possessed a raccoon's natural curiosity, and he investigated everything he didn't understand, but with greater caution. Also, he had four siblings to protect, and like his mother, he would not hesitate to sacrifice his life in their defense, should it become necessary.

The kits had discovered the honey tree on a new moon; that is, the moon was dark because the earth obscured it from the sun. Although the kits could still see in the dark, they could not see as well, and risk of predators and other dangers increased during that time. Some predators detect their prey by smell, and their nose guides them in the darkness. One dark night, the five kits stood off a wandering bobcat that would have surely killed a lone adolescent raccoon. Also, he was in familiar territory, and the kits were not.

As they returned home from their nightly hunt, they had spread out about twenty-five feet apart. The bobcat approached Becky downwind, thinking he could grab her in his mouth and disappear into a laurel thicket before the others realized what had happened. He underestimated the warning system Packy had established among them. He passed close enough to Mandy that she smelled him. She churred a warning, and the others responded immediately.

Becky never saw the cat; she only knew to react. She crouched low and ran toward Mandy. When the cat reached her, she had moved just enough to spoil his attack. Instead of grasping her body in his teeth as he intended, her thrashing tail blinded him and spoiled his aim. By the time he made a U-turn for a second attack, four other raccoons were closing in to defend their smallest sister. Misty and Cindy were closest and they moved in as a team. Mandy, normally the slowest of the group, moved with surprising speed and agility.

Packy, out in front, was farthest away. By now, he could run faster than almost any adult raccoon. He dodged bushes and plants as he charged in the pitch black of the night. Just as the bobcat reached Becky for the second time, four other kits rushed in from three directions. In a fearless rage to protect their sister, they bit and clawed as soon as they touched strange fur. Becky, went down on her back, but managed to get a grip on the cat's front paw. Like farmer Mason's dog, they taught the hungry wildcat that there is strength in numbers. It only took him a minute to realize he was no match for five scrappy kits. The surprise attack completely terrorized him, and he ran blindly into the night.

The kits had had enough excitement for one night, but they were to endure one more scare. Exhausted from a night of foraging and the bobcat fight, they had relaxed their normal vigilance. The road they had to cross to get to the river was a paved highway. There was little traffic during the night, but an occasional vehicle did drive by. Several nights before, they had seen an oncoming car just before they reached the pavement. They hid in tall grass and waited until the vehicle had disappeared around a curve down the river. This night, they all crossed the road at the same time, only a short distance from the upriver bend.

Suddenly, a speeding pickup truck came around the curve with its lights on bright. For a moment, they all froze where they stood in the road. Packy was the first to come to his senses, and he churred the danger signal. Four of them dashed to the edge of the road. When Packy looked back, he saw Cindy still standing where they had left her. He turned back and rushed to her. He churred the danger signal again, but her fear kept her from crossing. There was only one thing he could do, and he did it. Quickly dashing behind her, he bit her as hard as he could. She screamed in pain and dashed blindly ahead.

Packy had no time to follow her, so he raced to the other side of the road. The driver, in an apparent attempt to hit him, veered into the left lane. The only thing that saved him was his reserve of adrenaline that poured into his muscles. The truck was going so fast the pressure wall of air blew him over. Tumbling end over end, he landed in a drainage ditch. When he looked up, four concerned faces peered down at him. Becky made a light churring sound in her throat and Packy responded. Looking cautiously down the road, they crossed again. By the time they swam the river and walked across the fields, they were one tired family. The first light of day erupted into the sky as they passed the barn. They had a good day's sleep for the first time since Mother's death.

****

A few days later, Packy and his sisters decided to cross the road again. Undaunted by their close calls with the bobcat and the speeding truck, they set out. Refreshed from a good day's sleep and driven by their cravings for more honey, they left the elm tree under a brilliant, star-studded sky. A circle around the moon portended rain, but the kits had no knowledge of folklore. They felt energized, and they raced along the riverbank until they found a crossing to their liking.

As usual, Packy was the first to reach the other side, and he waited patiently until the others swam up to him. Learning from their mistakes, they walked below the road until they reached the middle of the straight-away. From their new vantage point, they could see down the road in both directions for a considerable distance. When they were sure no cars were approaching, they dashed across the road like soldiers patrolling in enemy territory. They all waited their turn until Packy churred for them to cross. When one started out, there was no turning back. They dashed headlong to the other side, confident their new technique would allow them to cross in safety.

Once on the other side, they began a methodical search for another honey tree. They were so intent on finding honey, they lost track of time. They inspected stumps, fallen logs, damaged trees and a myriad of other places where a wayward group of bees might take up residence. They made occasional stops to eat other things they found to their liking. At one point, they chased a half-grown rabbit for several minutes. They were a stubborn group, and it took them a while to admit the rabbit was too quick, and they were never going to catch it. Even a concerted effort to encircle the rabbit ended in failure. The frightened creature dashed between Becky and Mandy and disappeared into the night.

In the middle of a copse of blueberry bushes, they found a wild turkey hen with several chicks. Packy and Misty each captured a chick before the birds could find enough room to fly away. In a few moments, they could hear the mother hen calling to her missing offspring. Becky and Packy devoured his kill while the other three ate Misty's catch. Now, full of meat, the search for honey had lost some of its significance, and their thoughts turned to home. Instead of following their scent back, Packy decided to take a short cut. The waning moon told him the night was coming to an end. They were still a long way from home so he quickened the pace.

By the time they stopped for a short rest, they realized it would be daylight before they reached the river. From there, it was still an hour's walk to the elm tree. As they topped a ridge, they came upon a strange object in the middle of a small clearing. Tired as they were, raccoon curiosity dictated they investigate. They walked around looking and smelling. As soon as they got close, a delicious odor emanated from the object. Packy could detect a slight smell of human, but it wasn't enough to make him unusually suspicious. Upon approaching the object, they could see the food inside.

Packy churred for the others to stay back while he inspected for possible danger. He sat on his haunches, and using his sensitive fingers, touched the slats. The metal felt cold, and he recoiled momentarily. Nothing seemed to move, and he ventured another touch. Soon, he was feeling all around the object. He walked around to the other side and looked in again, this time from a different angle. Now, he was downwind from the food and the scent was almost overpowering. He salivated as he thought about how good it would taste. As he worked his way around to another side, he saw an entrance.

Approaching cautiously, he eased his head inside for a better look at the food in front of him. Still suspicious, he backed out and walked around the cage again. His sisters moved closer, also attracted to the smell. Again, he churred for them to stay back. Additional inspections revealed nothing dangerous, and he approached the entrance again. He went in and sat just inside the entrance. He edged closer to the food and sniffed all around it. Finally, he touched it with his tongue. The taste was as good as the smell.

Deciding the best plan of action was to take the food outside, he picked it up in his mouth and started to turn. As he did, he heard a snapping noise, and the metal door of the cage clanged shut. He laid the food down on the metal floor and pushed against the door with his head. It didn't give, and Packy knew the strange device had him trapped. His sisters approached the cage again, but he hissed at them to stay back. Intimidated momentarily by the strong warning, they backed several feet away.

Using his paws, Packy shook the bars of the door. When that didn't help, he tried each side in turn. For several minutes, he tried a variety of ways to escape from the cage, but nothing worked. Suddenly, he felt claustrophobic, and he shook the bars violently. Still, nothing helped, and he sat down to let the feeling pass. Finally, he marshaled his thoughts and began inspecting the door. He felt around the wires and springs trying to figure out how the door opened, but the solution evaded him. At the top of the cage, a long wire attached to a spring and pulley.

When Packy pulled, the door moved, but it wouldn't open. He tried using both paws but when he pulled on the wire, his fingers slipped along the smooth surface. He couldn't get enough grip to release the spring that held the door in place. When he looked up from his labors, he saw his sisters gathered around two sides of the cage. In their own minds, their concern for their brother negated his orders. Becky stood on her haunches, and reached inside, trying to help free her beloved brother.

Fearing she would become trapped, he hissed at her to move back. This time, she ignored him, defying his orders. Realizing he had no choice, Packy sat back and watched Becky. She had smaller paws and fingers, and she had better dexterity than Packy. She felt, pulled and pushed to no avail. Following Becky's lead, Misty and Cindy moved to the other side. Another wire ran across the top and attached to the other side of the door. Working together, they tried several times to make the door spring open.

As the kits worked, they failed to notice the night had passed. Beams of sunlight passed through the trees and illuminated the clearing. The metal of the cage gleamed in the sunlight. As Packy watched his sisters, an idea formed in his mind. He churred for Mandy to pull on the door. As Cindy and Misty played with the door mechanism, Mandy sat on her haunches and pulled with all her might. Still, nothing worked. Packy moved to the back of the cage for a better view of his sisters' efforts.

The sun climbed up in the sky, and the temperature began to rise. Tired and sleepy, the kits continued to work diligently. At one point, Misty and Cindy pulled on the wire, and Becky fooled with a mechanism in the back of the cage where the wire ended. Mandy continued to pull on the door. Just as they were about to give up and rest for the tenth time, Mandy pushed on the door instead of pulling. As Becky felt along a lever at the end of the wire, something snapped and the door sprang open.

The spring action was so strong it knocked Mandy backwards. The lever pinched Becky's paw, and the quick movement of the wire startled Misty and Cindy so badly that they lost their grip. For a moment, they all forgot the goal was to free Packy from his prison. He rushed through the door so fast he ran into Mandy who was just getting up from her fall. Collecting themselves, they all hurried from the clearing and ran into the woods.

When Packy was sure they were free of danger, he stopped so they could rest and calm down. They all churred, licked and touched. Packy knew they were too far from home to attempt a daylight journey. Together, they began to look for a place to rest for the day. They came to a small stream that ran down the mountain. Dehydrated from their ordeal, they drank their fill of water. Next to a small waterfall, Becky found a hole large enough to accommodate all five of them. They crawled in, made themselves comfortable and dropped off to sleep. For the first time in their lives, the kits slept the day away, two hour's walk from home.

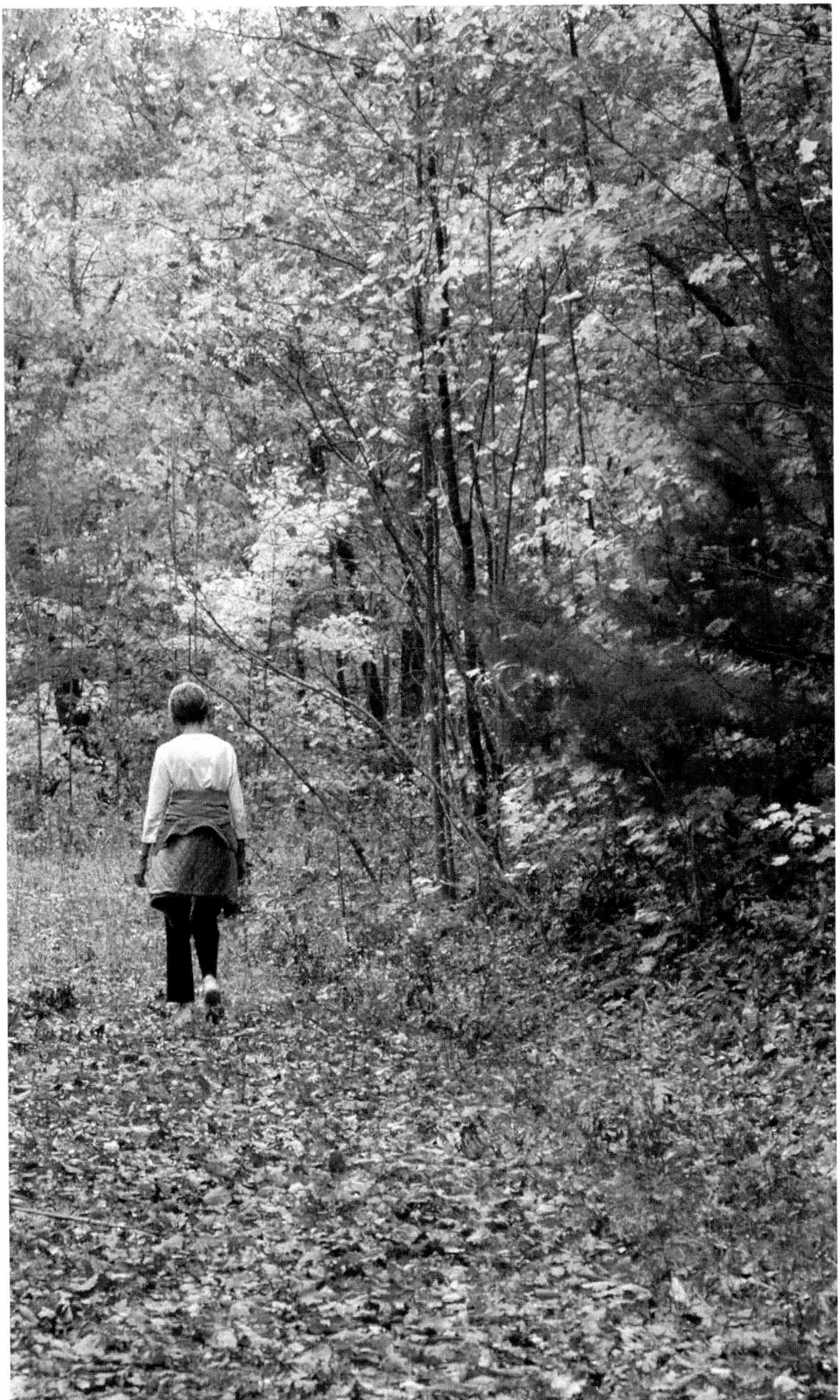

Chapter 08

PAYBACK

Autumn arrived with all its resplendent beauty and delightful smells. Heavy rains, followed by unseasonably dry weather, had combined to create unusually beautiful colors. Farmers and ranchers had cut, baled and stored their winter's supply of hay to feed their cattle and horses. Despite changing weather, a bountiful harvest had filled freezers and pantries with vegetables and fruits. Now, huge tractors crawled across harvested fields as farmers prepared the ground for next year's crops. For animals living in the wild, Mother Nature had begun the process of modifying their bodies according to their species. Without knowing why, raccoons, foxes and groundhogs began eating more, and their coats began to thicken and change color. Squirrels stored nuts at a furious pace, and birds gathered in flocks to prepare for long southerly flights.

Along with her animal projects, Juanita Dills had hired part-time laborers to clean up the Dills farm. Weeds had taken over most of the pasture land, and she set about to restore the grasses. She understood that large amounts of weed killer could be harmful to both plants and animals. She contacted the department of agriculture for help on how to achieve the most beneficial balance. She also determined to leave hedgerows and grain strips for protection and feeding of small animals. Each day she reserved a few minutes to study their habits, verifying what she had read in books and manuals represented a modicum of truth. Farming in its literal sense didn't interest her, except for the feeding of her animals, both domestic and wild. She believed this concept to be unique, a model for the future of animal husbandry.

On the first Tuesday morning after Labor Day, Luther Loggins showed up on Juanita's doorstep. When she came to the door, he respectfully removed his cap, and with a tremor in his voice, asked her for a job. After stuttering and shuffling his feet, he said her cousin, Bob Pendergrass, had mentioned she would be hiring someone to help care for her adopted animals. After several direct questions, she learned he had arranged for the young raccoons to climb down from the barn roof.

"Why did you have such a hard time admitting you helped them? Why do men have such a hard time admitting to kindness?"

"Well, ma'am, I spent time in prison, and in that institution, one doesn't show any sign of softness."

"Okay, let's just say for the sake of argument I believe you. Why do you want to work for me? You'll have to work hard, sometimes long hours without a lot of pay."

"Well, the truth is," he said, as he got redder by the minute, "because of my prison record, I haven't been able to find a permanent job. Your cousin, Bob, said he would vouch for me based on the temporary work I've done for him. I'm probably being presumptuous by coming here, but I want to start my life over, and I need a place to begin. Bob, er...Mr. Pendergrass, said you might be the best thing that ever happened to me."

"Well, I don't know about that, but I would hate to stand in the way of a man trying to restart his life. Let's see if you mean what you say."

For ten minutes, she fired one question after another at the embarrassed man.

"Okay," Juanita finally said, "I'll give you a try on two conditions. The first is that you do nothing to violate your parole. No guns, no hunting, no nothing. The second is that you stay away from that worthless friend of yours who fell out of my tree. You think you can agree to that?"

Luther broke out into a broad smile. "You have my word as a man, ma'am. I'll certainly agree to your conditions. When can I start?"

Juanita pointed across the yard. "You see that long chicken house over there?"

"Yes, ma'am."

"Go over there. I'll meet you in ten minutes. And stop calling me ma'am. You make me feel old. My name is Juanita, and you have my permission to address me by my first name. In fact, I insist on it."

****

At first, the appearance of humans on the Dills farm made Packy and his sisters nervous and apprehensive, but they adjusted quickly. After a few days, they concluded the woman who walked the farm at night did not pose any threat to them. One night, while digging for crayfish in the mud flat, Packy heard her singing as she sat in the barn loft. He stopped his digging and listened to her for a few minutes. Looking back, he saw that his sisters had stopped also. Something new had invaded their environment, and they didn't know what to make of it.

Although the kits could see her clearly, they didn't know she couldn't see them. After completing her third song, she stopped and listened to the night sounds. After a while, she climbed down and walked along the creek side of the barn. Intrigued by her singing, Packy decided to follow her. With his sisters trailing close behind, he rounded the barn just in time to see her walk up onto the porch of the farm house. Creeping along a few yards at a time, they climbed on a woodpile for a better view.

Juanita sat in her chair by the door and began rocking. Soon, she started singing again, and her clear soprano voice carried into the night. Drawn to her like a magnet, Packy inched closer to the farmhouse. Just as the kits reached the edge of the yard, the moon came out from behind its cloud cover. It only took a moment for Juanita to spot their movement. Continuing to sing, she watched them closely as they sneaked across the grass. Bolder than the others, Packy climbed the steps and sat on the end of the porch. Becky, Mandy, Cindy and Misty sat at varying distances in the yard.

Like a captivated audience who had paid to attend a concert, the kits watched and listened intently. Juanita was smart enough to know if she moved, they would panic and run. She was sure they were the same raccoons she had seen climb the elm tree. She wondered why the mother wasn't present with them. After a while, she stopped singing and just sat quietly. The kits continued to sit for a few moments, but they finally realized there would be no more music, so they turned and walked away.

Juanita resolved to make friends with them, starting with the bold one that sat on the porch. She didn't know if their visit was a fluke, or if they would return again. She had read that some raccoons liked music, and she wondered if it might be her singing. She would research what raccoons liked to eat and see if she could attract them onto the porch with food. At first, she had decided to buy a dog for protection against burglars and other such ilk. Now, she knew she wouldn't. Her desire to befriend wild animals seemed more important than owning a dog. She would buy a gun instead and get Bob to teach her how to use it.

****

With each passing autumn day, the kit's voracious appetite continued to dominate them. Driven by Mother Nature's mandate to gain weight for the coming winter, they increased their food hunting hours. They ate things hey might not have eaten in early summer. Field mice, voles, moles and other small animals came under fierce scrutiny, as Mother's orphans plied the fields searching for starches and proteins. They consumed nuts and berries where they grew, and ate fruits where they lay. Of course, they ate the best of everything, damaging briars, plants and vines in the process. Daylight often found them gorging on some delicacy at the edge of fields and gardens. Their wariness increased with age, and they rarely ate anything more than fifty feet from cover.

Packy weighed in at eighteen pounds, twice as much as Becky at nine pounds. The other's weights fell in between, with Mandy running a close second to Packy. Despite the drought, Mother Nature had provided an abundance, although fruits and berries were typically smaller than normal years. Oaks had weathered the season well, and as if returning nature's kindness, acorns littered the forest floor. The starchy fruit provided a back-up diet for the kits, giving them something to eat on days when they found little of anything else. They soon learned white oak acorns had the best flavor, and they scoured the forest looking for them. Misty and Cindy found a copse of the tall trees along the crest of a ridge, and it was there where all five kits congregated for their daily fix of starch.

Almost as if to exact vengeance, they made the Mason farm one of their favorite feeding grounds. Wary of the old man and his clumsy dog, they took turns at watch while the others fed on his harvest. In the middle of the night, they climbed his apple trees and pulled the ripe fruit from the stems where they grew. Half-eaten apples littered the ground under each tree. Just at the height of their ripening, they pulled his grapes from the vines on the night before he planned to gather them. The next night, he lay on the roof of his house, holding his twelve-gauge shotgun at the ready, hopeful that he could shoot the 'pesky critters' under the vines.

Fifty yards from where the old farmer lay in waiting, the kits raided his corn crib. Packy sat on the roof of the crib and watched, while his siblings foundered themselves on the wholesome kernels. Two days later, the farmer went to the crib with a wheelbarrow, as part of his plan to fatten his hogs before slaughter. When he opened the door to the crib, a large pile of half-eaten ears poured out onto the ground. That night, he decided to sit on top of the chicken house, hopeful to end the rampage of the raccoons. His vigil served no useful purpose except to keep the chickens awake. At dawn, he climbed down, sleepy and angry, only to find that the rest of his grapes had disappeared in the night.

The next night, the old man awakened to the sound of squawking chickens. Thinking this was the night to end the destruction, he rushed to the henhouse with Buster following close on his heels. He found nothing out of the ordinary except a building full of nervous hens. At daylight, he walked out on the back porch to stretch. As he looked at the thermometer nailed to a porch post, he glanced into the back yard. The tops of two of his beehives lay on the ground. He rushed up the hill to examine the damage, swatting his way through thousands of angry bees. When he brushed the bees away and looked down into the hives, he found that most of his honey had disappeared. The raccoons had devoured the lighter-colored sourwood honey, leaving the darker clover honey for the old man and the bees.

In farmer Mason's mind, this was the last straw and enough was enough. He called his son, who lived on Snow Hill Road. That evening, three men arrived in pickup trucks, with several dogs in the back of each truck. Just after dark, the men gathered in the Mason yard, and released the dogs. Raccoon scent abounded, and the dogs ran in all directions. After an hour of following trails, all of the dogs ended up at the same place, on the bank of Rose Creek. After much confusion and howling, the men directed the dogs down both sides of the creek all the way to the river. One man took six dogs and drove around the road to the other side of the river. Soon, the dogs picked up raccoon scent and followed it, only to end up back at the river again. At midnight, the hunters gave up and loaded the dogs back into the trucks. Between 3:00 and 5:00 a.m., Packy and his siblings finished off the last of farmer Mason's honey.

****

Somehow, it seemed ironic that the first animal to arrive at Juanita Dills' shelter was a four-year old raccoon named Scrappy. Agnes Norman had found him in a stump before he was old enough to eat solid food. Widowed and lonely, the aging woman had bottle-fed him until he could eat from her hand. Domesticated and happy, he had adapted to living in a house and eating food from her table. He was the nosiest animal she had ever seen, and she enjoyed watching his antics as he prowled around her property. Eventually, she gave him his freedom, thinking he would leave, but he didn't. She made a door for him to enter and leave the house. He often wandered off at night, returning at daylight to sleep the day away in the box she had provided. On those occasions when he awoke in the daytime, he followed his mistress around the property, nosing into everything that interested him. Sometimes, he would fall asleep in her lap while she stroked his fur. When she tired of holding him, she would lay him down on the couch. The only sound that seemed to bother him was the barking of her neighbor's dogs.

One day, the dogs got out of the lot, and Scrappy took offense to their presence on the Norman property. He took on all three dogs in a horrific fight. He killed the biggest dog with a bite to the jugular and mortally wounded another. The old woman beat the remaining dog away from Scrappy with a broom. Even though he had won the fight, the price he paid took a toll on his health and well-being. In addition to several scars, he lost one eye and his right front foot. Agnes took him to a veterinarian and then nursed him back to health. After that, his missing foot restricted his walking distance, and he stayed close to home. His name had been Prowler, but Agnes changed it to Scrappy in honor of his bravery in the fight with the dogs.

At the age of ninety-one, Agnes died in her sleep. After a futile effort to revive her, Scrappy wandered off in search of food. The old woman's daughter found her body when she came to see why Agnes wasn't answering the telephone. Due to his disability and domestication, Scrappy couldn't feed himself properly. He returned home to find his mistress missing. Sick and lonely, he lay down to die. The daughter found him one morning when she stopped by to check on her mother's house. Not wanting him, but not wanting him to die either, she drove him to Juanita Dills' farm after hearing about it from a friend.

Juanita pulled off the ticks, de-wormed him and cured his mange. She could do nothing about his old injuries, but she nursed him back to health for the second time in his life. She kept him in a pen especially designed for sick animals and fed him until he had gained several pounds. She tried to find him a home, but no one wanted a disabled raccoon. Having failed to adopt out her first animal, she turned him out of his cage to see what he would do. He followed her to the house and sat on the porch waiting for a handout. Soon, he had the run of the farm and she turned her attention to other animals that now arrived on a daily basis.

****

As much as Juanita Dills wanted to befriend Packy and his sisters, she decided digging crayfish out of their holes wasn't her cup of tea. Instead, she bought some catfish fillets at the market and kept them cold until she was ready for her experiment. To keep her scent off the fish, she wore rubber gloves while she washed them. At 5:00 p.m., she took them out of the refrigerator, cut them into small pieces, and then allowed them to come up to room temperature. At 10:00 p.m., she put several on the porch rail, placed one at the edge of the yard, and so on, until she had a trail of catfish back to the house. She turned off the lights, found a comfortable chair and watched out the window. At midnight, she went to bed disappointed, but not surprised. At daylight, she found all the fish had disappeared in the night. She thought the raccoons had eaten them, but she also knew an opossum, a fox, or a stray cat could have been the culprit.

She waited until the weekend to try again. On Saturday, she repeated her experiment, but this time, she took an early nap and placed the fish on the rail at midnight. Instead of going back into the house, she sat in her rocking chair on the porch and started singing. In the middle of her third song, she glanced to her left and saw all five raccoons sitting in the yard. By the middle of the next song, the largest one sat on the porch ten feet from her chair. Strangely, he didn't seem interested in the fish, and she wondered if he could smell it. As she looked left again, she saw the others eating fish in the yard. When they finished eating, they followed the first one onto the porch, and then sat down directly behind him.

She decided to stop singing and see if they would run away. Scarcely daring to breathe, she sat silently and waited. Finally, the smallest of the group climbed up on the rail and began to eat. Three of the others followed shortly, but the largest one continued to sit and watch Juanita. All four ate nonchalantly, as if the human on the porch didn't exist. It occurred to her the large one was standing guard to make sure she didn't harm the others. While the others ate, the smallest one climbed down, carrying a large piece of fish in her mouth. She stopped about halfway between her and the guard and dropped the fish on the porch floor. She made some kind of noise, and then walked to the largest one and sat down. He immediately turned around and went to the fish while the little one stood guard. Soon, the raccoons had eaten all the fish, leaving Juanita with nothing to keep them on the porch except her singing.

     She sang a song while they watched, then stopped and began talking in a quiet, low voice. As she talked, they cocked their heads and stared, but made no move to run away. She started singing again, then leaned forward and held out her hand. They backed up several feet, stopped and continued to watch her movements. Now, she realized she had brought them as far as she could in one night. She sat silently and waited. After a few minutes of mutual watching, the kits understood the food and singing had stopped. They turned and walked silently off the porch, and then disappeared through the boxwoods at the edge of the yard. The temptation to follow them was hard to resist. She wanted to confirm this really was the group living in the elm tree. After a moment's reflection, she decided it was too much of a gamble and could result in loss of trust she had gained so far. Happy she was making progress; she went inside and climbed the stairs for a short night's rest.

****

     Somewhat perplexed by the overtures made by Juanita Dills, Packy and his sisters enjoyed her presence, nonetheless. To date, their experience with humans had resulted in danger or death, so it seemed quite natural to have misgivings about the woman who gave them the delicious treats. Certainly, she seemed friendly enough, and they did like the strange, soothing noises she made. If only they could understand what she was trying to say, the relationship might go better. Still, she had no smell of fear or distrust, and she made no sudden moves that frightened them.

Also, she didn't have a dog around the house to chase or scare them. It seemed most other humans they had encountered owned at least one dog, and all of them disliked raccoons. Even if they weren't mean, they still raised a ruckus and alerted their human. At their worst, they ran in packs, barking and howling for hours at a time. They chased after raccoons purely for the fun of it or to please their humans. Regardless of their purpose, this posed a danger. The kits only understood killing for food. This was nature's way, the law of survival.

The next evening, Packy woke up early. His sisters were still sleeping, and not wanting to disturb them, he slipped out quietly. Besides, he wanted to check and see if the woman had put out any more fish. As he rounded the backside of the barn, he met Scrappy almost head on. On a couple of occasions, Packy and his sisters had met other raccoons on their feeding excursions. Contact was usually minimal, often a churr or two, and then going their separate ways. This was the first time Packy had met another raccoon on the Dills farm. Contrary to meetings in the wild, this one was friendly from the outset.

Packy sat down and stared, not sure what to make of this stranger. Scrappy churred a friendly greeting, and then limped toward him. Packy shrank back, but made no attempt to fight or run. Packy didn't understand about disabilities, but he soon figured out this stranger was no threat. Deciding his new found friend was hungry; Packy churred his best invitation, turned and walked toward the creek. He climbed down the bank, and then turned to see if Scrappy followed.

He didn't. Packy churred again, in his friendliest tone. Scrappy came to the bank and looked down.

He started down, but lost his footing and tumbled end over end. At the bottom, he stood up, and to keep his dignity intact, pretended nothing had happened. He followed Packy to the mud flat, then sat and watched while Packy dug up a crayfish and ate it. Packy churred for him to join in. Scrappy tried digging with his one foot. Without both feet, he couldn't scoop and soon gave up the effort. Now Packy understood. His friend couldn't dig, and he couldn't see well either.

Packy went to another hole, dug out another crayfish and brought it to his new friend. He set the crustacean down in front of Scrappy, backed away and waited for him to eat. Using proper raccoon protocol, Packy didn't kill his gift, but gave his guest the right to do it. As Scrappy reached out with his foot to hold it down, the crayfish made a dash for the nearest hole. The startled raccoons watched in amazement as the crustacean disappeared. Again, Packy realized that Scrappy could not hold down live food with one foot.

Not to be outdone, he went to the hole and dug out the crayfish again. This time he killed it before giving it to Scrappy. The happy stranger consumed it immediately. And so it went. Packy dug out several more and gave them to his friend. After a while, they both tired of crayfish digging and eating and lay down for a rest. Soon, the sky darkened, and thunder began to roll in the east. A large bolt of lightening startled them out of their reverie, and they headed back in the direction they had come.

Packy climbed up the bank near the barn and turned to watch his friend. Scrappy couldn't climb the bank. As rain started falling, Packy churred to encourage him. The bank was just too steep for Scrappy to climb. Packy climbed back down and churred for Scrappy to follow him. Leading his friend east along the creek, he soon came to a more gently sloping bank. Packy climbed up, and this time, Scrappy was able to follow. Turning south, they slogged through wind and driving rain.

By now, Packy knew Scrappy couldn't keep up with his normal speed, so he slowed down. Stopping every few yards, he waited until Scrappy reached his side. Soaked to the skin, both raccoons fought their way through the downpour. Upon arrival, they sat just inside the barn door and waited for their fur to dry. After a while, the storm moved on, and Packy decided he should check on his sisters. He stood up, churred a greeting to Scrappy and headed toward the elm tree. About half-way, Packy looked back. He saw Scrappy limping toward the chicken houses and wondered how his new friend had survived.

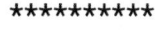

****

Juanita Dills and Luther Loggins had agreed his working hours would be from 7:30 a.m. until 5:00 p.m. This was the first time in his life Luther had ever had a say in the hours he worked. The woman expected him to be productive, but she was fair and kind and often brought him a dessert to go with his lunch. He tackled the job with enthusiasm, often arriving well before 7:00 a.m. On a recent trip to Atlanta, Juanita had bought a variety of cages and had them delivered. Luther built others as time and facility permitted. One end of the building served as an aviary, housing a variety of birds, from domestic to the exotic. Parrots, parakeets and canaries warbled, squawked and whistled. Strangers came and went, sometimes taking a bird home, sometimes not.

In the other end of the building lived a strange mixture of four-footed creatures. Pot-bellied pigs relaxed in their pens, ignoring a monkey that chattered and pulled at his bars. An iguana sat on a limb, shaking his head back and forth. An ocelot paced her cage, hoping for freedom that would never come. A German shepherd mother suckled six pups while she stared at a mixed Siamese and Persian cat three feet away. All of them had been someone's pet at sometime, and their loneliness and frustration showed on their unhappy faces. Ironically, Luther understood. He had been lonely all his life, and prison had been the worst. So it was understandable he developed a natural affinity for the plight of his charges. As luck would have it, Juanita had picked the right man for the job.

At first, she had trouble making him understand the importance of proper diets for each breed and species. Feeling sorry for them, he tended to overfeed, thinking they should have all they could eat. Patiently, she explained to him they were no different from people when it came to eating the right amount at the right time. As each new breed of bird or animal arrived, she developed a diet tailored to its specific needs, including the proper amount, based on its weight and general health. Once he understood, Luther followed her directions to the letter. She found a supply house that would deliver and taught him how to order by telephone and computer.

Luther became a quick study, taking over duties as fast as Juanita could teach him. With her encouragement, he enrolled in night school and began work on completing his high school education. Before long, he was instructing new owners in the care and feeding of their pets. Each person signed an agreement that he or she would care for the animal or bird and give it a proper diet. The agreement included the right to return the pet at any time with no questions asked. The new owners automatically became lifetime members of Juanita's pet recovery project, and she boldly asked them to volunteer time and money whenever possible.

Before long, Luther had two part-time assistants. Juanita developed a set of rules all volunteers had to agree to before she allowed them in the adoption buildings. She and Luther trained them to clean and care for the adoptees just as they would care for their own pets. The work was hard, and one of them quit. By the next week, another volunteer replaced her, and this one stayed on. Before long, it was obvious Luther had obtained one of his goals. He had a purpose in life.

****

Lately, Juanita had been too busy to play her fish game with the kits, but now that Luther had assumed many of her duties, she had more time for herself. She laid the catfish pieces out as she had done before, and sat in her rocking chair to wait. It came as no surprise when Scrappy showed up to dine on her bait. She gave him his fill, then took him to his cage and locked him up. She went back to the house, replenished the fish, sat down and began singing. By the third song, the kits showed up, and as usual, the bold one came on the porch first. This time, they were less nervous about her presence. They practically ignored her as they followed the trail of food toward her chair. Despite their increased boldness, she soon found they would come no closer than ten feet.

Having gained confidence, she created a new game to make them more comfortable in her presence. She decided to tie a piece of string to a fish and pull it toward her, hoping they would follow. As luck would have it, she couldn't find any string, but she did find a length of small diameter rope in one of the sheds. Omitting the use of her gloves this time, she punched a hole in the fish, inserted the rope end through the hole and tied it back. Again, she sat on the porch and waited. As Packy approached the fish, she pulled it toward her. Instead of following, as she hoped he might, he sat down and studied the situation.

Juanita pulled the fish a little closer to her. Packy made a sudden dash toward it, but instead of grabbing the fish, he grabbed the rope. As she continued to pull slowly, he pulled back. Surprised at his strength, she pulled him toward her. At about ten feet, he turned it loose and sat down again. When she pulled it all the way to her chair, he sat immobile, staring directly into her face. Trying not to make a sudden move, she tossed the fish toward the others, rope still intact. They made no move toward the fish, but Packy backed up, and grabbed the rope again. She had no way of knowing they had been feeding on crayfish and weren't hungry. They made no move toward the fish, but Packy backed up and grabbed the rope again.

Thinking he wanted to carry the fish further away from her, she let go of the rope. To her surprise, he walked down the rope to her end and pulled it almost to her feet. He dropped it, and then went back to the other end and picked it up, fish and all. She immediately realized he wanted to play tug rope. She picked her end up, and Packy began trying to pull his end away from her. She allowed him to back away a few feet, and then she pulled him toward her again.

After a few minutes, Packy dropped his end of the rope and churred something to the others. Becky immediately went to the rope and picked it up. She played the game with Juanita for a short time, and then dropped the rope. As soon as she did, one of the others picked it up. The game went on for two hours, and it seemed to Juanita they would never give up. Finally, she tired of the game and laid the rope down, hoping they were ready to quit, too. Leaving the remaining fish tied to the rope, they all turned and walked away. When they reached the steps, Packy turned and churred at her.

"Good night to you, too," Juanita said.

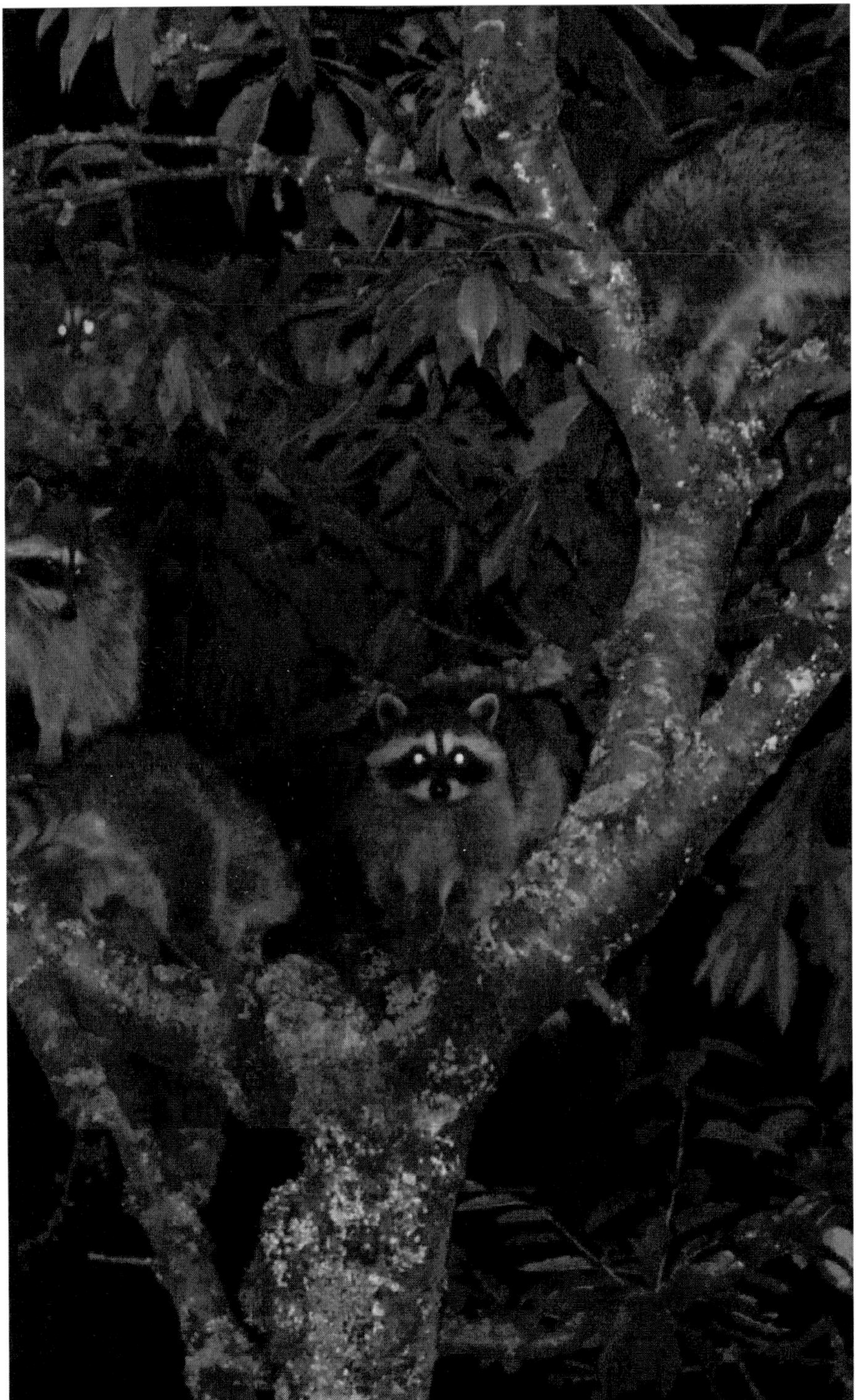

Chapter 09

DREAM COME TRUE

The previous night had been long and difficult for Packy and his sisters. They had left early and returned late. Daylight had found them still across the river, and for the second time in their lives, they swam across after the sun rose. By now, they understood the Dills' farm was a safe haven, a respite from predators. Juanita Dills liked them, and the three other people on the farm had made no attempt to bother them. On several occasions, Luther Loggins had left some food at the base of the elm tree. They had been suspicious at first, refusing to eat, but then Packy finally tasted it, and found it to be good. Now they looked forward to his occasional visit, although they waited in the tree until he left. They had met him once by the barn, where he had removed some food from his pocket and placed it on the grass. He had made a strange clucking sound, and then backed quietly away so that they could eat without fear.

The kits were also wary of strange animals living in the converted chicken house, although Scrappy didn't seem to mind. He came in and went out of the building at will, sleeping the day away in his open cage, oblivious to the barks, caws and squalls. His presence added to their feelings of security, and he had gradually become their friend and sometimes companion. While he seemed to be comfortable in the presence of humans, the kits were not. Juanita Dills was the only person they allowed to get close, but not close enough to touch. They did like her singing though, and would sit and listen as long as she would sing.

One night, they heard a different kind of music coming from inside the house. Juanita had finally found time to play the piano. They didn't know she played just to see if other kinds of music attracted them. She propped open the screen door and hoped they would come inside. She had turned the piano so she could see the front door, and she played the same songs she had been singing. As she expected, Packy was the first to appear in the doorway. Soon, all five sat with their heads cocked, listening intently. Unfortunately for Juanita, they came no closer, but still, they had come inside, and that was progress. Next time, she planned to put fish in a bowl halfway between the door and the piano. She understood that wild animals did not befriend humans easily, so she must be patient and give them time to adjust.

****

The kits slept around the clock. When they climbed down the elm tree, something strange coated the ground. They had never seen frost before, and they wondered what the cold, white stuff could mean. After a few minutes of sniffing and touching, they accepted its presence and continued on their way. Food was getting harder to find, and their voracious appetites only increased the difficulty. The occasional fish Juanita Dills left on the porch only whetted their appetites. Some nights, she didn't leave any fish, and they went away disappointed. Despite this added frustration, they managed to fend for themselves in an increasingly harsh environment.

As autumn rushed toward winter, the nights continued to get colder. The kits paid little notice, since Mother Nature had blessed them with thickening coats. Their inside hair remained virtually the same while the outside became thicker and longer. This, combine with increased fat, meant they could endure much colder air without discomfort. At some point, they would hole up in their tree and sleep for days at a time, although they would not hibernate. As they slept, their heart rates would drop, but not to a trickle like that of a woodchuck or a bear.

On this night, Scrappy had decided to come along, but when they reached the river, he balked at trying to swim to the other side. He knew his limitations, and the kits respected that. Packy churred a good-bye to him, and then led his siblings into the cold water. At mid-stream, he turned to count heads and realized immediately someone had disappeared. Looking toward the bunk, he saw Mandy climbing up toward Scrappy. For whatever her reason, she had decided to stay with the disabled raccoon. Packy drifted downstream for a moment as he watched them disappear into the field. Concluding that his sister was safe, he turned and swam in the direction he intended.

Packy had walked ahead of Scrappy, then stopped and waited, but Mandy walked beside him, maintaining his pace. Not even she was sure why she had turned back. At the last minute, it had just seemed the thing to do. As her siblings disappeared across the river, she had a moment's regret but soon lost the feeling. She watched as her companion limped along, understanding poor eyesight and a missing paw restricted his movements. In her own way, she had empathy for Scrappy, because she had always been the slow one in her family. Despite his disabilities, the older raccoon had physical strength, and his spirit remained strong. Always good-natured and friendly, he added joy to her daily life.

Now in his fifth year, he took life as it came, sleeping in his unlocked cage during the day and roaming about at night. Noise in the animal clinic didn't seem to disturb Scrappy, not even the raucous squawking of parrots or the howling of a frightened dog. Luther soon figured out the old raccoon had some kind of sixth sense and would wake up if anyone or anything come too close to his cage. Out of kindness, he found a big box and substituted it for the cage. When it became obvious Scrappy wasn't going to sleep in the box, he found a bigger box and put the cage inside it. Scrappy returned to his bed immediately. Why he preferred sleeping in the cage, Luther didn't know, because he had the run of the farm, coming and going as he pleased. Luther always fed him first and gave him an extra helping. Despite Scrappy's tameness, Juanita knew his metabolism increased with approaching winter, and she had told Luther to give him additional nourishment.

On this night, Scrappy decided to show Mandy around. She was wild, but he was not, and his presence comforted her as they explored the buildings and grounds. He took her to his cage and found that Luther had, as usual, left him an extra treat in his bowl. Even though there wasn't enough for both, he shared it with Mandy unselfishly. After they finished, they wandered around the building, looking for something else to eat. Standing just below the bird cages, they munched on discarded seeds and suet. Under the animal cages, they found an assortment of dropped food, and despite its dryness, they ate it anyway.

A pair of ferrets had dropped several small pieces of fish. The raccoons munched happily, until the ferrets began creating a ruckus. They moved away quickly, fearing their noise would bring down the wrath of Juanita Dills. Outside, they slipped through the moonlight, and walked across the field toward the barn. Always alert for predators, Mandy eyed the screech owl that sat atop a telephone pole. The owl watched the two raccoons for a short time before deciding that attacking them might not be in his best interest. Flapping his wings, he left the pole and glided north along the river, hoping for smaller prey.

When they reached the barn, they explored the ground floor. By now, Mandy knew it was not a good idea for Scrappy to try climbing into the loft. If she did, he would probably follow, risking a fall and possible injury. In one corner of a horse stall, they found a hen's nest. Few fowl laid eggs in cold weather, but chickens did, much to the pleasure of the raccoons. At first, it looked like the hen would defend her nest, but at the last minute, she ran clucking from the barn. They enjoyed two eggs apiece, leaving the cracked shells for the defenseless hen.

They continued their exploring until they became bored with the barn. A small harness shed behind the barn yielded nothing, and they soon found the old corncrib provided no sustenance. In a tool shed, they found an old leather belt. They chewed on it for a while, but soon decided the effort was more than the gain. They lay down in an empty tool box for a brief rest. When they went back outside, the first signs of daylight appeared on the horizon. After rubbing noses, Mandy headed for the elm tree, and Scrappy headed toward the animal clinic. At the base of the elm, Mandy turned and watched Scrappy disappear into the building. Half-way up to the den, she sat on a limb and watched the sun rise. The night had been good, and the mutual sharing with her friend had left her with a warm glow.

****

The kits never forgot the night that Misty and Cindy disappeared. As cold weather approached, the variety of food diminished to a few bland choices. With Packy in the lead as usual, they decided to explore the area north of the Dills' farm. They climbed down the elm tree just after dark, and followed the river on the east side. They had no way of knowing where the Dills farm stopped, and the Welch farm began. In late autumn, plowed fields became the norm, and large rolls of hay dotted the landscape. While plowed fields slowed the kit's pace, the rolls of hay provided cover to move from one point to the next. Ever mindful of the distance from cover to cover, the kit's stopped and listened after every movement. They didn't intend to get caught in the open by predators or people. Humans rarely ventured into the fields at night except to hunt, and when they did, they usually hunted raccoons. The occasional wandering hound posed the greatest danger, because he depended on small game for his food.

Packy had just decided to turn back when they topped a ridge, and saw a huge barn with three grain silos shimmering in the moonlight below. Somewhat in awe, the kits had never seen anything that large in their short lives. Raccoon curiosity immediately dominated their reason, and after exchanging a few churrs, they headed downhill. When they reached the meadow behind the barn, they worked their way around the field until they were downwind. From there, they approached the barn cautiously, suspicious that a dog might be on guard.

Once inside, they saw that stalls lined both sides of the barn, and dairy cattle stood quietly, occasionally munching on oats or corn. Accustomed to cattle, and not feeling threatened, they wandered along the aisle, looking and smelling. The barn was unusually clean, and finding something to eat proved difficult. Just before they reached the other end of the barn, they came upon a stainless steel tank mounted on four legs. After exploring and sniffing for several minutes, Becky climbed up on the platform. The tank was cold to the touch, but a tantalizing smell permeated the air.

Finally, Becky found a small wheel that extended just above the platform. After feeling around and under it, she tried to turn it, but it wouldn't budge. Refusing to give up, she churred for Packy to climb up and help her. Grasping the wheel from two sides, they turned together. Nothing happened, so they turned in the other direction. The wheel began to turn, and suddenly they heard something splattering just below them. They climbed down to investigate the source of the noise. A strange, white liquid poured out of a faucet onto the floor. It felt cold to their feet, and they backed away suspiciously. Soon, their curiosity got the better of them, and they moved carefully toward the flowing milk.

The smell was overpoweringly delicious, and the taste was even better. Packy churred to Mandy, Misty and Cindy, who were exploring a machine just behind the tank. They joined their siblings in the feast. The sweet taste brought up memories of Mother and the security they felt as they nursed at her breast. Standing in a circle around the puddle of milk on the floor, they lapped and licked until their stomachs felt bloated. Finally, with white feet and faces, they left the milk puddle and continued to explore along the back of the barn. It never occurred to any one of them to turn the faucet off. Milk continued to pour onto the barn floor and across a stall where it disappeared into a drain that ran down the inside of the barn.

Outside, they sat in the grass and stared upward at the stainless steel walls of the huge silos. To the curious raccoons, it looked like the shiny metal extended all the way to the sky. Somewhat in awe, they walked completely around both silos but couldn't find an entrance. Scratching the metal with his tough nails, Packy soon realized that digging through was not an option. Still, they were not a group to give up easily, so they sat on the ground and studied the matter. Seeing two large pipes extending from the silos into the barn, they went back inside and climbed a ladder into the loft.

After several minutes of looking, they found an open door in the side of one silo. Peering down into the vast container, they saw a sea of corn. At first, there appeared to be no way down. Metal support beams ran from side to side, staggered horizontally and spaced about one foot apart in the vertical direction. They soon figured out they could walk across one beam, and then climb down to the next one. They finally reached a beam partially submersed in the corn. Holding on to the beam, Packy began lowering himself into the loose kernels. When his hind feet could find no purchase, he pulled himself back onto the beam. Reversing his position, he stuck his head down in the corn. Breathing was difficult, and he began to sneeze. Pulling himself back up with his rear legs was not easy, but he managed it. He now realized if he stepped out into the loose kernels, he would sink in over his head. The possibility of smothering overcame his desire to swim in the corn. After churring to the others, he sat on the beam and scooped up kernels with his paws. Heeding Packy's warning, they all sat in a row and ate until they were sated with milk and corn.

Finally deciding to leave, they worked their way back to the door, and Packy discovered that he couldn't find anything to pull himself up with. Coming down had been easy enough, but the distance going back was just beyond his reach. He churred to the others who were directly behind him. They sat in a huddle and pondered the situation. Finally, they came up with a plan. The four sisters bunched up in a knot just under the door. When Packy climbed on top of them, he could grasp the ledge with his front paws. He pulled himself up and sat in the door. He churred for the others to come up, but they couldn't manage it.

He tried reaching down and pulling Misty up, but his hind legs wouldn't hold both their weights. He sat on the ledge and thought about the situation some more. Finally, he lowered his body down, holding onto the door with his front paws. This time, Misty pulled herself up by holding onto Packy. Mandy came up next, followed by Cindy. Becky, the lightest, came up last. After she crawled across Packy's head, he pulled himself up. Exhausted but happy, he churred for the others to go back into the barn loft. They all sat in a group and rested for a while.

Eager to explore some more, they climbed down out of the barn loft and went outside. On the other side of the silo, an empty milk truck sat, waiting for the next day's delivery. This was a strange object indeed, and it reeked of foreign smells. While Packy, Mandy and Becky checked out the tires, Misty and Cindy picked up a new smell and followed their noses, leaving the others behind to ponder the truck. About fifty yards away, they came to a dumpster, parked at the end of a ramp.

They walked up the ramp, sat down and looked down into the huge container. About half full, it emanated a variety of smells, some pleasant and some not. Having forgotten their near disaster in the silo, they climbed down to investigate. The smells and tastes of the dumpster captivated them. In one corner, they found three steak bones the Welch family had discarded. The bits of meat left on and around the bones tasted delicious, and the two kits momentarily forgot their siblings at the milk truck.

Without warning, a huge trash truck started backing up to the dumpster. The two kits were so engrossed in their eating; they paid little attention to the noise. As the truck began picking up the dumpster, loud noise, banging and shaking of the dumpster cause them to stop eating. They looked around for some means to escape quickly, but it was too late. The dumpster suddenly turned upside down, and its contents began falling into the hold of the garbage truck. Food, plastic and household items fell on and around them. Shaken but not injured, they began climbing on top of the trash heap in the back of the truck. A loud whirring noise began, the top closed and the pack cylinders began pushing the trash forward toward the cab of the truck. Panicky, the kits scrambled through the loose trash, finally coming out on top.

Fortunately, that had been the truck's last pick up, and the driver headed for the county landfill several miles away. The kits snuggled together in total darkness, shivering with fear as the truck continued its journey. At the landfill, the truck began backing up. More loud noises as the truck began its dump cycle. As the trash slid out of the truck, the kits again scrambled for their lives. When the trash finally came to rest, they wiggled and squirmed to reach the top of the pile. Misty reached the top first. She looked around to find Cindy, but she couldn't see her anywhere.

Suddenly, she heard her sister whining. She looked toward the source of the noise and started digging. She clawed and dug furiously until she saw the top of Cindy's head. Together, they managed to free her. They sat on top of the trash mountain, dazed and scared. As they returned to normal, they realized they were in a place they had never seen before. They understood enough to know they had to get out of this strange place and run into the woods.

As they began to clamber down, a voice suddenly yelled out, "Look, Jack, there a couple of raccoons."

"I see'em, Harvey, let's kill the little pests."

With that, the two attendants began to throw whatever objects they could find at the two kits. Something hit Misty in the side as she scrambled down the trash pile. Ignoring the pain, she continued to run with Cindy close behind. Fortunately, the two men were too lazy to give chase. The kits reached the woods and ran into the safety of the underbrush. They sat quietly for a long time. When they realized their enemies had lost interest, they drifted off to sleep.

As the sun dropped behind the mountains, they woke up in a strange location. They churred to each other for a short time before coming out of their hiding place. They peered at the landfill from the safety of the woods until they realized no humans or any other predators were present. They went back to the dump and hunted for food.

Once they had eaten enough to satisfy their hunger, they headed for home even though they had no clue as to its location.

****

Waking just after dark, Packy decided to go back to the dairy farm and look for Misty and Cindy. When they reached the barn, they found that someone had cleaned up the milk, and the smell of humans abounded. They prowled around the stalls until they were sure people were not lurking about to harm them. They helped themselves to the milk again, and then prowled around the barn and silo, still hopeful that Misty and Cindy could be found. After a fruitless search, they headed in the direction the garbage truck had gone, this time under cover of darkness. They bypassed the house where the dog had barked, making a circle into the woods and then back to the road. They continued to walk, churring every few minutes, hoping an answer would come out of the night.

Just before daylight, they reached the highway. Not knowing which direction to take, they turned to the right and walked until the sky began to lighten. They crawled into a culvert under the road to sleep the day away. By mid-afternoon, hunger and the sound of cars drove them out of the culvert and into the woods on the other side. By dark, they had eaten acorns, mushrooms and a few beetles. Again, the kits set out, this time, in the other direction. By midnight, Packy decided to give up the search. Just before daylight, they found a place to sleep a quarter-mile north of the dairy farm.

At the top of the ridge, they sat and waited, hoping for some miracle that would deliver their sisters to them. Finally, hungry and disappointed, they walked down the hill toward the river. As they swam across, Packy watched Becky and Mandy carefully; fearful that they, too, would disappear. At the barn, they met Scrappy, and after much churring, the older raccoon understood that two of his friends were missing. He led them to the chicken house where they found some extra food Luther had left by his cage. After the delicious meal, they bade Scrappy goodnight and headed for the elm tree. They bedded down close together and felt the ache of their missing sisters.

****

As Juanita Dills busied herself about the farm, she wondered what had happened to her newfound friends. She played the piano two nights in a row, but the kits didn't show. The third night, she sat in her rocking chair on the porch and sang, but still, no raccoons, except, of course, Scrappy. He lay quietly on the floor while she rocked and sang. After about six songs, she stopped and looked out over her farm.

"Scrappy, ol' boy, I wish you could talk," she said. "I don't know if you even know where they are. Why don't you go find them for me?"

Scrappy looked up at her, his big black eyes a mystery.

"You don't know where they are, do you fellow? If you did, you wouldn't look so sad. Well, if you find out, bring them to me, okay?"

With that, Scrappy stood up and walked across the porch. He stood on the steps looking into the night. He turned and churred to her, then limped down the steps and out in the yard. Juanita watched after him for a few minutes. Finally, she gave up and went into the house.

****

It had been six nights since the garbage truck had dumped Misty and Cindy into the landfill. In that time, they had eaten and slept little, and walked unceasingly. They had no idea in what direction they should be walking or how far it was to the Dills' farm. Some sixth sense guided them in a southeasterly direction, and they never questioned or wavered from it. November had arrived, and the nights had gotten colder with frost covering the ground almost every morning. Still, the weather didn't bother them as they continued on their determined path.

A new moon gave no light, and to add insult to injury, fog rose from the ground and covered the earth like a blanket. The ground was cold, and their feet were sore, but still, they kept going. On the birthday of their ninth month, and their sixth day on the road, they slept until after dark. They had found a hole in the back of a small building in an abandoned rock quarry. The fact they slept between two boxes of dynamite meant nothing to them. Dry wood shavings littered the floor, and it reminded them of home. When they woke up and went outside, a cold rain dripped from a darkened sky.

After considerable churring, they decided to stay another night. The building didn't leak, and it warded off the cold wind. They also knew no large predator could get inside. Dogs had been a perennial problem, but none seemed to be near the quarry. Hunger drove them to search for food, and they went out into the darkness. Although they had no way to convey it to each other, each wished Packy were there to guide them. Too, they missed the warmth of their sisters. After a fruitless search around the perimeter of the quarry, they found another small building near the one in which they had slept.

Just under the roof, they found a hole large enough to get through, and they climbed down inside. Metal cans of food lined the shelves from top to bottom, but they could find no way to get them open. In desperation, they chewed through a cardboard box in hopes of finding something edible. The box yielded a bonanza, inside were twenty-four plastic containers of beef jerky. They pulled one out onto the floor and ripped it open. Despite its staleness, the jerky tasted wonderful, and they consumed three containers. Now they had shelter and food.

The rain continued for three days, and on the fourth day, it turned to snow. On the sixth day, a warm front blanketed the area, and the snow melted as fast as it had come down. On the seventh day, the food ran out and the two raccoons set out to search for their family. The night was warm and a quarter-moon shone brightly from the sky. Their sore feet had healed, and they had each gained a little weight from all the beef jerky they had consumed. Just after midnight, they reached the Little Tennessee River.

They were still six miles north of the Dills' farm, but all they had to do was follow the river. They recognized nothing, but their confidence increased with each mile. Twenty miles of walking had not deterred them, and wind, snow and rain had only strengthened their resolve. In the deepest part of their hearts, they intended to go home, and they would stop at nothing to get there. At their age, three miles in one night was a stretch, but they made it. On the fifteenth night after the trash truck hauled them away, they recognized the Dills' farm. Exhausted and footsore, they churred their happiness to each other and increased their speed.

****

If raccoons could sweat, Packy would have done plenty of it. He lay in the den between Becky and Mandy. It had been a long night, and they had not found much food. For some reason, he could not bring himself to go to the farmhouse and look for fish snacks that Juanita Dills usually left on the porch. His missing sisters had changed his outlook, and his mood had been unusually black. First his mother, and now two of his siblings. Clearly, Becky and Mandy missed their sisters also. The death of their mother had bound them like glue, and they had stayed together as a group. Now, Packy feared he might lose Becky and Mandy also, and he watched them closer than ever.

Packy tossed and turned, and then finally went back to sleep. Now, he dreamed that all four of his sisters slept in a circle around him. Their warmth gave him such joy he churred in his sleep. Every way he turned, he bumped into one of his sisters. He put out a paw and felt Mandy, the Becky, then Cindy, and finally, Misty. He knew each one of them by the feel of their fur, but something was wrong. Misty and Cindy could not be there. He struggled to wake up, but in his dreamy stupor, the best he could manage was a half-waking, half-dreaming state.

He continued to struggle with his dream. Finally, he forced himself to open his eyes. Now that the elm tree had shed its leaves, light filtered in through the den entrance. He lay still for a bit, confused about a dream that seemed so real. He raised his head and looked around. There were four shapes scattered around the den. Coming fully awake, he sat up and felt each of the warm bodies sleeping next to him. As a number, four meant nothing to him, but in his own way, he could count. Misty and Cindy were certainly there, and it was no mistake.

Deciding enough was enough, Packy growled and churred until all five kits sat in the den looking at each other. Suddenly, Becky and Mandy realized their missing sisters had returned. In a few moments, they were all licking and touching. It was a grand family reunion, and they used the full range of their language, greeting touching and smelling. Their happiness knew no bounds. Too excited to sleep, they just sat and looked at each other in the half-light of the den. Cindy and Misty had returned, and Packy's dream had come true.

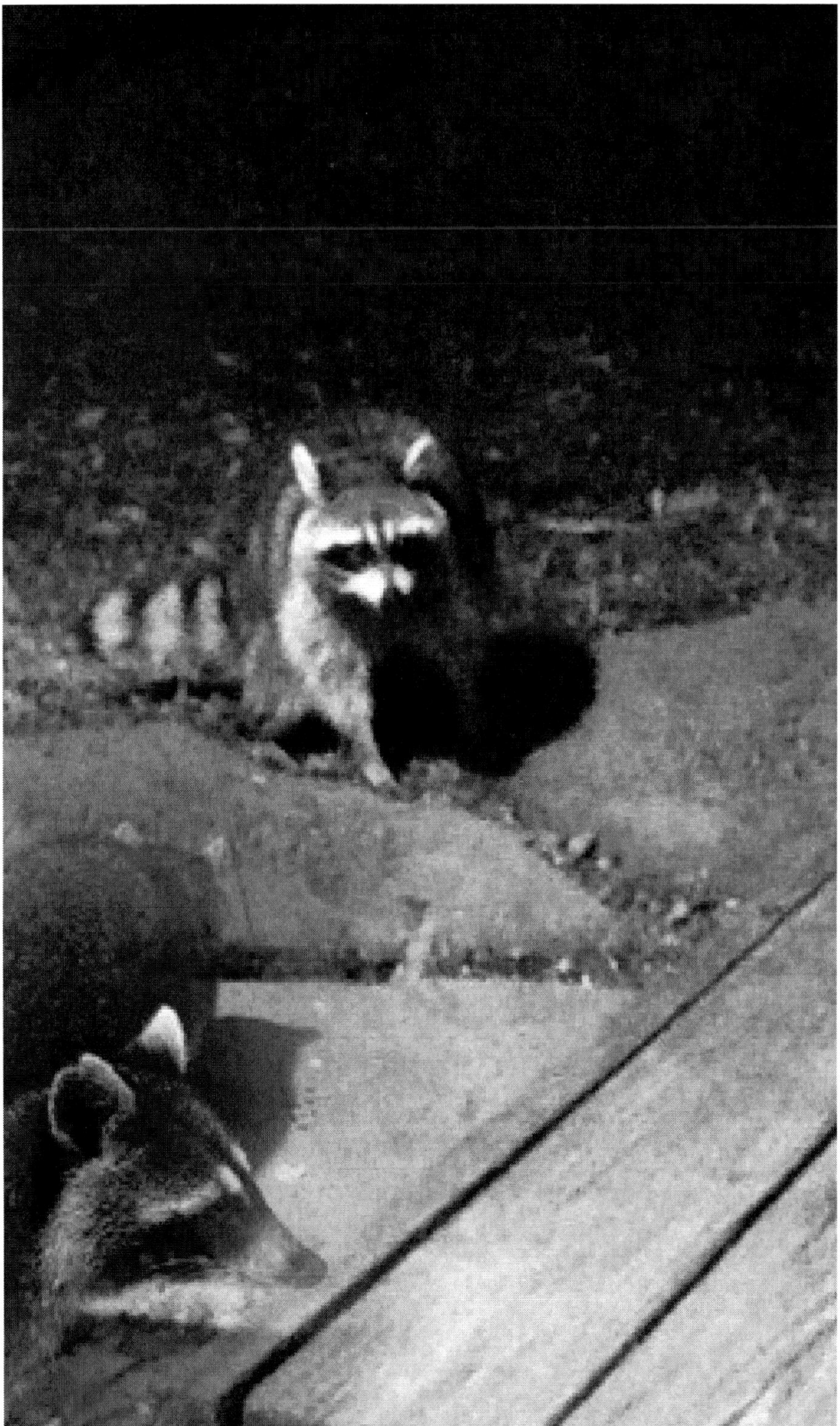

Chapter 10

A FRIEND IN NEED

Juanita Dills sat in her small office behind the stairs and concentrated on her ledgers. For the first time, adoption fees and donations had exceeded expenditures. Now, she had some extra money to spend on her latest addition. Also, Luther Loggins had surpassed all her expectations, and she felt a need to reward his efforts. Tired of balancing her books, she decided to go outside and get some fresh air. When she pushed open the screen door, she saw six raccoons staring directly into her face. She did a double take before she could think of anything to say.

"Scrappy, you little devil, you did it! I told you to bring them to me, and you did. Maybe you understand more than I give you credit for."

She started toward them, and then remembered they might panic, so she stopped in mid-stride.

"Stay right there," she said. "I'm going into the house, but I'll be right back. Now, don't go away."

In a few minutes, she returned, carrying a container of raw fish. She picked one up and held it out. Knowing Scrappy would come forward first, she let him have it. He quickly hobbled a few feet away, sat down and began to eat. She took another fish from the container and held it out. To her surprise, the biggest one came forward, took the fish and walked quickly to the end of the porch. One at a time, the others came forward also, and took a fish. Emptying the container, she went inside and brought out some more. Before long, they had eaten all her fish, leaving her with only one other thing to hold them.

"You know what fellows; I've got to give you names. I've observed all of you enough to know that the big one is a male and the rest of you are females. You there, the big one; I'm going to call you Packy, because you sure can pack the food away. The rest of you, I'm going to name after my best friends from high school. You over there, the little one, your name is Becky, and the two of you that always stay together will be named Misty and Cindy. You there by the porch rail, the shy one, I'm calling you Mandy. So there, all of you have names, so get used to it."

She sat and talked to them for a long time. Finally, they began to get restless, and Juanita knew their visit would soon be over. Reluctantly, she stopped talking. One by one, they got up and walked off the porch. Shortly, they disappeared through the hedge. Scrappy continued to lie close to her chair. She reached over carefully and picked him up. As she rubbed his fur, he purred like a cat, but louder. Lost in thought, Juanita looked out into the yard. Finally, she spoke to Scrappy.

"What do you think, ol' boy? Wouldn't it be wonderful if animals could talk?" She sat silently for a few moments. "Come to think of it, they can. People just can't understand their language."

****

On Thanksgiving Day, something unusual happened at the Dills' farm. Juanita hosted a Thanksgiving dinner for her friends and members of her animal adoption group. Several people spent the night on Thanksgiving Eve and more drove in the next morning. Assisted by her volunteers, she baked three turkeys. Luther surprised her by demonstrating his prowess at cooking. It was a grand luncheon, validated by the quantity of food consumed. Good natured banter and laughter ebbed and flowed around the house, porch and yard. Juanita proved to be an excellent hostess, and several new people joined her animal adoption group.

She had expanded into the second outbuilding and added another part-time volunteer. Luther Loggins acted like the proud father of a new-born child. He bubbled with enthusiasm as he explained their adoption process. When Juanita introduced him as her foreman, he almost dropped his coffee. Unaccustomed to public recognition, the promotion gave his ego a much needed boost. She went on to explain that he had been a significant part of her success. A private man; nonetheless, he soon disappeared and went out to check on his charges. Obviously impressed with the many accomplishments on the Dills farm, many of the guests adopted animals before leaving for home.

The kits didn't know what to make of all the commotion, so they stayed well away from the house. Intimidated by all the people and noise, Scrappy holed up in his cage and refused to come out. The buildings were so quiet Luther felt as if he had lost some of his best friends. Even so, he knew many more would arrive in the coming weeks. He wondered what the place would be like with four buildings full of animals. Scrappy came out and begged for a handout. Luther filled his dish to overflowing and gave him a couple of scratches before retiring for the evening.

So many strangers had wandered about the farm that the kits had refused to hunt on Thanksgiving Eve. They sat in the elm tree all night wondering at all the commotion. Thanksgiving Day was even worse, and they slept fitfully, waking often to strange and wonderful smells that drifted on the wind. By dark, the noises had stopped, and they prepared to climb down and hunt. As they came out of their den, an overpowering smell drifted up to their sensitive nostrils. They scrambled down the tree, hurrying to locate the source of the delicious odor. When they reached the ground, they found five large bowls of turkey spread out around the tree. Despite their hunger, they approached the food cautiously, but quickly decided no danger lurked in the bowls.

They attacked the food with much enthusiasm and noise. The turkey, cooked to perfection, had a wonderful taste and smell. The dressing had a strange odor, not at all to their liking. They refused to eat it, but they did eat the cranberry sauce. When they had finished, there was still enough turkey left for another meal. Now that they had no need to go out and search for food, they decided to check out the barn and house. Between the animal house and the barn, they met Scrappy, who had come out of the building to look for them.

With all the people gone, curiosity drove them toward the house. When they arrived, they found the lights were out and the porch was bare of treats. They were too full to eat anyway, but they had a yen to hear some of Juanita's singing and playing. Exhausted from all the cooking and hosting, she had gone to bed early. They all sat on the porch and waited for at least an hour. Finally realizing their new friend would not come out of the house, they left the porch and headed toward the elm tree. About half-way, Scrappy churred his good-byes and returned to his cage in the box. For the first time in weeks, the kits went to bed early.

****

The day after Thanksgiving, Juanita woke up early. She lay on her back and stared at the ceiling, hoping sleep would return. She found herself wondering how Luther would like living on the farm.

With some extra money, she could build an apartment in one end of the third building. With that thought in mind, she got up and made breakfast. After eating, she stashed her dishes in the dishwasher, and then went out on the porch. Even though it was still dark outside, she felt energized and decided to go for a walk. A blue moon, poised to drop below the mountains, still gave a brilliant light. She had given Luther and her three volunteers the weekend off. About half of her animals had been adopted out, and she felt she could manage by herself. Luther had broken out into a broad smile when she told him he would get paid on Friday, his first paid vacation day.

She crossed the yard and walked toward the barn. She intended to climb into the loft and watch the sunrise, by her figuring only thirty minutes away. About half-way to the barn, she saw an owl sitting in top of a dead tree. Deciding to take a closer look, she took a right turn into the field, hoping she could ease up to the tree without frightening the big bird. She had taken her flashlight, but she decided not to use it, lest she scare the owl away. She knew owls were raptors and subsisted on small animals for their food. She hoped the young raccoons living in her tree were too large for the owl to hunt.

As she walked quietly through the dead grass, she zipped up her jacket to ward off the cold air. She slowed as she approached the tree, watching the owl through dead branches. At about ten feet from the dead tree, she heard a snapping noise, and without warning, the ground gave way under her. Instinctively, she grabbed for the tree, but it was too far away. She saw the ground pass before her eyes as dirt and rotten lumber fell with her. She hit the bottom of the hole with a thud and for a few moments, she knew or remembered nothing. When she regained consciousness, she lay at the bottom of an old well, about ten feet down. Her grandfather's house had stood only a few feet away. Later, her uncle had torn it down, partially filled the old well, and then covered it. Over time, the wooden covering had rotted to the point that it would hold very little weight without caving in.

Not one to panic under normal circumstances, she felt around her body to see if she had any broken bones. She had scratches on her arms and one on her side, but no broken bones she could find. She touched her head carefully and found a bruised place on her scalp had already started to swell. She stood up and leaned against the dirt wall. She could see a few stars and the beginning of dawn. She held her hand up as far as she could, and immediately determined there were at least three feet of dirt between her hand and ground level. She tried jumping to see if she could reach the top, and quickly realized she couldn't.

Trying desperately to fight off panic, she sat down to rest. The bruise on her head began to throb, and she felt dizzy. She leaned back against the wall of the well and closed her eyes. She needed time to think. Then she remembered there was no one on the farm but her. She began to cry. After a few minutes, she opened her eyes and saw daylight. Feeling a little better, she decided to evaluate her situation. She was standing in a hole about five feet across and ten feet deep. The sides were straight up, and she could see nothing that would serve as a foothold. Several pieces of rotten wood lay on the ground by her feet.

She examined them and decided on one that looked like it might hold her weight. She leaned it against the wall and tried using it for a step. As soon as she took the other foot off the ground, the old plank broke with a sickening snap. She tried using two at the same time, but that approach didn't work either. She stopped to think again. It occurred to her she might dig holes in the dirt wall and climb up that way. Using her fingers, she began to dig. The soil was hard, and she broke off several nails in the attempt. By the time she had removed an inch of dirt, blood oozed from her fingers. She picked up one of the rotten planks and tried using it as a shovel, but pieces broke away with each dig. With a cry of despair, she gave up. Screaming for help seemed to be the only option left for her to try.

She began to yell, "Help, help, I've fallen into a well. Help, help, will someone help me?" She screamed until her throat was sore. Finally, she gave up. She removed one of her shoes and tried scooping dirt out of the wall with it. All she succeeded in doing was damaging her shoe and filling it with dirt. She sat back down and removed the dirt from her shoe, then put it back on. Again, she leaned against the wall and closed her eyes. As she sat fighting panic, she heard a churring noise. She opened her eyes and looked up. Packy sat at the edge of the hole, looking down at her.

"Packy, my little friend, where did you come from? You're supposed to be sleeping."

She stood up so that she could see more clearly.

Packy churred again, and then began walking around the hole, apparently looking for a way down. Dirt fell down as he worked his way around. She turned as he walked so she continued to face him.

"Dear God, Packy, right now I wish you were human. You could pull me up from here."

Packy churred again, and then she saw four other heads peering down into the hole. One after the other, they churred down to her.

"I know you guys can't do anything, but I sure am grateful for the company." With that in mind, she talked to them for a long time. Finally, she could tell they had lost interest. She sat down again. When she looked up, they had disappeared.

"Oh Dear Lord, I'm in a heck of a mess. It'll be Monday before anyone misses me, and here it is Friday morning. I'll probably freeze to death before then."

Even as she spoke, she felt the chill creeping into her bones. She stood up, and then jumped up and down to warm herself. After a few minutes, she began to tire, so she stopped. She found the exercise had taken the chill away. It occurred to her that without food and water, she would tire out and slowly freeze to death.

Her heart pounded in her chest, and she started yelling again.

"Help, help, someone please help me. Can anyone hear me out there, help, please help?"

Her throat began to hurt, and it dawned on her that she must not ruin her voice before Monday or no one would hear her, even then. She stopped yelling. She knew in her heart it was a wasted effort anyway. Pacing herself as best she could, she sat for a while, stood for a while and exercised when she felt chilly. Although there was no water in the well, the ground was damp, and her feet began to get cold. She sat on the ground, removed her shoes and began to rub her feet. Soon she had a routine going. Somehow, she had to hold out until Monday.

Time seemed to drag on forever. Sometime in the afternoon, she dropped off to sleep. When she woke up, she was shivering. She stood up and began her routine again. After what seemed like days, darkness began to fall. Now she was afraid. She gave herself a pep talk. Finally, she began to sing.

> "When you walk through a storm,
> Hold your head up high,
> And don't be afraid of the dark.
> At the end of the storm,
> Is a golden sky,
> And the sweet, silver song of a lark."

Her soprano voice rang into the night. In the middle of the

third song, she heard churring. She looked up. Outlined against the night sky stood five raccoons.

"Dear Lord, I'm glad to see you guys. I'm so lonely down here in this hole."

She began to sing again. Suddenly, dirt began to fall. Packy started down the side of the hole, and then fell to the bottom with a soft thud.

"Packy, you crazy fool; you shouldn't have come down here. Now you can't get out."

She could barely see him in the bottom of the hole, but she could tell he was standing up. She reached forward to pet him, but he shrank back.

"I'm sorry; I forget, you aren't Scrappy. You're a wild animal; a warm and friendly wild animal, but still wild."

Just as she finished speaking, she heard dirt falling again. Becky fell into the hole, followed by Cindy and Misty, and finally, Mandy. Now Juanita sat in the bottom of an abandoned well, surrounded by raccoons.

"I can't keep singing, guys; I'll lose my voice, and I have to preserve it. How about if I talk quietly to you?"

At 10:00 p.m., the moon rose in the sky and cast enough light for Juanita to see the kits much better. After a while, Becky decided to climb out. She started up the sheer wall of the hole, only to fall back. Angry, she tried again, and then gave up. Taking a cue from Becky that the wall was impossible to climb, they all sat down, close together. Juanita leaned against the dirt wall and closed her eyes. Mental exhaustion consumed her mind, and she couldn't think.

When she opened her eyes, the moon stood directly overhead, surrounded by a circle of clouds.

That's all I need, she thought. If it starts raining, I really will freeze to death, but at least I'll have some water to drink before I die.

Finally, mental fatigue caused physical exhaustion. She lay down on her side, and shut her eyes. Almost immediately, she dropped off to sleep. Sometime in the night, she woke up and pulled her jacket tightly around her. Her feet felt like popsicles, but the exhaustion was greater than the cold, and she went back to sleep again. Finally, she had rested enough that the cold woke her up. She began to shiver.

Suddenly, she felt a warm body move up next to her back, and then another one. Packy and Becky had moved against her. Whether because they were cold or because they were trying to warm her, she didn't know. In a minute or so, she felt warmth against her feet. Slowly and carefully, she removed her shoes, and then put her feet back against Misty. Soon, Cindy lay against the back of her knees. In another minute or two, she felt warmth against her stomach as Mandy snuggled against her.

Carefully, and cautiously, she began stroking Mandy's fur. Soon, Mandy began purring, sounding much like a satisfied kitten, but louder. Soon, Juanita began to feel warmer. She lay half-awake for a while, wondering at the miracle. She thought about a story she had read in the newspaper, about two elk that had kept a child from freezing to death in the snow by lying next to her all night. She had doubted the veracity of the story at the time she read it, but now she didn't. As she tried to think about other animal stories, she dropped off to sleep.

When she awoke, sunlight bounced against the dirt walls of the old well. Five raccoons sat looking at her. She stood up and tried to exercise. The kits shrank against the wall like she intended to harm them. She stopped and stood still.

"Look guys, I'm not going to hurt you. Far be it from me to harm the only friends I have in this God-forsaken hole."

She talked to them quietly for a few minutes, and they appeared to relax. Suddenly, Packy tried to climb the dirt wall. He made it up about two feet and then dropped back. He tried several more times to no avail.

"Packy," she said, "hold still for a minute."

He stopped and looked at her. Gradually and steadily, she moved her hands down to him. She stroked his fur for a few moments, and he didn't resist. Gently, she put her hands under his stomach and slowly picked him up. Surprised he didn't move, she tensed her muscles and quickly tossed him up and out of the hole. He landed on the ground, just out of sight. In a moment, he looked back down and churred. The others churred back to him. They continued for a few moments, using their voices in a variety of tones, including growls and grunts.

"I'd give a million dollars to know what you guys are saying."

Thinking the others wanted out, she reached for Mandy. She shrank back and moved to the other side of the hole. One by one, she tried to touch them, but they wouldn't allow it. She finally gave up, and looked to see what Packy was doing. He had disappeared without a sound.

"So what do you think, girls? Your brother has left us alone here in this hole. Why the rest of you are staying, I can't fathom, unless you just don't want me to touch you. But you didn't mind last night. So what gives, huh?"

Like raccoon statues, they sat and stared at her. Again, she sat with her back to the wall, and returned their stares.

"I don't know about you girls, but I'm hungry and thirsty. What I wouldn't give for a hot egg sandwich and a cup of orange juice. I wonder what happened to your brother. Do you think he has abandoned us? Wouldn't it be nice if he went over to the next farm and brought someone to rescue us? Yeah, sure, the first thing they'd do when they saw him coming would be to shoot at him."

As she continued to talk, the kits sat up and started looking up at the top of the hole. Juanita heard a slight noise above her head, and suddenly something dropped across her face. She screamed in surprise and jumped up. The end of a rope hung down into the well. She immediately recognized it as the one she had played tug rope with the kits on the porch. Packy looked down over the edge and churred.

"Oh, Packy, my fine furry friend, this is no place to play tug rope."

Packy churred again. She reached out and grasped the rope with her right hand. As she did, the other end of the rope came down into the well.

"Good Lord, Packy, Don't be in such a rush. I'm going to play with you."

Instead of grabbing the rope with his mouth, he sat at the top and looked down at her. She pulled on the rope with her hand. There was resistance at the other end. She pulled harder, and it didn't give.

She reached out and grasped the other end of the rope with her left hand. There was resistance there also. Suddenly, a light bulb came on in her head. She pulled on both ends of the rope with both hands. It didn't give. She seesawed it back and forth between her hands. It had hung on something, but what? Did she dare to hope?

"Dear God, Packy, did you knowingly catch the rope on something, or is it just an accident? It has to be a root, there's nothing else up there, I don't think."

She tied a knot in both ends of the rope, then put her feet against the side of the well and pulled with all her weight. The rope held. She stopped for a moment to think it through.

The tree is dead, so the roots are dead also. Are they rotten, or do they have strength left? Will the rope hold where it is, or will it slip off? Will I fall and break my arm, or worse, my neck?

"Juanita, ol' girl, your nerves are shot," she muttered aloud. "You've got nothing to lose, so why not go for it?"

Standing on her tiptoes, she reached as high as she could and tied the two ends of the rope together. She tied another knot about a foot farther down. When she finished, she had six knots in the rope. She rested for a few moments. Looking around, she saw that the raccoons in the well were watching her intently. She turned around and looked at the rope.

"Okay; now is the moment of truth."

She put her right foot in the knot at the bottom where she had joined the two ends of the rope together. Grasping the rope as far up as she could reach, she pulled up with her hands and pushed with her leg. Now, she hung suspended, about two feet above the bottom of the well. She repeated the process. At each knot, she stopped and rested. Fear overtook her, and she began to shake.

"Stop it, Juanita, you idiot," she admonished herself.

She breathed several deep breaths and waited. The shaking

subsided. When she lifted herself up to the next knot, her head was above ground. She could see the rope wrapped around the trunk of the dead tree. With a final effort, she pushed up on the last knot, and her chest and stomach lay across the ground. Fearing she would fall at the last minute, she seemed unable to move. Packy walked around in front of her and churred, scratching at her hand. With a final effort, she crawled out and away from the well.

She sat up and looked around. She could see the barn of to her right and the house directly ahead. Suddenly, she was aware that the ground was damp around her. Packy sat a few feet away, looking at her curiously.

"Packy, old buddy, I'm going to owe you the rest of my life. You and your sisters have a permanent place to live. If anyone ever tries to hurt you, they'll have to deal with me."

She stood up and walked to the edge of the well. She got down on her knees and looked down.

"Hang on girls. I'm going to get you out of that hole before you know it."

With that, she began looking around for something the kits could climb out on. She walked around the dead tree, but could find nothing that was long enough. She walked toward the tall grass where the creek flowed. At the edge of the creek, she found a fallen limb from the dead tree, and it appeared to be about fifteen feet long. She picked it up and tested it for strength. Deciding it would hold four raccoons at one time, she began dragging it by one end. Weakened from her ordeal, she had to stop and catch her breath twice. She finally reached the well. Working carefully, she pushed one end down until it touched the bottom. About five feet stuck out above the ground. She stepped to the edge of the hole. Four faces looked up at her.

"Okay, ladies, time to climb out."

They still sat motionless, looking up at her. Finally, Packy walked to the edge and churred down to his sisters. Becky immediately climbed on to the limb and began working her way up. Juanita held the end so the limb wouldn't turn and throw Becky off. In a few moments, she jumped onto the ground. Mandy came next, working her way slowly along. Finally, Misty and Cindy made the journey up the limb, one right behind the other. At long last, they all stood on the ground together. Juanita looked down at the five faces who sat waiting for her to do something.

"Okay, guys, let's go to the house and eat some leftover turkey."

****

Juanita's narrow escape from the well turned out to be a greater miracle than first met the eye. On Saturday afternoon, the temperature began to drop, and by midnight, it started to snow. An early winter storm dumped six inches of snow on the western half of the state. Had she remained in the well, she would surely have frozen to death. The kits had followed her, single file, back to the house. She had warmed a large pan of turkey and set it in the middle of the living room floor. She had been in awe at the amount of food her small guests consumed.

Despite her fatigue, she played the piano for half an hour. They listened attentively, cocking their heads from side-to-side as a piano tuner might, trying to discern the notes. After she stopped playing, she sat on the floor and coaxed them to her side. Still wary of humans, they sat in a bunch, just out of reach of her hands. After a few minutes, Mandy got up and walked to her. Juanita picked her up gently, then held her on her lap and stroked her fur. When Packy started toward them, Mandy growled, stopping her brother in his tracks. Packy sat down and waited. He watched them intently but made no move to intervene.

Finally, Mandy decided to get down. When Juanita reached down and picked Packy up, Mandy churred her approval. He sat quietly while she stroked along his back. After a few moments, he returned the affection by licking her arm. Tired to the bone, she eased him to the floor and lay on her side.

Soon, all four raccoons were lying in a huddle next to her stomach. As she stroked each one in turn, she dropped off to sleep. After napping for an hour or so, she awoke to find Packy scratching gently on her arm. Groggily, she sat up and saw the other four standing by the door. Sleepily, she got up and let them out. Barely half awake, she watched as they crossed the lawn toward the elm tree.

Now, she sat in the living room, looking out at the snow and wondering about her friends who had saved her life. She shivered as she thought about the possibility of still being in the bottom of the well. Donning her coat and boots, she waded through the snow toward the animal shelters. Once inside, she went about giving each of the adoptees food and water. Finished with the others, she walked over to feed Scrappy. Remembering that raccoons often sleep around the clock in bad weather, she sat the bowl down so as not to disturb him. Glancing inside, she saw a huddle of raccoons.

"Scrappy, old buddy," she said quietly, "when you have company, you go all out."

Chapter 11

CHURCH CALIMITY

New Year's Day brought more snow. An Arctic cold front drifted down over the land, bringing wind and freezing weather. Raccoons, by nature, become lethargic when the temperature drops below twenty-six degrees, and kits are no exception. Proving the theory that there is no place like home, they returned to the elm tree. Although they didn't hibernate, their metabolism slowed, and their need to void and excrete was minimal. While most animals in the wild huddled in ravines and thickets to ward off cold, the kits stayed warm and comfortable, basking in each other's body heat. For several days, they slept without end, refusing to come down, even for food.

Like a mother with quintuplets, Juanita Dills worried about her furry friends. Since they had saved her life, she felt responsible for them. In her mind, they were her best friends, and she believed they had sacrificed their own safety to help her at the most dangerous point in her life. Despite all this, they were wild animals, and she must not interfere with their freedom. To do so would compromise their friendship, a concept she didn't intend to risk. She had read everything she could find about raccoons, but still, she made a daily trek to the elm tree. When she found no tracks, she used Luther as a sounding board, drawing comfort from his assurances. The builders had started his new apartment, and she looked forward to having someone on the farm at night. Falling into the well had changed her outlook, and for the first time in her life, she felt mortal and vulnerable.

Raccoon intelligence intrigued her to the point she launched a quest to learn everything possible about the subject. With the exception of dolphins, she now believed them to be smarter than any other animal. The question foremost in her mind regarded Packy's looping the rope around the old dead tree. Did he do it on purpose, or was it an accident? She wanted to believe he had reasoned out a way to get her and his sisters out of the well. Too, she wondered if he would have done the same, were she alone, or did he do it for his sisters, knowing she would save them after she got out. Even that concept was a stretch, giving rise to the possibility he had simply hoped for a reward of fish or other food.

Realistically, she had to conclude on the side of an accident. She went back to the old well and studied the possibilities. When she looked from the well in a direct line to the house, she saw a line of rocks left over from the old house. About twenty feet from the well, the rocks could have created difficulty for Packy while dragging the rope. If that were the case, he might have taken an easier route and dragged the rope around the tree. After dropping one end into the well, he might have found he couldn't pull the rest of it, so he decided to pull the other end, and looped the rope around the tree by accident. In any event, the act for a reward concept gave her food for thought, an idea she couldn't eliminate.

She finally concluded it didn't really matter. Whether by accident or design, Packy, with the help of his sisters, had saved her life. The event had created even greater resolve she must succeed in her animal rescue mission. They were God's creatures, too, and not enough people cared about their welfare. It was one thing to quickly and mercifully kill an animal for food, but it was a completely different matter for them to go hungry or suffer. She had learned a valuable lesson from five adolescent raccoons. Maybe animals weren't so dumb after all.

****

The mating season for raccoons occurs in the middle of winter. In their first year of life, the males are not sufficiently mature to mate. Females, on the other hand, may or may not mate during their first winter, and is solely dependent on individual maturity. The females rarely wander far from their dens, preferring to stay close to home. Sometime in December or January, the more mature males wake up from their long winter's nap to realize they have a strong preference for female companionship. The desire for food takes a back seat, as they search forests and fields as part of their mating ritual. A male, for the most part, will mate with any female that receives him, but the female is much more selective. She will refuse to mate with all males except that special one. Mr. Right may be the first, the tenth, or the last male that makes romantic overtures, and only she knows the qualities he must possess. Sometimes, there is no eligible bachelor to her liking, and in this case, she must wait until the next winter when suitors again seek out her company.

As soon as the snow melted down to a reasonable depth, Scrappy began making frequent trips to the elm tree. On several occasions, he tried to climb up, but his disabilities prevented him from reaching the first limb. He often walked in circles around the tree, whimpering and growling. From all outward appearances, his efforts went unnoticed, because the kits ignored him, preferring to slumber away in their den. Finally, he would give up and go away, returning to his cage in the box.

In the second week of January, as Scrappy sat on the ground looking up into the elm tree, he heard scratching noises. Soon, Mandy came into view, and in a few moments, she sat on the ground with Scrappy. Excited to see his best friend, he churred happily, and they began playing around the tree. They chased each other through the snow, romping like children. Patient to the extreme, Mandy waited on Scrappy when he fell behind. Eventually, both of them tired of the play and lay down in the snow for a well-deserved rest.

The next night, when Scrappy arrived at the elm tree, he found Mandy patiently waiting for him. She churred happily as he approached, and he returned the greeting. The winter storm had passed, and a star-studded sky stretched from mountain to mountain. The moonlight shone through a gap in the mountains and cast a ribbon of light along the waters of the Little Tennessee River. The evening was still young, and the two raccoons left the safety of the elm tree and headed across the field toward the barn. The warning hoot of a screech owl sent them scurrying for cover. Once inside the barn, they sat quietly, waiting for the predator to fly away. Soon, the hoots came from across the river, and they resumed their normal activity.

On the backside of the barn, they discovered a ramp that had a gradual slope, and for the first time, Scrappy managed to get up to the barn loft. Any new territory always required exploring for a raccoon, and the barn loft was no exception. Like a hostess in a new home, Mandy showed Scrappy around, looking and sniffing at the many secrets kept hidden by the old barn. The passing years had not eliminated the many odors a raccoon's sharp nose could detect. They investigated one scent after another, basking in the glow of each other's presence.

Old horse harnesses, plow lines, and leather aprons hung from the walls. Antique tools, oil cans and wagon parts littered the floors. Boxes of seed corn and beans, relegated to forgotten locations, invited rats, mice and other vermin to crawl in and dine. Hay, stacked in years past and kept dry by a well-constructed roof, occupied an entire corner of the loft. None of this deterred the happy raccoons from their mission. It was just something new and different, providing an outlet for their curiosity. Scrappy took it all in wonderment, following Mandy from one part of the loft to another, stopping here and there to examine items of special interest.

The passage of time meant nothing as the two friends roamed throughout the loft, stopping occasionally to rest and enjoy the still of the night. So engrossed in each other the outside world became a blur, they temporarily forgot food, friends and family. Somewhere in the recesses of their minds, the flowers of love flourished, and for a short time, passion ruled their emotions. Daylight found them relaxing on an old horse blanket in the southwest corner of the barn. The rising sun cast bright beams across the loft, causing them to squint until they moved to a darker location. Tired from a full night of exploring, they crawled back under the hay and dropped off to sleep.

****

The other kits slowly adjusted to Mandy's strange behavior. At first it was subtle, and almost unnoticeable. In the middle of the night, she would disappear for an hour or two, then rejoin the others in their nocturnal pursuits. A close-knit family unit, the kits had learned to sense each other's moods and emotional changes. Within their normal hunting range, they could track each other without difficulty. When they became separated, they regrouped easily, and they had the ability to communicate meetings at pre-arranged locations.

As the days passed, Mandy's absences became more frequent, but Packy didn't worry. He had seen her with Scrappy often enough to be reasonably sure of her safety. Even though Packy was the undisputed leader, raccoons do not defer to each other in a hierarchy as wolves do. Under raccoon rules, Mandy could defer to Packy or go her own way. It all depended on her degree of maturity and emotional inclination. Even so, Packy kept an eye out for her presence, knowing Scrappy's limited mobility forced them to stay close to home. Still, the kits missed their sister, and her disappearances interrupted their routine. Despite this, life went on, and when weather permitted, the four other siblings foraged for food in the usual places.

Juanita had told Luther not to feed them all the time because she didn't want to rob them of their natural pursuits. After a while, she settled into treating them twice a week. That was enough food to keep them from starving, but not enough to appease their appetites. They also noticed Mandy was spending more time with Scrappy, but paid little attention other than to keep an eye out for their safety and well-being.

A week later, Mandy moved in with Scrappy. Now, they both slept in his cage in the box every day. They divided his food Luther left for him, and then searched for more as their hungry dictated. The barn became their preferred haunt, and catching mice became their favorite pastime. They weren't faster than mice; they just became adept at rooting the tiny rodents out of their hiding places. On some instinctual level, Packy, Becky, Misty and Cindy stayed away from the barn. Why they did wasn't clear, not even to them. Even though it would be temporary, Scrappy and Mandy had become a unit, separate from the others and with a new purpose.

On the first day of February, Mandy moved out of Scrappy's cage and went back to the elm tree. The sound of her claws on the tree bark woke Packy up, and he knew without looking Mandy had come home. By late afternoon, the temperature had dropped to twenty degrees, and it began to snow. Happy to have Mandy back, the other four snuggled against her, and they slept peacefully. For eight days, they never left the den. On the ninth day, they climbed down the tree to find a tantalizing meal of fish and chicken waiting for them.

After completing their meal, they went back up, but Mandy continued to climb until she located a satisfactory den in the third layer of limbs. The hole went back under two adjoining limbs, and then curved back under a third limb. Over the years, wind and water had rotted wood on the inside of the hole until it became soft and pliable. With her claws, Mandy scratched the rotten wood until she had enough for a comfortable nest. Using her paws, she moved the shavings about until she had them arranged to her satisfaction. Immediately upon finishing, she lay down and dropped off to sleep.

Concerned about her strange behavior, Packy climbed up to investigate. Peering inside, he saw Mandy was sleeping. He churred to get her attention. Much to his surprise, he encountered ferocious growling and the showing of teeth. He sat still, waiting for Mandy to calm down. When she stopped growling again, he attempted to enter again, only to be met with the same ferocious resistance. In raccoon language, he tried to reason with her, but he soon figured out he was wasting his time. Mandy had no intention of allowing him or any other raccoon to enter her den.

Perplexed and disappointed, Packy climbed back down to join his other sisters. Every two or three days, weather permitting, Mandy climbed down to forage for food. Although she passed right by her old den, she made no attempt to enter. She went straight to the animal shelter to look for Scrappy. Whether he was home or not, she ate the remaining food in his bowl. On the occasions when he was not home, she ate first, then went outside and looked for him.

One night, she couldn't find him, although she looked all over the farm. Finally, she figured out he was in the house with Juanita Dills. She climbed up on the bedroom window and looked inside. She could see him lying at the foot of Juanita's bed. She whined and growled until he got up and came to the window. In a few minutes, they sat on each side of the window looking at each other.

Finally, the churring and scratching awakened Juanita, and she got up to investigate. As she rubbed sleep from her eyes, she saw Mandy standing on her hind feet and holding onto the screen. Even though she feared Mandy would run away, she unlocked the window and raised it. When Mandy didn't move, Juanita unlatched the screen. As soon as she pushed it open, Mandy dropped down, and then crawled under it. When she turned around, she saw both raccoons standing at the door waiting for her to let them out.

Before Juanita opened the door, she reached down and picked Mandy up. Surprised she didn't resist, Juanita held Mandy in her arms and stroked her fur. She sat down on the floor, picked Scrappy up and snuggled them both. As she ran her fingers along Mandy's stomach, a light bulb came on in her head. Now she understood Mandy's strange behavior that Packy and his sisters did not. Mandy, not yet fully grown, was expecting a family of her own.

****

Many wild animals are born with ability to sense changes in the weather, and the raccoon ranks among the best. Their ability to sense changes in barometric pressure is uncanny, and their bodies prepare for seasonal changes without any conscious thought. Given this knowledge, it is surprising all the kits, except Mandy, got caught in a snowstorm two miles from home. The middle of February brought a warming spell that lasted almost two weeks. One week, they were lethargic and sleepy, and the next, they were active and hungry. When the temperature drops, their body chemistry reduces their appetite. When the temperature rises, hunger pains return in full force.

Not foolish enough to try a river crossing, Packy, Becky, Misty and Cindy decided to pay another visit to the Mason farm. They found a hen's nest in the barn, and each of them devoured one egg. After that, the pickings were slim. They did find some corn, hardened by winter weather and bland to the taste. Farmer Mason had nailed additional wire around his chicken house, and of course, nothing grew in the garden in the middle of winter. Still hungry and disappointed, they decided to try their luck in a residential neighborhood farther to the southeast.

Keeping an eye out for dogs, they managed to raid a couple of trash cans. Unfortunately, the noise generated by rolling the cans had unwelcome consequences. Almost immediately, lights came on in nearby houses, and in moments, homeowners appeared on decks and porches. Still wary of humans, and for good reason, the kits dashed to the woods at the first sign of trouble. They sat quietly until all the people turned out the lights and went back to bed. Like kids at Halloween, they dashed from one house to the next. By now, they could differentiate between house pets and hunting dogs, but even so, they had no intention of getting too close to man's best friend.

Finding there were too many dogs for comfort, they turned back toward home.

Returning at an angle in a northwesterly direction, they came upon a large wooden church sprawled across their path. Not as frightened by people smells as they had been in the past, they explored the grounds around the church. Failing to find anything to eat, they turned their attention to the forest of strange looking stones in back of the church. At the edge of the cemetery, they found some discarded flowers. The roses exuded a delicious scent, but the taste failed to measure up to the smell. Even worse, the plastic flowers had no smell but tasted worse than the roses.

Climbing on top of a large tombstone, Packy tried to make sense of the surrounding landscape. He had seen stones before, but this made no sense at all. Worst of all, no food seemed to exist anywhere in the stone forest. From his vantage point on top of the monument, he could see a light inside the church. Remembering a light stayed on in farmer Mason's henhouse, he churred a signal to his sisters. Returning to the church yard, they started looking for an entrance. Everything they tried resulted in failure until Becky found a broken window in the basement.

Despite the sharp edges on the glass, they managed to crawl through without incident. Once inside, they began looking for the light, thinking chickens or eggs could be their reward. After several false starts, they found and climbed a set of steps that led directly up into the sanctuary. The lights, mounted high up on the ceiling, cast a dim glow onto the aisles and pews. They worked their way through the pews, sniffing Bibles and songbooks. Walking along on the back of a pew, Misty slipped on the polished wood and landed on the carpet with a thump. When she realized she had hurt nothing but her pride, she decided to try it again. Soon, they were all climbing and jumping from one pew to the next.

Arriving at the altar, they found a large decanter filled with wine. While Becky held it, Cindy pulled out the glass stopper. Overwhelmed by the pungent odor, Becky dropped the bottle. Wine spilled down the side of the podium and out onto the floor. Easing along the floor, they approached the liquid cautiously. Outside the bottle, the wine lost its pungency, and a delectable odor rose from the liquid. Finally, they had found something with a taste that matched the smell. Not one to be shy, Becky started lapping the wonderful liquid. Packy and Cindy joined in while Misty sat back and watched. A little farther along the floor, she found a puddle all her own and attacked it with gusto.

After about thirty minutes, all four kits felt the effect of the alcohol in the wine. They didn't understand the change in their disposition, but they all felt light-hearted and full of mischief. They climbed up on the choir chairs and jumped off on the carpet. When they tired of that game, they searched for something else to do. Cindy climbed on top of the podium and churred to the empty pews. Becky and Misty turned over a music stand and it landed with a bang in the aisle below the altar.

In short order, Packy found the baptismal pool, which contained about six inches of water. Unlike the river, the water was cool but not icy cold. He churred for his sisters to join him. Soon all four of them were splashing and swimming in circles. Becky found the steps leading into the pool and leaped off into the water. The others joined in and they played at this game for at least an hour. Soaking wet, but happy, they finally tired of the water and wandered back down the aisle, leaving a trail of water as they went.

As their alcoholic befuddlement dissipated, hunger followed in its wake. Again, searching for food became their priority. Crossing over into the west wing of the church, they found a kitchen. It took a while, but they figured out that if they stood on top of the counters, they could get the cabinet doors open. Becky climbed up on Packy's back and pulled herself up onto the first layer of shelves. One by one, she pushed the cans out, and they landed with thumps and bangs onto the counters and floor. Despite their best efforts, they couldn't find a way to get any of the cans open.

Finally, Cindy found a bag of pretzels. She ripped open the plastic, and they all gathered around to sample the contents. The pretzels themselves weren't that good, but they all liked the taste of salt. After consuming the pretzels, they prowled about the kitchen in search of other morsels. Misty found a box of pepper and turned it over. It only took her a moment to work the lid open, and suddenly, she began to sneeze violently. The others came to see what was wrong with Misty, and soon all of them were sneezing and coughing. They quickly left the pepper and went to the other end of the kitchen where they sat until the sneezing spasms passed.

On the trail of more food, Packy found a liter of cola someone had left on another counter. Failing to get the cap off, he pushed it over the side. It hit the floor with a plop, and the lid popped off. Cola spewed all around the kitchen. When the spewing stopped, the kits found that the frothy liquid had a wonderful taste. When they had lapped all the cola that had spilled out on the floor, Becky and Misty played with the bottle until they managed to pour out the remains of the syrupy liquid. Finishing that, they chewed the bottle apart and licked the plastic.

Still not satisfied, they began a new search. In another cabinet, they found a carton of eggs with only one egg missing. Removing the delicacies, one at a time, they ate the contents and scattered the shells all over the floor. Renewing their search, Cindy found a box of cereal. They pushed the box over and ripped the sides out. Soon, they had sugary flakes scattered all over the counter and floor. Finally satiated, Packy decided it was time to go home.

Outside, the temperature had dropped, and feathery snowflakes fell from the sky like salt from a giant shaker. As dawn lightened the sky, Reverend Wiggins and his wife decided they should go over and adjust the heat in the church. When they turned on the lights in the sanctuary, they immediately saw the mess left by the kits. Thinking vandals had broken into the church during the night, they began a methodical search of the building.

When they turned the light on in the kitchen, four raccoons sat transfixed on the counters. The pastor's wife reacted first. Reaching behind the door, she grabbed a broom and took out after the kits. As she ran toward Packy, the others scurried by Reverend Wiggins and headed for the basement. As the angry woman closed in, Packy stood on his hind legs and growled ferociously. Momentarily startled, she delayed long enough for Packy to dash between her legs. Recovering quickly, she turned and ran after the recalcitrant raccoon. Packy reached the stairs about three steps ahead of the broom. He ran down the steps with Mrs. Wiggins in hot pursuit.

As she swung at Packy, he dodged left and right, convinced the woman was out to kill him. By the time he reached the floor under the broken window, the others had managed to crawl out. He made three circles of the room as air from the broom fanned his fur. Finally, the minister's wife became too tired to run, and her fury abated. She sat down in a chair, and Packy hid behind a box of songbooks. In a mirror on the wall directly behind Packy, she could see him huddled on the floor. A kind woman at heart, she began to sympathize with her prey.

"I'm sorry fella," she said, "it's just you made such a mess."

Packy peered around the corner of the box.

"I'm not mad any more, and I'm not going to hurt you."

She stood up and started walking slowly toward Packy. He seized the opportunity and jumped up to the window ledge. Realizing she would reach him before he could crawl out, he jumped back to the floor and ran behind the box again.

The woman stopped and turned toward the door a few feet from Packy. Walking slowly, she crossed the floor and opened it. Outside, snow fell heavily from a charcoal sky.

"Okay, little fella, I'm going to leave the room. You have two minutes to disappear, and then I'm going to chase you with the broom again." She smiled as she said it.

Packy had no way of knowing what she said, but the tone of her voice sounded soothing. He watched her leave the room. He waited a few seconds and dashed for the door. Outside, he began to look for his sisters. He found them huddled under a hedge about twenty feet from the building. With Packy in the lead, they headed for home. By now, the snow was two inches deep with no letup in sight.

They didn't like the snow, but they had no choice but to continue. By the time they reached the ridge above the Mason farm, Packy knew they could not make it home. Their stomachs were now dragging in the snow, leaving a trail that quickly disappeared in the deluge of falling flakes. Both Misty and Cindy began lagging behind, and Packy had to churr several times to get them to continue. In desperation, he began to look for shelter.

Finally, he saw a hole under a rock outcropping. The others waited while he crawled inside to investigate. The hole was damp and cold but large enough to hold them all. He went back out and churred for them to go in. Packy got behind and pushed with his head. Finally, they were all inside, packed tightly in the hole. At first they were cold and uncomfortable, but soon their bodies began to warm each other, and they dropped off to sleep.

The snowstorm lasted three days, and the temperature remained below freezing for the duration. On the first of March, the kits crawled out and headed for home. The snow had melted enough so they could travel. When they reached their tree, they found a large bowl of perch and chicken waiting for them. Still warm, the taste was splendid, and they emptied the bowl in short order. With full stomachs, they climbed the elm and snuggled in for a well-deserved rest. Two hours later, a worried Juanita Dills found the empty bowl. She examined fresh claw marks on the bark, and then looked up into the tree and smiled.

****

  Calvin Cooke's broken arm had healed, but his anger still burned. Forgiveness was not part of his nature, and forgetting was impossible. He had sat on his porch for days on end, the cast on his arm a grim reminder of his misfortune. Not only that, but his rescuers had made him look like a fool, poking fun at his predicament. Adding insult to injury, Luther had disowned him, taking up with the woman who owned the property where he had fallen from the tree. In all the months of healing, it never occurred to him the whole incident was his fault. In fact, in Calvin's way of thinking, nothing was ever his fault.

  Now, he walked along the river on his uncle Chad Mason's property. One way or another, he had decidedhis enemies, the raccoons, had caused his injury. Feeding them to a pack of dogs became his goal, and Luther Loggins and that uppity woman would also pay. In Calvin's mind, retribution had no meaning, vengeance was all that counted. Over his uncle's protestations, he had decided to use the Mason farm as his staging ground for his final strike at the raccoons.

  The field along the river was almost a mile long, and it was level enough to cross with a pickup truck. In fact, if all his friends showed up, there would be a half-dozen pickup trucks. It was an easy passage through the gate by the barn, then an easy drive along the barbed wire fence that ran along the river. The only question was whether he could make the rest of the trip along the old logging road that ran into the Dills' property.

He stood by the fence at the property line. He didn't know which side owned the fence, but he didn't care. When he made his move, he would simply cut the fence and drive across. He could fix it later if it belonged to his uncle Chad. He climbed through and walked along the old road. He saw immediately that trees had grown in the road to the point that driving it would be difficult, if not impossible. Anyway, he didn't want to damage his truck. He walked back across his uncle's field and returned with a large bowsaw and a set of vice cutters.

He figured it to be about a half-mile to the open field on the Dills' property. He began to saw and cut a swath wide enough for a pickup truck to pass comfortably. He gave no thought to the fact he was both trespassing and destroying property without permission from the owner. His shoulders began to ache as he continued to saw and lop small trees growing in the road. He wanted to be able to drive right up to the creek, which ran close by the elm tree. He had also made arrangements to borrow a chainsaw with a thirty-inch cut, which he would use to cut down the tree before the woman could figure out what was happening.

When the time came, he would move suddenly, cut the tree down quickly and be gone before the sheriff's department could arrive. After that, it would be his and his friends' word against that of an outsider. His uncle would see nothing, and his story would be that six of them had played poker all night at his cabin on Chestnut Creek. He would move in at dawn on a Sunday morning. That way, the raccoons would be back in the tree, and response time by the sheriff's department would be the slowest. He knew better than to involve his brother, Jerry, a deputy on the sheriff's department, but he also knew

Jerry would defend his own blood.

Six hours later, he chuckled as he walked back to his truck, parked at the fence that joined the two properties. It had been hard work, but it would be worth it in the long run. They could now drive within fifty yards of the elm tree without difficulty. He hoped the Dills woman didn't discover what he had done. Even if she did, his uncle would tell her a couple of fishermen had probably been trying to get better access to the river. All in all, he had a well-thought-out plan.

"I should have been in the military," he said to his truck as he unlocked the door.

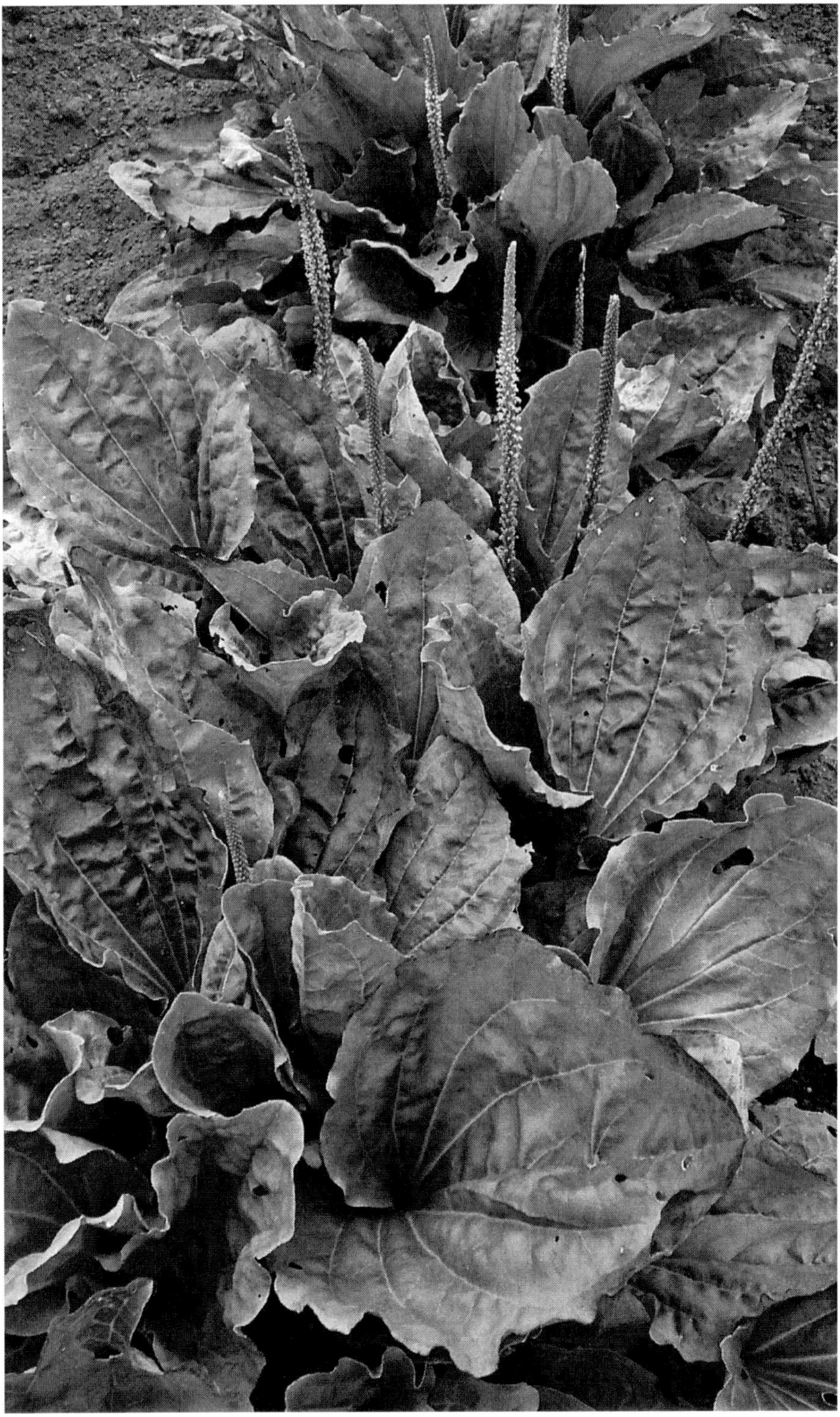

Chapter 12

BECKY'S PLIGHT

Accidents are among the most unpredictable events in nature. Both people and animals suffer from this misfortune. There are occasions when people injure themselves on purpose, but animals never do. On a conscious level, they live their lives one day at a time; but instinctually, they prepare for the future in a methodical way. When animals get hurt in the wild, they either get better or die. Typically, there is no in-between, for a lame animal is subject to dying a slow death or being devoured by predators. In fact, predators themselves will often devour their own kind at the slightest sign of weakness.

And so it happened that Becky was well and happy one minute, and disabled the next. Early March had been cold and blustery, but mid-March brought a warming spell. Snow and ice melted at a rapid rate, and early spring plants started budding prematurely. For a short time, the kits became vegetarians, eating new plant growth for much needed vitamins and minerals that normally dissipate from their bodies during long winter months. Most of the food that Juanita Dills had given them contained their needed nutrients, but the kits didn't know it. They simply followed the directions embedded in their genes.

Driven by their instinctual cravings, the kits climbed down the elm and began searching the fields for tasty green shoots that hidunder dead leaves and grass. Behind one of the outbuildings, they found a plethora of early plantain. Similar to people in many respects, they chose to dine on the darker, tender leaves that sprung out of the acidic sections of soil. Keeping a few feet apart, they scratched away leaves and twigs that covered the hidden delicacies. Munching happily, they moved from plant to plant, all the while, keeping eyes and ears open for predators.

In years past, Juanita's uncle had stacked a large pile of wood against the outbuilding where the raccoons were now foraging. The old man never burned the wood, and as it deteriorated, the stack leaned away from the shed. Later on, he had propped it up with a 2 x 4 by sticking one end in the ground and the other end against the top layer of firewood. Over time, the end in the ground rotted, allowing the woodpile to lean outward away from the building. Juanita had used a few sticks from the pile, but the wood was so old it burned up almost as fast as she could throw it on the fire.

Becky, in her eagerness to get at the tender leaves, pushed against the stick that braced the pile. Without warning, the wood began to topple, and Becky failed to understand the danger. About twenty feet away, Packy had just started toward Becky, when he saw the wood start to fall. He churred a warning, and Becky reacted immediately. Unfortunately, she ran parallel with the woodpile, instead of away from it. With a resounding crash, the wood hit the ground, burying Becky underneath the pile. For a few moments, she lay unconscious; but worse, a heavy stick of wood had broken her left front leg.

Forgetting for the moment danger might still lurk, Misty, Cindy and Packy rushed to her rescue. They pushed and pulled with their paws until they uncovered Becky. She lay on the ground, whimpering and groaning. Raccoon medicine could not repair a broken leg, but they tried anyway, licking her wounds and providing moral support.

As she lay among the sticks and plantain leaves, her breath came in short gasps, and her eyes refused to focus. Her leg, temporarily numbed by the accident, lay at an odd angle. Still in shock, she stood up on her other three legs and began to hobble toward home.

Daylight revealed the group about halfway between the outbuildings and the elm tree. Every few feet, Becky had to stop and rest. By sunrise, she could go no farther, and she lay down on the dead grass. He three siblings hovered around her, helpless to do anything. Finally, they lay down beside her, trying to keep her warm and comfortable. About noon, she rallied enough to continue on her strenuous journey. In three attempts, she only managed to travel about fifty yards, and it became certain she would not make it to her den.

About 2:00 p.m., Luther Loggins decided to take a break from his animal husbandry. Needing to stretch his legs, he walked toward the barn. About halfway, he saw movement in his peripheral vision. Looking to his left, he saw the kits milling about, with one of them down on the ground. Knowing it was highly unusual for raccoons to be out in the open in the middle of the day, he went to investigate. By now, the kits did not run when they saw him, but they usually kept their distance. At this point in their life, Juanita Dills was the only human they trusted.

This time, they didn't move away when he approached. As he stood looking down, he tried to ascertain the extent of Becky's injuries. He squatted down closely, but he made no attempt to touch her. He could readily see she had broken her left front leg. As he watched, she lay on her side panting; but otherwise, she made no attempt to move. Packy, Misty and Cindy stood about ten feet away, and Luther could tell Becky's injuries troubled them greatly. Careful not to frighten them, he stood up slowly and walked toward the house. In less than ten minutes, the kits saw two people walking across the field.

Immediately upon arrival, Juanita got down on her hands and knees and inspected Becky's injuries. Right away, she knew Luther was right. Becky had a broken leg. Being careful not to frighten the injured raccoon, Juanita talked to Becky in a soothing tone. At the same time, she reached out and gently stroked her fur. Becky began to whimper, and then moved slightly. Juanita knew if she touched her leg, Becky would probably bite her.

Without looking up, she spoke quietly to Luther. "Go to the animal shelter and bring me the tranquilizer gun and two of the smallest pellets. Do you have your keys with you?"

"Yes, I do," he replied. "I'll be back in a flash."

Without another word, Luther headed across the field. Juanita continued to stroke Becky, as she watched for Luther to return. Becky's siblings moved in closer, and Juanita reached out and stroked them with her other hand.

"I know you guys are worried. I'll take care of your sister for you, but you may not understand what I do. I'll have to take her to town to Dr. Martin. He's the local veterinarian, the nice doctor who visits your animal friends in the shelter."

As she talked, she continued to watch for Luther. In less than five minutes, she saw him round the corner of the third building. He hurried across the field, but he didn't run. As he walked up, he handed Juanita the tranquilizer gun.

"I loaded it," he said. "And I made sure I inserted a small pellet. I have the other one in my hand in case you need it."

She took the gun from Luther's hand and backed away about three feet. She aimed it at Becky's rump.

"This will only hurt for a second, ol' girl."

Without another word, she fired the gun. They heard a swish, pop, and Becky jumped slightly. She handed the gun to Luther, then stood and quietly waited. In less than five minutes, Becky was sleeping soundly. Juanita got down on her knees, eased her hands under Becky and picked her up. Standing up, she cradled Becky to her chest and walked slowly toward the house. The other three kits walked close behind, running when necessary to keep up.

When she reached her van, she opened the door and laid Becky down on the passenger side of the front seat. Before she could close the door, three other raccoons sat on the seat beside Becky. Startled for a moment, she looked thoughtfully at Packy, Misty and Cindy.

"Okay, guys, when I get back, we've got to have a heart-to-heart."

She turned and looked at Luther. "Keep an eye on them while I go into the house. I'm going to call the vet and get my purse and keys."

She walked to the house while Luther waited. In a few moments, she returned. The kits still sat on the front seat with Becky.

"Okay, guys," she said for the second time. "You can't go. I can't turn three raccoons loose in the doctor's office, and you can't stay in the car. I'll probably be there at least two hours, if not longer. Now, scat. I'm going to take care of Becky, and I promise, I'll bring her back to you."

She hardened her tone of voice. "Now, out, out, out."

Packy cocked his head and looked at her. Standing up on his hind legs, he growled, and then suddenly jumped off the seat onto the ground. Misty and Cindy followed him. They walked a few feet away from the car and lay down on the grass.

"Well, I'll be darned," Luther said.

Juanita smiled at him. "I'll call you." She closed the door, started the engine and drove down the farm road.

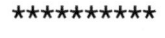

****

"You're right, Juanita," Dr. Martin said. "Her leg is broken. I'll have to put a cast on it. You'll have to keep her in the house or in a cage. If she's outside, she may wander off and get lost. Also, I'm going to put a plastic collar around her neck to keep her from chewing the cast off. She's not going to be happy with it, but it's for her own good."

"That's fine, Bill. I know a raccoon's teeth are sharper than a dog's. It's not going to be easy. Raccoons are nocturnal and I'm not. The first few days are going to be tough."

"Are you sure you want to invest that much time and energy in a wild animal?"

"Now, Bill, you know why I'm so fond of Becky."

"I'm sorry. I'd forgotten these little guys saved your life."

"That's right. And now, it's my turn. I'll always be indebted to them."

"I understand. Would you like to sit in the waiting room while my assistant helps me? It's going to take a while."

"Absolutely not; I know more about this than your assistant does. And besides, I'll go nuts just sitting out there. I don't know who buys your magazines, but you should have a talk with them."

"I'll do that. Now, you shave her leg while I gather and mix the proper materials."

In a few minutes, Dr. Martin was ready. Even though Becky remained unconscious, Juanita stroked her head while the veterinarian worked. She thought about all the times she had helped her husband work on cats and dogs. Deciding not to dwell on the past, she changed the subject.

"Have you ever set a raccoon's leg before, Bill?"

"No I haven't, but I did patch one up about two years ago. I had to remove one of his feet. He had been in a fight with a pack of dogs. I believe it's the same one I saw in your animal shelter, Juanita."

"I'll bet it is," she replied. "His name is Scrappy."

"That's a good name for him. As I remember, he killed three of the dogs."

"Well, I'll be darned," Juanita said. "I never did know the full story of his injuries. The rascal is about to be a father."

"And how do you know that, Juanita?"

"It's Becky's sister, Mandy. I expect she'll be a mother in a couple of weeks."

"Well, let me know if you need a good obstetrician." His blue eyes sparkled beneath his shock of unruly white hair. "It looks like we're done. Do you want me to help you carry her to your car?"

"Not for a few minutes, doctor. I want to run to the pet store and pick up a couple of items. I don't want her waking up in the car and finding out she's alone. She's going to be difficult enough with me there with her.

****

As Juanita drove down the farm road, she could see the river sparkling in the moonlight. Becky lay on the seat beside her. She thought about how small and helpless Becky looked with her leg in a cast. Directly in front of her, a full moon hung low in the sky, reminding her how long it had been since breakfast. She reached out with her right hand and stroked Becky's fur.

"Well, ol' gal, it's going to be a tough time for you for a while, but the first thing I'm going to do is get something to eat."

As she turned back to her driving, she saw an opossum crossing the road in the glare of the headlights. She slowed the car to avoid hitting the scurrying marsupial.

"All right, get on with it, ol' boy. I'm not in the mood to take another animal to the vet tonight."

She stopped the car for a few seconds and watched the opossum climb down the bank to the river.

It's amazing, she thought. People worry and fret about everything from the important to the ridiculous. Animals just take it one day at a time. No worries, no responsibilities, no time clock.

She looked over and saw Becky jerk in her sleep. "I'd better get you home, little one."

As she came out of the final curve just before her house, she saw Luther standing in the yard. All three outside lights were on. He had a rope in one hand and at the other end, three raccoons tugged vigorously. She pulled to a stop in the driveway, and for a moment, watched their game. From out of the shadows, Scrappy and Mandy walked toward the car.

"Hmm," Juanita mused, "Word sure gets around."

Almost simultaneously, Luther and the kits turned loose of the rope and walked toward the van. Luther opened the door and held it while Juanita got out. Immediately, he walked around and opened the passenger door. He squatted down on one knee and looked at Becky. In a few seconds, the front seat was full of raccoons. They all crowded around and began to lick Becky's fur. Becky stirred and opened her eyes, groaning slightly.

"Your patient is awake, Juanita," Luther said.

"Help me carry all this stuff in the house, please, Luther."

As she went around to the passenger side, Luther opened the cargo door.

"All right, you guys, get out of my way so I can carry your sister into the house."

Luther brought in a plastic doghouse without a bottom and a comfortable looking dog bed.

"Juanita, this house and bed is big enough for a Saint Bernard. Do you expect Becky to grow a lot while she's healing?"

She turned around and smiled at Luther. "No, I don't. But I expect some of her family members will sleep with her if I let them."

"What's in the box?" Luther asked.

"It's a doggie door. Would you mind installing it in the back door of the kitchen? I don't want to spend half my time letting raccoons in and out."

As Luther went to look for his tools, Juanita set up Becky's bed in a corner of the living room. When she was satisfied with the location, she placed the injured raccoon in it. Slowly, Becky sat up and stared around the room with a dazed look. Juanita warmed a small amount of liver pate' and folded it around a small red pill. She held it out to Becky. As the smell hit her nostrils, she licked it. As Juanita held it between her thumb and forefinger, Becky took it with her teeth. In a moment, she swallowed it.

"Good," Juanita said. "I wasn't looking forward to stuffing it down your throat, what with those sharp teeth of yours."

Luther returned with a saw, hammer and other tools. Juanita went with him to the kitchen and showed him how she wanted the door installed. When she returned to the living room, she saw Becky had laid back down, surrounded by five other raccoons. As Becky slept, the others lay quietly, providing comfort and solace to their injured sister. Mandy and Scrappy lay together on one side, while Misty and Cindy lay on the other side. Packy lay at the end in a position that allowed Becky to use his side as a pillow.

"Luther," Juanita called out. "I hate to interrupt your work, but would you come in here and look at this."

There was a moment's delay, and Luther walked into the room. He stared at the raccoon family. "Well, I'll be darned. They could teach people a thing or two."

After Luther walked back into the kitchen, Juanita carefully placed the plastic doghouse down over Scrappy and the kits. She understood raccoons slept better when they were surrounded by something solid. She got down on her knees and looked through the door. They were all still in the same position. She stood up, went into the kitchen and started preparing something to eat. She insisted Luther join her before he finished the doggie door.

****

Impressed at how quickly the raccoon family learned to use the doggie door, Luther affectionately dubbed it the "procyon portal."

"You've learned a lot, Luther," Juanita said when she first heard him use the term. "You really are using those books I gave you."

One evening, over coffee, he told her about his life, his struggles to return to society, and the difficulty of putting his prison record behind him. His classes at the community college were going well, and he had made the Dean's List. For the first time in his life, he saw his name in the newspaper in a good light. Juanita framed a copy of his letter of congratulations and hung it on her living room wall. She had made arrangements for him to alternate his work schedule so he could attend full time. She knew it was a difficult load for him, but she believed he was up to it. There was definitely more to the man than she had thought when she first met him. When he asked her about future classes, she refused to advise him.

"Far be it from me to decide your future life, Luther. I'll be happy to listen, but I won't tell you what curriculum to pursue."

He had accepted her answer and selected his courses. Now, it seemed the more he learned, the more motivated he became and the harder he worked. One night, she saw his lights on at 1:00 a.m. She knew he was studying for an exam. At 6:00 a.m., he was at work in the animal shelter. The next morning, forgetting her rule not to advise him, she did caution him not to burn himself out.

As time passed, it became obvious Luther was a jack-of-all-trades. He could carpenter, wire, plumb and build anything she asked. Together, they had decided to repair the outbuildings one at a time. As she watched him work, she admired his strength and dignity. The muscles in his arms rippled as he mixed mortar to repair a rock wall. Suddenly, it dawned on her she had developed feelings for the man. The realization shocked her to her toes.

"Nah, just friendship," she muttered under her breath.

"I'm sorry," Luther said, looking up from his work. "I didn't understand what you said."

"Nothing; sometimes I think too much. I'm going to the house for a while. Let me know if you need anything."

****

Winter decided to get in one last blow before surrendering to spring. The comfortable March temperatures suddenly dropped, brought on by a cold front that drifted down from Canada. For several hours, heavy snow poured from a sable sky, masking the farm with an alabaster blanket. The sturdy old house stood strong as heavy winds buffeted the walls and gables. Despite the fact the new heating system worked perfectly, Juanita kept a roaring fire going in the huge rock fireplace. Luther came and went in the performance of his duties, carrying wood, making entries into Juanita's computer, and helping with Becky.

Given her new feelings, Juanita became more distant with Luther, causing the man to wonder about the subtle change. Finally, he chalked it up to the stress of running a business, looking after Becky and the weather. His heavy schedule at school didn't allow him much idle time, and he soon accepted the change as part of his daily life.

Being an intelligent woman, it soon occurred to Juanita she might alienate the man who had helped her more than anyone else. The next day, she invited him over for dinner. She prepared her special pot roast followed by homemade apple pie. After they finished eating, Luther refused to sit down until he had helped clear the table and pack away the dishes. Later, they ate popcorn and watched a movie. At 11:00 p.m., Luther walked across the packed snow to his apartment, scratching his head and mumbling about the vagaries of women. He showered and went to bed, but soon found he couldn't sleep. He got up, dressed and went out to check on the animal shelters.

As he passed Scrappy's box, he decided to look in. Not surprised to find the aging raccoon missing, he figured he was out making his nocturnal rounds. Even though Mandy had moved to the elm tree, Luther saw the two together from time-to-time. He smiled as he thought about the many common characteristics animals and people shared. It occurred to him if Scrappy and Mandy were people, they would be the subject of hearty gossip.

Finding things in order, he decided to go back to bed. Just outside the door, he met Becky limping across the snow on three legs, holding her injured leg as high as she could. Juanita had convinced him to shovel a path from the buildings to the barn and the elm tree. Without that, Becky would not have been able to travel. Deciding not to interfere for the moment, Luther stayed well back and followed her. At first, he thought she was going to the barn, but he soon realized her destination was the elm tree. Hoping she didn't harm herself, he continued to follow.

Arriving at the foot of the elm tree, Becky immediately tried to climb up. She made it about two feet, and then fell to the snow covered ground with a soft thump. She lay still for a moment and then sat up. She began a soft wailing churr that Luther had not heard before. After a few moments, he heard scratching noises. In the dim light, he saw Packy coming down the tree, followed by Misty and Cindy. As they crowded around Becky, she stopped her strange noise and lay down in the snow. Soon, the others joined her.

Luther stood silent for a while, mulling over the situation. He knew Juanita would get upset if she found out Becky had left the house. They had discussed the possibility and decided her cast would keep her in. Now, he knew better, having witnessed first-hand, the courage and determination of the smallest raccoon. Even Dr. Martin had agreed Becky's recovery had been remarkable. Just as Luther concluded he should get Becky and carry her back to the house, he saw Packy stand up and start walking in that direction. When the others didn't follow, he stopped, turned and growled at them.

In a few moments, Becky stood up and started hobbling toward Packy, flanked by Misty and Cindy. As Luther watched in fascination, the four siblings continued to walk toward the house. On four occasions, Becky stopped to rest, and the others waited patiently until she felt strong enough to continue. At long last, they made it to the back of the house. When they reached the doggie door, Packy went in first, followed by Becky and then Cindy and Misty.

Luther stood by the porch and wondered what he should do. Finally, deciding it was best to check, he used his key and slipped in quietly. As he walked toward the living room, he saw Juanita sitting on the floor in her nightgown, cradling Becky in her arms. The other three sat on the floor, watching their friend and sister. Unaware Luther stood in the shadows of the kitchen, Juanita sang quietly as her soft soprano voice filled the room. He stood for a moment longer, then slipped out quietly and locked the door. He walked with his hands in his pockets as his feet crunched on the packed snow. Back in his apartment, he found his harmonica and began to play the same tune he had heard Juanita singing to the kits.

****

Luther's nightmares about prison life had finally abated. The worst one had been a recurring dream where he stood in a courthouse listening to a harsh judge recite endless prison sentences. When that happened, he usually woke in a cold sweat. He would get out of bed, sit in a chair and stare out a window. Sometimes, he didn't go back to sleep for hours. Now, his nightmares had receded to the depth of his subconscious. A few pleasant dreams began filtering through his psyche, and for the most part, he slept soundly. The healing process brought positive results, among them, the need to care for people again.

Juanita Dills had certainly been a positive influence on him, although his achievements were the result of his own efforts. His was a classic case of a good man who had temporarily gone bad, and would spend the rest of his life trying to right the wrongs he had committed. Recognizing his progress, Juanita had invited his family, with his permission, to tour the farm. When he insisted on helping, she stopped him.

"No Luther," she said. "This is my treat, and I intend for you to enjoy your family. Besides, I'm having it catered; I just haven't told you."

So Luther acquiesced, and sat in the living room, entertaining his mother and sisters with stories about school and the farm. Juanita could see the pride in his mother's eyes as she watched his every move. At dinner, she stayed in the background, preferring for Luther to have center stage. After dinner, Luther built up the fire in the fireplace, and then insisted each family member bring him up to date on family life and events. Juanita became the final event when he asked her to sing and play the piano.

Caring for Juanita's adoptees had become a way of life for Luther, and he shuddered to think what would happen if he suddenly lost his job. In a way, it seemed as if he had been Juanita's foreman forever. Seven days a week, he rose at 6:00 a.m., ate a bite of breakfast, and then went directly to the animal buildings. Working quietly and efficiently, he prepared all the varieties of food he would feed the birds and animals. When the part-time employees and volunteers came in later in the morning, he assigned their daily duties and then left for school.

Traffic had increased up and down the farm road, so Juanita decided to have it paved as soon as weather permitted. So many clients came and went that damage to the road became an impediment to traffic. It had gotten to the point Luther and his helpers couldn't get their work done without constant interruption.

Due to abandonment and neglect of the Dills farm, local farmers and hunters took the privilege for granted and trespassed as they saw fit. Many of them hunted and fished out of season, believing their long family histories preordained certain rights. On one occasion, three deer hunters drove right up to the barn, got out and started across the fields. In less than an hour, Juanita heard the sound of gunfire. When they returned carrying a large buck, she told them not to come back. Even so, other hunters continued to come and fishermen cut trails along the river.

Finally, she decided they were ignoring her because she was a woman. She went to the courthouse and filed for posting, and then hired two teenagers to put up signs every fifty yards around her property. Many of the hunters ignored the signs. On a Saturday morning, she found six of them strolling casually across the north field. She called the sheriff and filed trespassing charges. When one of them threatened to burn her house down, she filed another set of charges. Eventually, word got around and most of the trespassing stopped. Life returned to normal, and Juanita went back to running her business.

At the end of March, the Asheville Citizen-Times did a feature article on the farm and Juanita's animal adoption business. In addition to Juanita, they interviewed Luther and quoted him on several occasions. Thankful they didn't delve into his past, he gave the reporters an excellent tour of the buildings and grounds. They left impressed, and their stories reflected their admiration. Juanita's and Luther's social standing rose in the community, and for the first time, many local people came out just to tour the farm. One hunter, whom Juanita had run off the property in November, came out, apologized and volunteered his services.

One afternoon, Luther told Juanita he didn't much care for all the publicity

"Don't knock it, Luther. You and I may not need it, but the animals do. Adoptions have increased by twenty percent since the Citizen-Times ran their article. Also, I can now afford to give you a raise in pay. I don't suppose I'll ever be able to pay you what you're worth, but I'll bet you could use a newer car."

Chapter 13

A NEW GENERATION

Calvin Cooke drove north on Highway 28, his aging Ford F150 locked in four-wheel drive. Dry snow drifted across the road, and clandestine patches of black ice lurked on shaded curves. Icicles dangled from overhanging rocks, suspended in space and time, waiting patiently for warmer temperatures to release their trapped energy. On the mountains above, frozen fog clung tenaciously to ancient oak and hickory, dovetailed into the cold, steely sky. In the valley below, the Little Tennessee River meandered between hills and peaks, drawn ever downward in its watery march to the sea.

At Allen Cliffs, Calvin pulled onto an overlook, killed the engine and climbed out of the truck. Nerves taut as a piano wire, he leaned against the steel railing and looked down onto the westward march of the river. The grandeur of the panoramic vista meant nothing to him as angry thoughts roiled and burned in his head. Below and to his left, several deer stood clustered in a meadow, pawing at the frozen ground in hopes of finding green shoots that had sprung up during the warm spell. Calvin watched them for several minutes, then went to his truck and removed his 30-06 rifle from the gun rack.

Returning to the railing, he dropped down on one knee and sighted along the barrel of the rifle. Still shaky from a late-night drinking bout, he had to use a post to steady his gun. His vision blurred as he tried to focus on the largest of the hungry animals. Calvin had needed glasses for several years, but believing they would make him less of a man, he had steadfastly refused to go in for an examination. Squinting as best he could, he fired at the deer's chest. Swinging the barrel quickly, he fired at the other deer until he emptied the magazine.

Checking the gun, he stood and surveyed the scene below. Two deer had fallen to the ground, and another dragged its injured body toward the trees at the edge of the meadow. The others disappeared into the forest like wills-of-the-wisp on a foggy night. Calvin watched the wounded deer until it became a still form on the frozen earth. He felt no sympathy for the dead and injured animals. To him, it was sport and nothing more, an unadulterated joy in destroying something that couldn't fight back.

He walked back to his truck and placed his gun back in its rack. Strangely, he felt better. The tension had drained away and his agitation had disappeared. He smiled as he cranked the engine, the deer slaughter forgotten. He looked up and down the road, and then pulled back onto the pavement. At highway 74, he turned west and drove toward the Nantahala Gorge. At Needmore Road, he turned left, and then followed the road for about a mile. Finally, he turned left again and drove up Wildcat Creek.

The road, snow covered and icy, followed an ancient Cherokee trail. Calvin see-sawed the steering wheel, forcing the tires in and out of slippery ruts. As he passed dilapidated mobile homes, dogs bayed and howled at his passing. Old cars, tires and empty drums littered every yard. Firewood, stacked haphazardly on rickety porches, gave the appearance of an abandoned sawmill. Smoke drifted up from home-made chimneys, announcing the owner's presence. As Calvin rounded the last turn, the pickup skidded dangerously. He fought the steering wheel until the truck corrected itself, leaving him breathless and shaking.

Finally, he pulled into a snow-covered yard and cut the engine. An unshaven man in a pair of overalls walked off the porch and out to the truck. Reaching under the seat, Calvin extracted a pint of bourbon whiskey. Removing the cap, he swallowed a couple ounces of the burning liquid, and then handed the bottle to his cousin.

"A little hair of the dog, Ralph?"

"No thanks, Calvin. That stuff would kill a grizzly bear."

"Suit yourself. Let's go out back and look at the dogs."

"I swear, Calvin, I think you like dogs better'n people."

"Nah, I hate the smelly things; they just serve a purpose."

"You mean like getting a bunch'a coons out of a big ol' elm tree? You don't give up, do you, Cal?"

"It ain't my nature, Ralph. You still in or not?"

"Shoot yow, man. Me and the boys are aching for some action."

"Good, then, let's go look at'em. I want to make sure you're starving them enough to make'em real hungry when the time comes."

****

In early April, the kits had their first birthday. Of course, they had no way of knowing that, and life went on as usual. The fact all five of them still lived was a miracle in itself. The first-year survival rate for raccoon kits born in the wild is less than fifty percent. Their mother had taught them well, and Packy's leadership had been a major factor in their survival. Along the way, they had learned some humans could be kind and helpful and some could be mean and cruel.

The loss of their mother had matured them more than the average yearling raccoon. As difficult as it had been, they benefited from their hardships. Even though their intelligence was more primitive than that of humans, they learned from their mistakes, and they grew in their ability to cope with their environment. Instinct alone did not account for their survival, but combined with intelligence, it gave them an edge most raccoons did not possess. They never ceased to astound Juanita and Luther, and many of their antics came off as a sense of humor.

Juanita and Luther began carrying a tape recorder, and Juanita started a log of raccoon sounds. The kits amazed them with their ability to communicate, and they compiled more than thirty different churrs. Juanita soon learned the kits repeated specific sounds for specific events. She and Luther tried imitating the sounds, but for the most part, they couldn't do it. Juanita did imitate their food sound and soon wished she hadn't, because every time she did it, they expected a snack.

They had figured out some time ago Packy was the leader of the group. They spent considerable time trying to figure out if Packy's churrs sounded any different than the others. They did decide Packy's sounds were a little deeper, but they knew that could simply be the difference between male and female and have nothing to do with the leadership role. Juanita went on line with some other raccoon enthusiasts, but none of them knew any studies about leadership among raccoon families other than that of parent and offspring.

One chilly Sunday morning while most of the farm slept, Juanita sat in front of the fireplace and wrote impromptu in her journal: "Their antics are often funny to humans, and they love to play and have a good time. They can communicate with each other better than almost all animals except dolphins. They have a known vocabulary of at least thirty distinct churrs, and this gives them an edge over all of their predators except one; the human. They can easily outsmart dogs, evade humans and hide from guns, but they can't defeat all three at the same time."

"In the wild, grown raccoons are adept at outsmarting their

predators, and they are fierce and unforgiving in a fight. They are predators themselves, hunting and eating mice, voles, small rabbits and birds. In the same vein, they often eat berries, apples, grapes and other starchy foods such as acorns and plants. Their first love is aquatic food such as crayfish, clams, oysters and fish. Their second love is fresh corn, and they have an uncanny ability to know when this vegetable is at its peak of ripeness. It is not unusual for a gardener to go to bed with a full patch of corn and wake up to find a family of raccoons has ravaged his entire crop.

"Given the opportunity to socialize with humans in a non-threatening way, they quickly lose many of their feral traits. Once they realize a family of humans won't hurt them, they become panhandlers, begging or stealing food at every opportunity. They have insatiable appetites, especially in the fall when Mother Nature is preparing their bodies for winter. A fifteen-pound raccoon can gain ten pounds in sixty days, and then lose it all during the winter months.

"Unless they are born in captivity, feral raccoons will never become tame to the point they lose their wildness. Nevertheless, they will quickly learn to go into a house with people present, if they think food is available. They often allow friendly humans to pet them, sometimes picked up and held, but if startled, they may scratch and bite. Under certain conditions, they will move into a house with people as long as they can sleep in a box or something similar. It is essential they have an exit from the house they can use at their own discretion.

"Unlike dogs, they can readily return to the wild if it becomes necessary. Even a raccoon raised in captivity can adjust to forest living in a short time. Their resourcefulness is legendary. When one of them can't accomplish a needed task alone, they will enlist help if it is available. They will combine their talents to open jars and cans or pick locks. One will watch while the other steals food and sound an alarm if danger approaches.

"During their second year of life, most of them will become loners, but not all. Sometimes they will live as a family unit for years, reaching the point that several generations will be living in the same place such as a tree or abandoned barn. When a female becomes pregnant, she will sometimes live with the father for a short time, but before birthing her young, she will find and move into her own den. She will not allow any other raccoon to live in the den with her until her kits are able to fend for themselves. If she is part of a family unit, she will stay close but not in the same nest.

"Notwithstanding the fact that I owe my life to five of them, they are the most interesting and lovable creatures in all the animal kingdom. Contrary to dogs and cats, they have an insatiable curiosity about everything. It is obvious they enjoy music, but I don't know why. I suppose it's for the same reason humans do, because the sound is pleasing to the ear and calms the soul. Packy, of course, is special. Not only did he save my life, but the lives of his sisters as well. I am still perplexed as to why he did it, but it really doesn't matter, the end justifies the means.

****

And so it was with Mandy, that despite her illness, her maternal instincts forced her to live alone, even though her den was only ten feet above her brother and sisters. Scrappy couldn't climb the elm, so she didn't have to deal with the issue of driving him from her den. She had even ousted her own brother when he tried to visit. Her instincts controlled her actions, and although she understood she would be a mother, she did not consciously think about it. Shortly before her time, she scratched additional shavings from the den walls, and then layered them into a soft bed.

Mandy had been slow ever since she had gotten sick when the kits lived with their mother in the groundhog's den. Since that time, she had never felt as well as the others, even though she led a normal life. She rested more often, and whenever possible, she made shorter trips than the others. Had she been human, she would have voiced her discomfort, and someone would have taken her to a doctor.

Given the circumstances, her pregnancy had gone well. She actually felt better than she had in a long time, even though her energy level remained lower than that of her siblings. Several days before her due date, her sluggishness returned. To compensate, she rested more and slept longer. In typical raccoon fashion, she kept more to herself as her body prepared for the delivery of her unborn kits. She stopped meeting Scrappy, and looked for food by herself.

She didn't find much to eat, and despite her perpetual hunger, she stayed away from the farmhouse. Sometimes she ate from the bowl Luther left at the base of the tree, but even then, she did it when the others were not present. Because she didn't feel well, she ate sparingly, and this complicated her condition. By the time of her due date, she became so weak she had difficulty climbing the elm tree. Even so, she persisted, and one week after her first birthday, she felt her body stir, and she knew her time was at hand.

One more time, she raked her wood chips into a neat pile, and then used her paws to arrange them to her satisfaction. A new moon crawled up a star-studded sky, giving no light. Midnight came and went, and Mandy lay quietly as birth pains racked her body. An owl hooted in the top of the great elm, but she didn't hear it. Mother Nature manipulated Mandy's body in the same way she had for a million raccoon generations. Despite her condition, her bodily functions worked as they should, one step at a time. There was nothing Mandy could do but suffer and wait.

When the first kit passed through her birth canal, she whimpered, but only for a moment. Five minutes later, a tiny blind and deaf body lay quietly on the shavings. Mother Nature had programmed him also, and his instincts told him to do nothing for a time. In less than an hour, he would feel hungry and search for a nipple, but for now, the innate time delay allowed for the births of his brothers.

Mandy's womb started contracting again, but this time, she felt it vaguely. Her pituitary gland had dumped a natural narcotic into her bloodstream, but later than normal because of her illness. Even so, it worked, and the pain of the second birth was less than that of the first. She began to pant, the human equivalent of sweating. No one was there to wipe her brow and give her encouraging words. Like her mother before her, she endured her pain alone.

For a short time, her bodily functions came to a halt. Her natural mechanism called for a rest. Her energy level was too low to continue. The third kit had to wait until her body marshaled strength for the final push. The delay was long, and the two new-born siblings began to feel hungry. They smacked their lips and started to move. Blindly, they groped around in total darkness, seeking a source of nourishment. In their blind search, they couldn't feel Mandy's nipples, and they began to panic. Finally, they crawled into each other, and the warmth of the other body calmed them. Snuggling together, they dropped off to sleep. Now, Mandy had time to recover before feeding time. Outside the blackness of the den, daylight started burning away the dark. Somewhere in the distance, a rooster crowed, and the tropical birds in the animal shelter began to shrill to one another.

Finally, Mandy's body decided it could handle a third birth. Glands began to function again, setting the birth process back in motion. Her body had consumed the natural narcotic, and pain returned with the birthing. Mandy moaned low in her throat as the third kit began to move. She whimpered as contractions consumed her, but finally the third kit lay on the chips behind her. No strength remained to deliver a fourth kit, but nature had provided, and the third was the last.

Driven to the limit of endurance, she passed out, and didn't move for several minutes. After a brief rest, she awakened to the sound of almost imperceptible whimpering. She sat up and searched for the tiny bodies she knew lay next to her. Her nocturnal eyes gathered minuscule bundles of light out of inky darkness, and she could see them. She summoned her strength, and licked them, one at a time. The taste didn't matter; it was her assigned duty to clean them up and prepare them for nursing.

The kits accepted the washing without complaint, and the feel of their mother's tongue passing over their bodies gave them contact with the world. For a while they dropped off to sleep, and then one by one, they crawled until they found a nipple. Dissipated but happy, Mandy lay on her side and accommodated them. Like all mothers since the dawn of time, she felt love for her tiny offspring. A tightness welled in her chest, and her body struggled to deliver the milk required for their survival. Unable to stay awake, she slept while they nursed, not knowing that her sickness had reduced the flow of milk. Still, for now, she had enough, and they suckled eagerly, not yet understanding a universe waited to greet them.

Down below, in the foggy morning, Packy, Misty and Cindy returned from a night of feeding. Becky still resided in the house, living the good life, despite the cast on her leg. They visited Becky regularly, but they still missed Mandy, and every time they entered their den, they sniffed the air to search for her presence. They knew not to climb up, Packy had experienced the ire of an expectant mother, and the others had learned from his mistake.

Misty and Cindy went into the den, lay down and waited for Packy. He had a duty they didn't have, passed to him from Mother, and his sisters understood in their own way. He sat on a large limb, and looked up into the tree. He knew Mandy was there, and his chest ached to fellowship with her. He listened quietly, and his sharp ears could hear Mandy panting. He had a vague feeling something was wrong, something intangible and out of his reach.

After a while, the panting ceased, and Packy felt better. The need for sleep suddenly alerted him to his tiredness, and he crawled into the den. In the darkness, he could see Misty and Cindy looking at him. He crept closer and lay down, basking in their warmth. Finally, he heard their shallow breathing, and he understood they had gone to sleep. He lay awake in the darkness, again, bothered by some vague uneasiness. For a moment, he heard a small, whimpering noise.

He remembered the days in the den with his mother, and he recognized the sound immediately. He moved his lips in the equivalent of a raccoon smile. He now knew Mandy had kits, but he didn't know what gender or how many. Uncle Packy dropped off to sleep as his three nephews suckled in the darkness of their den. Early spring had brought a new generation to the elm tree, a new family, filled with wonder and curiosity. Three new faces to romp and play, blessed by ignorance of an uncertain future, no worries and no fears, just love to share and seasons to grow.

****

Spring arrived in all its splendor, early by the calendar, causing tantalizing plants to spring from the ground and display their many shades of green. Nature adheres to its own schedule, often ignoring man and his calculations. A warm front had crept in on the prevailing winds, neutralizing winter's frigid moods, and spreading joy throughout the land. Birds twittered in the trees as they worked furiously to prepare their nests for the laying of eggs. Bears and woodchucks woke up from their long winter's map, leaving their dens to search for starches to replace nutrients lost during hibernation. Raccoon mothers searched along streambeds, looking for crayfish and pollywogs to satisfy their lactating bodies.

Packy, Misty and Cindy panhandled from Juanita and Luther when they could, and hunted in the fields and along the river when they couldn't. Becky could now put her foot on the ground without feeling pain, and although she walked with a limp, she could walk on all four feet. Juanita would fuss when Becky went out with the others, and then return with a dirty cast. Becky would sit quietly while Juanita cleaned it, peering out through her black mask at the kind woman who had rescued her.

She had learned from her failed experience she couldn't climb the elm tree, so she didn't try. She had adjusted to living in the house, and the free meals had spoiled her. Juanita and Luther stuck to their code of not feeding the others all the time because they didn't want them to become dependent. They figured Becky would join the others when her cast came off. Scrappy, already domesticated when he arrived at the farm, came and went at his own calling. Knowing Scrappy couldn't survive in the wild, given his disabilities, they fed him regularly. Juanita tried to be sure he had a healthy diet containing vitamins, protein and starches.

Sometimes, he and Becky would wander around the buildings together, but they never developed the closeness he and Mandy had accomplished. Becky had reached the point her speed would not increase until her cast came off. Her slowness caused her to gravitate to Scrappy, and their friendship grew. Still, she would not sleep in Scrappy's box unless Packy, Misty and Cindy accompanied her. When they finished their night of exploring, Becky returned to the farmhouse and crawled into her doghouse for a good day's sleep.

On the second night after Mandy's kits were born, Packy, Misty and Cindy went to the mudflat behind the barn. There, they dug for crayfish until the sun began to lighten the sky. The night had been fruitful, and they had full stomachs. They rested from their digging for a few minutes, and then headed for the elm tree. As they approached the tree, Packy's uneasiness about Mandy returned. They climbed up, and again, Packy sat on the limb and listened. This time, he heard a chorus of whimpering and crying. His ears told him it wasn't Mandy, but her kits that were making the noise.

He listened for a while, and then crawled into the den to join Cindy and Misty. Tired from digging, he lay down and immediately dropped off to sleep. About two hours later, he woke up from a deep dream about being chased by dogs. He sat up and shook off the fear, looking around the den for comfort. He understood nothing about the nature of dreams, but in his own way, he knew they weren't real. Again, his ears picked up the whimpering and crying of Mandy's kits. It came to him in a vague sort of way he hadn't seen Mandy come out to look for food, and this realization disturbed him.

He listened for a few more moments, and then decided to go up and investigate. Slipping out of the den, he blinked at the bright daylight, and then sat still until his eyes adjusted. He climbed the short distance to Mandy's den, and then peered inside. From the outside, he couldn't see much, so he decided to risk Mandy's wrath and go in. Once inside, his eyes readjusted quickly, and he could see well in the dim light. Mandy lay still, but the kits were crawling around, trying to nurse at dry nipples.

Packy churred for Mandy to get up, but she didn't move. Finally, he went to her and shook her with his paw. Still, she didn't move. He shook her with both paws and churred loudly, but that didn't help. Still blind and deaf, the tiny kits felt, rather than heard, the churring noise and thought it to be their mother. They immediately crawled to Packy and started feeling for nipples to nurse. Packy shrunk away to the other side of the den and continued to churr to

Mandy. He finally realized she wasn't going to move.

For several minutes, he sat in deep concentration, trying to fathom the situation and what to do about it. He left the den and climbed down the tree. Crossing the field at a dead run, he headed for the farmhouse. He went in through the doggie door and found Juanita preparing lunch in the kitchen. He sat on the floor, looked at her intently and churred loudly. When Juanita looked at him, he churred again. He went back through the door, sat on the porch and waited for her to follow. When she didn't come out, he went back in, walked close to her and started churring again. Juanita finally understood that Packy was trying to tell her something.

"What is it, Packy, what's wrong?" she asked.

Packy churred again, and then went back through the doggie door and into the yard and churred again. As soon as she walked into the yard, Packy walked a few yards toward the barn. He looked back at her and then stopped and churred.

"All right, Packy," Juanita said, "I understand you want me to follow you. Lead on, and let's see what's happening."

When she started toward him, Packy turned and began to walk at a rapid pace. Juanita hurried to keep up. When Packy got too far ahead, he would stop and wait on her. Finally, they reached the elm tree. He climbed up the tree a few feet looked down and churred at her.

"Now, Packy, old boy, you know I can't climb your tree. I know something's wrong, but I don't know what."

When she finished speaking to him, he climbed on up the tree and disappeared among the limbs. The leaves had not yet come out, and she caught glimpses of him as he continued to climb. Finally, he disappeared. She stood on the ground and waited, wondering what had happened. Shortly, she saw him coming down with something in his mouth. When he reached the bottom, he turned and gently laid a tiny kit at her feet. Packy sat staring at her while the kit wiggled and whimpered. She looked at Packy and then at the kit.

"What's wrong with Mandy, Packy?" she asked. "Why isn't she with you? Is she sick?"

Suddenly, it occurred to her Mandy might be dead. She reached down and picked up the small, furry creature. Very carefully, she put it in her sweater pocket, but continued to hold it with her left hand. Packy churred something, turned and climbed the tree again. In a few minutes, he returned, carrying another kit. Juanita picked it up and put it in her pocket with the other one. Finally, she had three kits in her pocket. Packy went back up the tree, leaving Juanita to wonder how many kits he would bring down.

Back in Mandy's den, he went to her still body and tried to pick her up by the neck. Finally, he got a firm grip and began to drag her. When he reached the hole, he couldn't pull her through. He tried several approaches, but it just wouldn't work. She was just too big and heavy for him to carry. He placed her gently back on the wood shavings and climbed back down the tree. At the bottom, he began walking in circles and churring to Juanita. She watched his movements and listened to his churring, trying to decipher his intent.

"What is it now, Packy? Is something wrong with Mandy? God, Packy," she said, "I wish you could talk. Tell you what, let's take these little guys to the house and make them comfortable, then we'll find Luther."

On the way back to the house, she tried to figure out how she would feed three newborn kits. She had fed tiny puppies and kittens before, and she knew it would be the same principle. Inside the house, she found a basket, ripped up some cloth and made a bed. She placed Mandy's kits inside and covered them. They continued to whimper, and she knew they must be fed soon. She went to the animal shelter and found Margaret, one of the volunteers, and then she looked for and found a small bottle she had used to feed an abandoned puppy. She saw it was a little large, but it would have to do. In a cabinet where she kept medications, she found a medicine dropper.

Back at the house, she warmed some milk and instructed Margaret in the fine art of feeding a tiny animal without strangling it. Satisfied Margaret understood, she went to look for Luther. She found him working behind one of the outbuildings.

"I can't climb that elm tree," Luther said. "Look what happened to Calvin Cooke."

"I know, but he's stupid, and you're not. And besides, it's the middle of the day. You can see what you're doing."

"I don't know," Luther said. "It's still risky."

"Okay, then, you hold the ladder and I'll do it."

"No, you won't. You'll break your neck. I know you're not bluffing, so I'll do it."

"I'm sorry, Luther. I don't want to put you at risk, but you know how important these little guys are to me."

"I know. I like them, too. I've got an idea, can we delay the climb for half an hour or so?"

"Okay," Juanita said. "I've learned to rely on your judgment. Tell me you idea."

"I will, but let me make a telephone call before I tell you."

Taking his new cell phone out of its pouch, he punched the numbers. He talked for a minute, and then hung up the phone.

"Okay, here's the deal. My friend, Roger, has some climbing equipment. He's going to run it right out."

"Good idea, you go to the house and wait on him, and I'll go back to the elm tree."

As she passed the barn, she saw Packy sitting under the tree. She walked up to him and dropped down on one knee.

"You know what, Packy? I think you knew I would be back. Let's be patient for a few minutes while we wait on Luther."

Packy cocked his head and looked at her. Without a churr, he climbed back up the tree and disappeared. In a few minutes, he returned. He climbed the tree and returned three times while they waited on Luther. Finally, Juanita saw Luther and Roger coming across the field. When they arrived, Roger helped Luther fasten on the climbing spikes and adjust the belt. He gave Luther very specific instructions.

"You got it, Luther?" Roger asked.

"I've got it," Luther said.

Luther hung one of Juanita's old purses across his shoulder by the strap, letting the bag hang down against his side. He clipped a construction flashlight onto his belt.

He turned and Roger helped him strap the climbing belt around the tree.

"Be careful," Juanita said. "I don't want anything to happen to you."

She said it with such conviction and sincerity Luther turned and looked at her strangely, searching her eyes for meaning.

Without a word, he began to climb, hesitantly at first, and then as his confidence grew with each step, he moved along at a faster speed. Even so, he moved slowly, stabbing the climbing spikes deeply into the thick bark of the elm tree. When he reached the first row of limbs, he unloosened the belt and hung it on a limb. Still digging the spikes into the tree, he used his hands to balance himself as he climbed.

At the first hole, he shined his light inside, but saw it was empty. He continued to climb. At the fourth hole, he saw Mandy lying inside. He positioned himself carefully, and then shined the light all around Mandy. She didn't move.

"I hope she isn't dead." Luther mumbled.

He reached in and touched Mandy with his gloved hand. She didn't move. He shook her gently. She stirred slightly and moaned. Not knowing any other way, he grasped her by the skin of her neck and lifted. She moaned again, but didn't resist. Working her outside the hole, he held her for a moment and stroked her fur. He could readily see something was seriously wrong. He worked her carefully into the old handbag and started back down.

When he reached the bottom row of limbs, he found he couldn't reach around the tree with the climbing belt. Knowing he was at risk, he used the bark for hand holds and moved slowly down the tree. The thirty feet diminished to twenty feet, and then ten. Juanita held her breath as she watched. Roger called up encouragement. Finally, Luther stood on the ground. He handed the bag to Juanita.

"You'd better get on with it, Juanita. Mandy's still alive, but she's in bad shape. You hit the road and I'll call the vet. Also, I'll help Margaret with Mandy's kits while you're gone."

Chapter 14

FOR THE LOVE OF MANDY

Dr. Martin smiled. "This is getting to be a habit, Juanita," he said. "I've got to give it to you, though; you sure are loyal"

"They're my friends, Bill," Juanita said, "and I take care of my friends."

"So which one have you brought me this time? I don't think I can tell them apart, even though I'm a veterinarian."

"This is Mandy. She just had three kits, and one of Luther's helpers is at home feeding them. Mandy has a white splash on the crown of her head, and she has five rings on her tail, while all the others have four.

"Okay," Dr. Martin said, "let's place her on the examination table and have a look at her."

Juanita carefully laid Mandy's still body on the table. She held her gently and stroked her. Dr. Martin placed his stethoscope on her chest and listened to her heart. He moved it to a slightly different location and listened again.

"She's alive, Juanita, but just barely. You don't have any idea what's wrong with her?"

"I'm afraid not, Bill. Packy found her and brought it to my attention."

Dr. Martin looked skeptical.

"I swear, Bill, Packy brought her kits down out of the elm tree, and then churred until I got Luther to climb up there and bring Mandy down."

"I know raccoons are smart," he said. "Let's see if we can find out what Mandy's problem is before it kills her."

He opened Mandy's mouth, looked inside, then felt along her sides and stomach. When he pushed in on her abdomen, Mandy jerked and groaned.

"Do any of the others act sick or listless?"

"Not that I can tell. They're all a bundle of energy, even Becky with her broken leg."

"Okay," Dr. Martin said, "I'm going to draw some blood and take a stool sample. I think I know what's wrong with her. She jumped when I pushed her stomach. She could just be sore from having babies, but I think it's more than that. She's very touchy in her upper abdomen, not as area likely to get sore from kitbirth. So, dear lady, let's get busy. We've got a life to save."

Dr. Martin retrieved a syringe and three slides from a cabinet under the examination table. Juanita watched patiently while he drew Mandy's blood. He placed the sample in the centrifuge, then returned to Mandy. Holding a large cotton swab in one hand, he lifted Mandy's tail and pushed the swab into her anus. Withdrawing carefully, he placed a small sample on each slide. Walking to a microscope, he sat down and studied each slide carefully. He pulled a large book from a shelf and leafed through it. He finally stopped at a page that interested him, then studied it for a few moments. Returning to the examination table, he sat down.

"It's just as I thought. She has a severe case of Baylisascaris."

"Worms!" Juanita exclaimed. "She has worms? That's all?"

"It's not a simple case, Juanita. She has a severe case of raccoon roundworms. Her intestines are full of the things, and the larvae may be encysted in her organs. Left untreated, raccoons invariably die from them. I don't know how long she's had these things, but I'll bet it's been a long time. I'm surprised that her intestines haven't ruptured."

"So, what's the next step, doctor? Don't worry about the expense, just treat her."

"Well, Juanita, several drugs have been developed in recent years to treat worms, and as you probably know, they're called anthelmintics. The only one I have on hand is Piperazine, but we're in luck, it's the best one for short-term treatment. I'll give her the maximum dosage I can without killing her. I'm going to order some Dichlorvos for long-term treatment. I should have it by tomorrow. All the others will require treatment also, because I'll bet they have these roundworms, too. Then, as a precaution, I'll need to come out to the farm and take samples from your other animals. Chances are, they don't have them, since you keep them off the floor and in cages. Oh, and by the way, I'll need to check all the people who work on your property, including you and Luther."

"I understand, Bill. I'll do whatever needs to be done, so let's get on with it."

Dr. Martin went to the back, and in less than two minutes, he returned carrying a syringe. Slowly and carefully, he pushed the needle into Mandy's rump. Juanita held her breath until the syringe had emptied.

"There we go," Dr. Martin said. "I'll need to keep her in my animal hospital for at least twenty-four hours. Do you want to stay with her?"

"Absolutely. Luther can manage the farm without me."

"I thought you would. Mandy may not make it through the night, Juanita. You need to be prepared for that."

"She'll make it, Bill. I just know she'll make it. These little guys are tough."

"Good," Dr. Martin said, "but we've got to find a quiet place to keep her. I don't want barking dogs scaring her to death."

****

Mandy lay in an unconscious state for several hours. Every few minutes, Juanita checked to see if she was still breathing. In the early morning hours, she dozed off for a short time. She awoke to find Mandy staring at her, but not moving otherwise. Juanita walked over to where Mandy lay and began stroking her head gently. Mandy closed her eyes, but her breathing had improved. She appeared to be conscious, but now sleeping. She jerked occasionally and then slept fitfully. Juanita gathered Mandy into her arms and carried her to the rocking chair. She rocked gently and sang quietly.

Daylight came, and still she rocked. Finally, she dropped off to sleep, while Mandy slept peacefully in her arms. Juanita awoke to find Dr. Martin standing in front of her.

"So, how is the patient today?" he asked.

"She's regained consciousness, but she's still one sick raccoon."

"Well, I hate to do this," Dr. Martin said, "but it's time for another shot. We need to get her revived enough so that I can give her a laxative. She's got to pass all those worms that are making her sick. It won't be a pretty sight, Juanita. Are you sure you're up to it?"

"Not to worry, Bill, I can handle it."

The day passed slowly, while Juanita worried. Amazed by the number and size of the worms Mandy passed, she collected them as instructed by Dr. Martin. By evening, she felt comfortable enough to leave the room for a short time. Upon returning, she found Mandy sitting up in her cage, staring out through the bars. Juanita opened the door, picked Mandy up and carried her to the rocking chair. Again, she rocked and sang. Soon, Mandy slept gently, stretched out across her lap. Just before daybreak, Juanita awakened to find Mandy sitting up. Knowing the strange surroundings could frighten Mandy, Juanita stroked her gently while she talked softly. At mid-morning, Dr. Martin came in and examined Mandy again.

"I think she's going to live," the white-haired veterinarian said. "I'm going to send the two of you home so that you can get some real rest. Make sure Mandy takes her medication on time and keep an eye on her. If she gets worse, bring her in immediately. She's going to be weak for several days, but she should revive quickly after that. I'm going to give you a weak solution of Dichlorvos to put in her baby's milk. We want to be sure those little fellows don't come down with worms. It would kill them for sure.

"As soon as you get situated, let her kits sleep with her. If you wait too long, she may reject them. Continue to feed them, though, until you're sure Mandy has enough milk of her own. You have the touch, Juanita. Your mothering instincts are excellent. Have you ever thought of having one of your own? You're still young enough, you know. Sorry, there I go, meddling in your business. Bring Becky in next week, and I'll remove her cast."

****

A scattering of billowy clouds passed across a brilliant moon as the final remnants of a spring shower rushed to join their darker cousins. Neonate plants and flowers drank greedily from crystalline drops before evaporation returned them to mist. In the trees and bushes, nesting mothers covered their young and waited for sunlight to dry their feathers. Peep frogs sang a tune along the creek bank, and a lone heron stood on one leg trying to ignore the noise. In the barn, several owls maintained defensive positions, prepared to defend their young against five raccoons prowling below.

A checkerboard pattern of moonlight played across Juanita's bed, illuminating her bedspread into an artist's dream of pastel browns and steely grays. She lay propped against several large pillows, unmoving, but listening intently for a repeat of the noise that had awakened her. She heard the flip-flip of the doggie door, and she knew one or more of her raccoon friends had either come in or gone out.

From her position on the bed, she could see the doghouse she had bought for Mandy on the way home from her stay at the animal hospital. A few seconds later, she saw Mandy go into her den, and just as quickly, she came out, carrying a kit in her mouth. Again, she heard the flip-flip of the animal door.

She reached across, picked up the telephone, and then dialed Luther's cell phone number. Luther answered on the second ring.

"Are you awake, Luther?"

"I am now," he mumbled.

"Listen, Mandy's moving her kits. Would you mind checking on her? I think she's taking them back to the elm tree, but I want to be sure. If she goes somewhere else, she might disappear before her regimen of medication is finished."

"I'm on it, Juanita. I'll call you back shortly."

Juanita lay quietly and waited for Luther's call. She wanted to get up, but she knew it wasn't wise to interrupt Mandy in the middle of moving her kits. So she waited. She heard an owl hoot in the distance, and she was glad the kits were too large for the owl to handle. Time lingered on, and finally she heard Mandy return for the third time. Again, Mandy went out, carrying a small, furry bundle in her mouth. Again, Juanita waited. She drifted off in her thoughts, thinking about Luther. The telephone startled her out of her reverie.

"Are you awake?" Luther asked.

"Not funny, Luther, of course I'm awake."

"You can rest easy. Mandy took her kits to the elm tree. I put out a bowl of food for her. I think it's best she doesn't do a lot of hunting on her own yet."

"You are a dear man. I'm sorry I had to drag you out of bed."

"Hey, no problem," Luther replied. "It goes with the territory."

****

After Becky had her cast removed, Juanita brought her home, and then closed the doggie door for two days. She wanted to be sure Becky's leg had normal usage before she returned to the tree. On the morning of the third day, Juanita set her free. Becky made a beeline for the elm tree. As Juanita and Luther watched, Becky climbed up. She took her time climbing, but she made it up without difficulty.

Packy, Misty and Cindy had just returned, but had not yet gone to sleep. Becky churred when she reached the den, and Packy answered. Becky crawled in, and they all snuggled up close. Just after noon, it began to rain, and it continued on into the night. About midnight, boredom drove them out, and they headed for the barn. Once inside, they decided to climb up to the loft and raid the barn owls' nests.

As they sat pondering the situation, they heard Mandy climbing up and immediately recognized the noise. Happy to see her, they rubbed noses and churred. After they managed to convey their intent to Mandy, she surprised them all by climbing a rafter and began working her way across to a nest. The rain had kept the owls in, and they defended their nest with sharp beaks and talons. In a short time, the kits decided the reward wasn't worth the effort and gave up.

As they sat in the loft wondering what to do next, they heard a noise on the floor below. Mandy immediately recognized Scrappy's churrs and climbed down to join him. They explored the ground level of the barn for a while, and then returned to the animal shelter. They ate the rest of Scrappy's food, and then took a nap in his box. At daylight, Mandy returned to her den and lay quietly while her kits suckled their breakfast.

****

Just before daylight on Sunday morning, Mandy dug for crayfish in the mudflat while Scrappy watched. One mile south, five men in three pickup trucks drove along the river on the Mason farm. At the property line, Calvin Cooke jumped out of his truck and cut the barbed wire fence. They drove slowly along the old logging road, making as little noise as possible. The low sound of truck engines growled along the riverbank. They came out of the woods onto the Dills farm, drove a few yards across the field and stopped.

Moving quickly, they jumped out of their trucks, ran to the back and opened the tailgates. By agreement, each man would handle three dogs, which would presumably make the operation more efficient. They had muzzled the dogs to keep them from barking and baying until Calvin gave the word. For easier access, they dragged two of the cages off the trucks and set them on the ground. Now, each man could remove his dogs from their cages at the same time. Each of the men carried a gun except Calvin because he had to carry the chain saw.

After a few minutes of whispering, Calvin said go, and each man rushed to release the dogs. As they removed the dog's muzzles, barking and baying broke the silence of the morning. In less than three minutes, they had released all the dogs.

The trail on the bank was sloped enough for Scrappy to climb. Despite the rush to escape from the dogs, Mandy waited on Scrappy.

By the time they reached the top of the bank, the dogs had reached the other side of the creek. Knowing he couldn't climb the tree, he churred for Mandy to run. When she balked, he bit her hard on the rump. Mandy squalled and rushed toward the elm tree. Torn between Scrappy's safety and her own, she stopped to look back. Scrappy churred at her in his angriest tone. Suddenly remembering her kits, she turned and rushed on toward her den. Scrappy looked for a defensive position to fight the dogs.

The aging raccoon had never run from a fight in his life, and he didn't intend to start now. When the first dog reached the top of the bank, Scrappy grabbed him by the throat. Killing the hound instantly, he looked up and saw the others top the bank. As he went down on his back, he made his second kill, then grabbed another by his front paw. Scrappy shook his head, and the sound of cracking bones filled his ears. In less than thirty seconds, six dogs ganged up on Scrappy, while the remaining six headed for the elm tree.

Scrappy fought valiantly, killing one more dog and maiming two others. Despite his kills, the other three dogs overwhelmed

Scrappy, chewing and biting his head and legs. When the fight was over, Scrappy lay dead on the creek bank. He had stalled the onslaught long enough for Mandy to reach the elm tree and climb out of the dog's reach. She was twenty feet up the trunk when the first hound reached the base of the tree. In a short time, nine dogs milled around the tree, barking and baying to signal their masters.

When Calvin and his friends crossed the creek, they found three hounds dead and three more wounded to varying degrees. Among them lay one dead raccoon with a missing foot. Calvin began kicking the dead dogs into the creek. He laid the saw on the ground, grabbed a gun from one of the men and shot the wounded dogs. He then pumped three shots into Scrappy's body.

"Wow," one of the men said, "there must have been five or six raccoons in this fight."

"Yeah," Calvin said, "and now they're all in the elm tree. We've got'em fellas, let's go."

Handing the gun back to his buddy, Calvin picked up the saw and hurried toward the tree. By the time they reached the tree, the first glimmer of daylight began to lighten the sky. While two of the men held flashlights so Calvin could see, he squatted down and prepared to start the chain saw. When the saw roared to life, the dogs scattered away from the tree.

Revving the saw several times, Calvin placed the speeding chain against the bark of the elm. The roaring of the saw reverberated across the Dills farm. The chain began to eat into the tree trunk, throwing chips all over Calvin and onto the ground. The tree was huge, and Calvin soon realized that cutting the tree down was going to be harder than he thought. The chain began to bind, and the saw stopped. Calvin pulled on the saw, intending to restart it. He pulled harder, but the chain wouldn't come out of the cut. Cursing, he directed one of the men to come and help. Suddenly a woman's voice cut through the semi-darkness.

"Just what do you people think you're doing!"

Calvin looked up to see Juanita Dills pointing a .38 police special directly at him. He released his grip from the saw and stood up. He made a quarter turn to face the woman directly. Finally, he found his voice.

"Put the gun away before you hurt somebody."

"You people are trespassing and destroying my property," Juanita said.

"Don't matter. We're here on a mission, and we intend to finish it."

"You're not going to finish anything. You're going to leave my property immediately."

Calvin took a step toward her. "Put that gun down. If you don't, I'm going to take it away from you."

"You take another step and I'll shoot you," Juanita said.

"I don't think you have the nerve, lady," Calvin said. He began advancing toward her.

The clear sound of two metallic clicks interrupted the morning. No one had seen Luther Loggins walk up. He stood ten feet away, a cocked, double-barrel, twelve-gauge shotgun held firmly in his hands.

"You take one more step toward her, Calvin, and you're history."

It was now light enough to see that Calvin's face had suddenly turned a chalky white. He hesitated, as he looked from Luther to Juanita and back again. Summoning his courage, Calvin started to advance on Juanita again.

"Calvin," Luther barked, "Juanita may not have the nerve to shoot you, but I do, and you know it."

Calvin stopped again, then looked around for help.

"Don't just stand there," he said to his buddies, "do something!"

Luther swung the shotgun just enough to point toward the other men.

"Which two of you want a face full of buckshot?" Luther asked.

No one moved.

"It's not our fight, Calvin," the tall man standing nearest to Luther said.

"What a bunch of cowards I've brought with me," Calvin said. He turned to look at Luther again.

"You know you'll go back to prison, Luther. All I have to do is tell the sheriff that I've seen you with a gun."

Juanita spoke sharply. "You're a low down skunk, Calvin, and stupid, too. Luther's not on probation anymore, and besides, he's allowed to protect his own property. He lives here. I've talked to the sheriff myself. Now, get off my property."

Giving Luther one last look of hate, Calvin started toward the creek.

"Not that way," Juanita said. "Down the road."

"But our trucks are over there across the creek," the tall man said.

"That doesn't matter. You skunks are going to walk down the road. Maybe two miles of walking will bring some sense to you. I'll call the sheriff and ask him what to do about your trucks, and take these dogs with you. If I ever find you on my property again, I'll see that you do jail time, Calvin, and your deputy sheriff brother won't be able to help you, either."

****

Juanita and Luther followed the men as far as the farmhouse. Luther didn't uncock the shotgun until they were well down the road. They watched the men until they disappeared around the curve. Finally, Juanita turned and looked at Luther.

"Why would you risk going to prison for me, Luther? I'm just your employer."

Luther stared at her until she began to blush. Clearly, he was having difficulty finding the right words.

"Because I'm in love with you," he finally blurted out."

Now, it was Juanita's turn to stare. Now, Luther blushed.

"Do you really mean that, Luther?"

"Of course I mean it. I wouldn't say it if it weren't true."

"Why haven't you said something before?"

"Because you're untouchable; you're a successful woman with money, and I'm an ex-convict. Not exactly the best match in the world."

"Luther, Luther, Luther," Juanita said. "As long as you think of yourself as a convict, you're going to be one, at least in your own mind. You have a lot to be proud of. You're a capable foreman who runs a successful farm and animal shelter, and you're making straight A's in college. Given time, you could build a house by yourself and pass all the codes. You can repair car engines, lawn mowers and farm machinery. Even more important than all that, you have honesty and integrity, and you care about people and animals. Now, for God's sake, put your prison record behind you. I don't ever want you to refer to yourself as a convict again."

Finally, she ran out of words and stared at Luther. She thought he would speak, but he said nothing.

"Luther; it might interest you to know that I'm in love with you, too. Now, don't just stand there, do something."

For a moment, Juanita thought Luther would walk away. Then suddenly, he stepped toward her, pulled her into his arms and kissed her. The danger they had just faced drew them even closer together. They hugged, kissed and embraced for several minutes, until both of them became embarrassed with their passion. Finally, they stopped, then just stood and looked at each other.

"I really do love you, Juanita. I think about you every hour of every day."

"I love you, too, Luther, but I've been having trouble admitting it. I guess that's why I've been acting weird lately." She reached out and took him by the hand.

"I think we could use a hot, home cooked breakfast," she said.

****

Juanita and Luther buried Scrappy about twenty feet from the elm tree. Luther made a small cross out of pine lumber and Juanita painted it white. They buried the dogs in a mass grave across the creek where they had buried a parrot, two canaries and a rabbit. Juanita insisted that they, too, should have a small cross.

"You know, Luther, we might as well fence an area specifically for an animal cemetery. It's inevitable that some of the animals we adopt are going to die. Some of them are in terrible physical condition when they arrive."

"I agree," Luther said. "I'll buy the fencing tomorrow."

They went to the elm tree to survey the damage. Luther found a couple of wedges in the tool shed and used those to help remove the chainsaw.

"The cut is about a third of the way through," Luther said. "I don't know enough about trees to know if it will die or not."

"I sure hope it doesn't," Juanita said. "My great-grandfather brought this tree from Ohio as a sapling and planted it here. I found some old letters in the attic. This tree is 121 years old. It's probably the oldest tree in Macon County."

"I'll call the forest service," Luther said. "Maybe they'll have some ideas on how to save it."

"Poor kits," Juanita said, "they're probably up there huddled together, too terrified to come down. I just hope the dogs didn't get one of them."

"I don't think so. I made a thorough search of the area while you were cooking breakfast. I think they're all up in the tree."

They stood and talked for a long time. Finally, Luther went to the shelters and fed the adoptees. As he finished up, he looked out and saw Juanita standing by the old well where she had fallen in. He knew that something troubled her, and he decided not to interfere. After a while, she went back into the farmhouse. Sometime after noon, she found him working at the barn.

"I've brought you some lunch, Luther. Now that our relationship has changed, I feel a need to pamper you."

"Speaking of pampering, I have something for you." He handed her a sketch of five raccoons staring out of a hole in a tree.

"Wow, Luther, this is good. There's just no end to your talents."

Luther sat down and unwrapped his sandwich. "Okay, Juanita, let's hear it. There's something heavy on your mind."

"I've been thinking, Luther. Even though raccoons can be tamed, they're not like dogs. Dogs bond themselves to their owners, but raccoons rarely do. They're children of the forest, and they love to be free."

"So where are you going with this, my dear woman?"

"Every time I turn around, some coon hunter is trying to kill them. When Becky, Misty and Cindy start having kits, there's going to be a lot of raccoons living here on the farm. Every coon hunter for twenty miles is going to want to shoot at them. There's no way I can protect them all. Now, I have a ranger friend over in The Great Smoky Mountains National Park. She has agreed to help relocate the kits. If we took them about twenty miles into the National Forest, all in all, they'd stand a better chance of survival than they'll have here on the farm. What do you think, Luther?"

"Well, I hadn't thought about it, but it sounds like a good idea. Are you sure you can deal with it, though?"

"I don't know. I sure would miss the little guys, and I never forget I owe them my life, especially Packy. And I wouldn't get to see Mandy's kits grow up. I promised them they would always have a home here, but that's a people concept. Real love is not selfish, and I need to do what's best for them."

"So, when do you want to do this, Juanita? I know you well enough to realize your mind is made up."

"I think in about six weeks. I want to make sure they're free of worms, give them all distemper shots and that sort of thing. Also, Mandy's kits have to be big enough to climb down a tree by themselves."

Chapter 15

HOME AWAY FROM HOME

A series of warm nights in May enticed Luther and Juanita to go camping. Juanita called her friend, Margie Douthit, a ranger at Deep Creek Campground in Swain County. Given the circumstances, Margie agreed to let them drive Juanita's van inside the Great Smoky Mountains National Park. She and Luther packed the van full of camping gear and headed out. They drove north on Highway 28 and then east on Highway 74. Upon arrival, Margie unlocked the gate so they could drive up the forest service road. About five miles in, Luther engaged the four-wheel drive, and then they drove slowly for another ten miles until the road ended.

They carried their gear as far as they could, and then selected a clearing near a rushing stream. After setting up camp, they spent the afternoon looking for a place to settle their raccoon families. Like a woman possessed, Juanita dragged Luther from one place to another. When darkness came, she still had not found a location that satisfied her idea of raccoon heaven. At daylight, they ate breakfast, and then packed a lunch to carry in their backpacks. Relying on forest service maps, they followed one hiking trail after another. In the early afternoon, they left the hiking trails and found a suitable place to eat lunch near the junction of two creeks.

As they ate, Juanita studied the area from her seat on a fallen log. The two creeks cascaded down individual waterfalls, forming one large pool at the bottom. Downstream from the pool, the larger creek spread out into a flat area, and a swamp had formed on both sides. Upstream from the pool, the land rose sharply, with rhododendron thickets growing along the streams. Farther out from the stream on the left, huge oak trees dominated the landscape. On the hill to the right, old-growth beech trees blotted out the sky, holes clearly visible in many of their trunks.

Juanita stood up suddenly. "This is it, Luther," she said. "This is a raccoon paradise. Everything they could possibly need is here; food, water and plenty of places to make dens."

"I think you're right, Juanita," Luther said. "The only predators here are owls, hawks and bobcats, and they won't bother full-grown raccoons. The mothers will protect their kits."

"Now, I feel better, Luther," Juanita said. "It sure takes a load off, knowing my furry friends will have a good place to live."

****

Early June brought beautiful weather. Rain had been plentiful in May, and the Dills farm had reaped the bonanza. Luther ran the farm with finesse, and Juanita gave him a free hand. A proper combination of fertilizer and weed killer had made the fields a veritable oasis of greenery. Luther's work crew had planted multiflora rose in just the right places to provide cover for rabbits, foxes, opossums and birds. Corn, wheat, rye, sugar cane, potatoes and beans dotted the fields, giving new life to the farm. Luther had promised Juanita the farm would be entirely self-supporting in three years.

Juanita had made the final arrangements with Ranger Douthit, and now the time arrived. She put on a brave face as she and Luther gathered the kits for the trip. Juanita hated to put them in cages, even for a forty-mile ride. As the big day approached, she spent more time spoiling them. Mandy had brought her kits to the house, and Juanita gave them a special feeding of rainbow trout. She cut the fish into tiny pieces and watched while they wolfed down the tasty morsels. She noted they had beautiful markings and each of them had five rings on their tails, just like their mother. She thought about giving them names but decided against it. Such an action would just make it harder to leave them.

She didn't know about the midnight hours Mandy had spent sitting by Scrappy's grave, nor did she know about the sacrifice Scrappy had made for the only mate he ever had. Raccoons grieve in their own way, and Mandy had been no exception. All of them missed Scrappy, humans and raccoons alike. He had been a pleasure to all. In the autumn of his life, when raccoons usually become defensive and grouchy, he had exhibited none of those characteristics. His good nature had become legendary on the Dills farm. Mandy's kits would never know their father, nor know anything about him, but through them, Scrappy's fighting spirit would live on for generations to come.

****

    Juanita and Luther spent two nights with the kits in their new home. On the eve of the first night, they made a small campfire near their tent. After dinner, they decided to relax for a while before turning in for the night. Knowing the kits were afraid of fire, they found a comfortable spot about fifty feet away. Juanita sang while Luther played his harmonica. For a while, the kits sat in a semi-circle and listened attentively. In about an hour, Mandy and three kits slipped away. A few minutes later, Packy, Misty and Cindy stood up and crept into the underbrush. Becky climbed up on the portable camping table, stretched out and went to sleep.

    Upon retiring, the couple found Mandy and her young curled up on Juanita's sleeping bag. Gently, she move them enough so she could crawl inside, leaving them between her and Luther. Humans and raccoons drifted off to sleep. At daylight, Luther got up to prepare breakfast. A few minutes later, Juanita started the coffee. The kits had disappeared during the night. One by one, they reappeared, attracted by the smell of cooking food. Luther gave each of them two strips of bacon. Seeing no more food was forthcoming, they slipped away. Thinking they had found a new place to sleep, Luther found all eight of them snuggled up in his backpack. He shooed them out and closed the flap.

    Finally, the raccoons all followed Packy into the woods. Luther pulled out his binoculars and scanned the trees in the direction they had gone. Just as he was about to give up, he saw Packy climbing the trunk of a huge beech tree. One by one, the other raccoons followed until they disappeared into the foliage. Luther and Juanita took turns watching through the binoculars until they realized the kits had bedded down for the day. As they cleaned up their campsite, Luther heard Juanita crying. He went over to comfort her. She pulled away and sat down by a tree.

"Good Lord, Luther, I feel like such a heel. I've taken them away from their home, and they don't understand. Mandy looked so upset. I could almost see emotional pain in her face. I'm about ready to load them up and take them back home. Every time I look at them, I think about that night in the well. They never abandoned me for a minute. Oh, Luther, what am I going to do?"

"This is not like you, Juanita," Luther said. "You're always so decisive."

"I guess so, but there's a moral issue here. I don't know if I'm doing this for them or for me. I thought it through and decided this is the best place for them over the long term, and I still believe that. But now, I realize they didn't get to vote on it. Clearly, their preference is to stay on the farm. So...do animals have rights or not? Should they have a choice in their future? It's all so confusing because they can't talk. Now, I have to weigh what they want against what they should have. It's like making a choice for a child. We can't always give children what they want, because inevitably, they will make some bad choices."

"I think you just answered your own question, Juanita. You're on this guilt trip because you promised them down in the well they would always have a home on the Dills farm. Life isn't perfect, no matter where we are, not for people and not for animals. I might doze off on your upstairs porch, fall and break my neck. Packy might fall out of that tree he just climbed and break his leg, and then some predator gets him. Anyway you go at it; life is about choices and the outcome of those choices. Everybody and everything makes good choices and bad choices. So, my dear lady, you're at a crossroads. You can still take them back, or you can leave them here."

"What would you have done, Luther?"

"Well, my dear woman, you never asked my opinion. You made your decision without any input from me. That's your right, of course; but interestingly enough, you consult me on just about everything else. I think you were afraid I would disagree with you."

"Would you have disagreed with me, Luther?"

"Yes, I would have. But with the gift of hindsight, I can see I would have been wrong. Five years from now, there are going to be a hundred of these guys. They will either overrun the farm or you will have to start adopting them out. Whether they're here or there, some of them will die a natural death, and some of them will get killed. On the farm, they will start interbreeding and become more susceptible to disease and predators. Here in the Great Smokies, they will breed with other raccoons and become a stronger, healthier group. Whether the Dills farm would be a better place for your special five remains to be seen, but their progeny will be better off here.

"Now, back to your moral issue, Juanita. Do you honor your promise to the five of them or do you do what is best for the next several generations? I'll tell you what I think. If they could talk, their choice would be for their offspring. Case in point. Mandy would die to protect her kits. In that respect, animals are no different from people. Decisions should be made on what is right, not on promises. I hate to see them leave just as much as you do; I'm just not as emotional about it. And besides, they don't know you promised them anything. At that point, you were just so grateful to be out of the well you let your emotions rule your head. Assume for the moment they unselfishly did what was best for you. Should you not do the same for them? In a few weeks, they will be just as happy here as they would be on the farm.

"So now, would you leave them here, Luther?"

"Yes I would, Juanita, because it's the right thing to do."

Luther turned and walked back to the campfire. He added a few sticks, and then stood watching as the flames increased. In a few minutes, he felt, rather than heard Juanita's presence.

"I'm okay now, Luther. Let's stay the night, and then leave in the morning. It's easier to say good-bye in the daylight.

****

Packy and his family didn't understand why Juanita and Luther had brought them to the Great Smokies National Park. They had no idea where they were or why they were there. Even so, they soon figured out the raccoon family would have to fend for themselves. For raccoons, that simply meant finding a suitable den and an abundant food supply. At no point did they consider striking out for home. They seemed to understand the futility of such a venture and set about to make the best of their new surroundings. Unlike dogs and cats, they had an innate ability to adapt to the wild.

The first night after Juanita and Luther left, they gathered in a circle and discussed the matter through a series of churrs, growls and chirps. As usual, they looked to Packy for leadership. Putting first things first, he led them to the swamp where they found a plentiful supply of crayfish, frogs and minnows. Fruits, nuts and berries proliferated on the hillsides, and the creek provided an abundance of fish. Instinctively, Mandy and her kits stayed a short distance away from the others. Packy, Becky, Misty and Cindy understood Mandy's need and made no attempt to interfere with her motherly duties. As time permitted, they searched for more comfortable living quarters, because the holes in the old beech tree were small and uncomfortable.

A short distance from their temporary den, Packy found another beech, old and gnarled, with roots interlaced into the shallow soil of the rocky hillside. As Packy explored a hole in the trunk, he found the center had rotted out. He followed that passage and soon found himself in a cave that circled back under the falls. Try as he might, he could find no other entrance into the cave. At the south end, a window opened under the falls. The sides were solid rock and vertical, precluding the possibility of any predator entering or leaving through that opening. On one side of the window, water trickled through a small hole in the rocks and formed a small pool of fresh water that circulated continuously.

Returning to the others, Packy invited them into his new found home to look around. Mandy hung back, but soon followed, and became the first to select a spot for herself and her kits. After a night of hunting, they all returned to the cave for a day of sleeping. Continuous and permanent, the sound of the waterfall lulled them to sleep. Unlike the previous nights, they slept peacefully, secure in the knowledge no predator could enter their cave.

Over time, the hunting dogs in Packy's dreams disappeared to be replaced by more pleasant visions of the forest's bounty. On several occasions, he dreamed about a woman who sang beautiful songs and gave him tasty fish treats. As it always does, summer passed, and autumn burst forth with dazzling colors. The kits hunted, played and grew. The forest was not without dangers, but the family survived, and winter arrived in all its splendor.

Sometime in January, Packy awoke with an urge to mate. Just south of the swamp, he met a female who liked his attention. They played in the moonlight, and Packy brought her special treats of fresh crayfish. In a few days, he returned to the cave to join his siblings. On the last day of March, they had a visitor who made her own nest in a crevice high up in the cave. On the tenth day of April, a new sound mingled with the babble of the waterfall. Nature had come full circle, and Packy had become a father.

****

Two years had passed since Juanita and Luther had carried the Blue Ridge Bandits into the Great Smoky Mountains National Park. They still basked in the memory of their wedding on the Dills farm and their honeymoon in the Swiss Alps. Luther had graduated community college and now attended the university. They had purchased the Mason farm from the aging owners and "60 Minutes" had featured their animal shelter in a ten minute special.

As they sat on their screened-in back porch having breakfast, Juanita in her usual fashion, surprised Luther.

"I want to go check on my furry friends in the Park," she said suddenly.

Luther understood immediately. "Are you sure you want to do that?"

"Yes, Luther, I'm sure. I need closure and now I'm ready for it. If we can't find them, I can accept it. A year ago, I couldn't."

"When do you want to go?" Luther asked.

"Today. Right now. We'll drive up, load up the backpacks and hike in. We'll stay for three days. If we don't see any sign of them, we'll come home, and that will be the end of it. Call your mother and see if she'll keep little Luther, and then we'll get ready."

"On one condition," Luther said.

Surprised, Juanita asked about the question.

"You help me write a book about your little guys."

"Are you serious, Luther?"

"I sure am. I've thought long and hard about it."

"It's a deal. Let's get ready. When we return, you start on your book, and I'll help as needed."

Of course, Luther's mom was excited to keep the child as she always was. In less than an hour, he returned.

"You know something, Juanita. That woman treats little Luther better than she did me."

"No she doesn't," Juanita replied. "She just spoils him more because she's a grandmother. There's a difference."

EPILOGUE

It took Luther and Juanita three hours to pack in from the van. They picked a spot near a large, flat rock to set up camp. The creek babbled fifty feet away, and the sound of twin waterfalls provided a forest soliloquy. By twilight, they had finished their meal and washed their pans and other utensils in the creek. They spread a blanket on a rock and sat quietly, listening to night sounds. A bullfrog grumped from the little swamp, and an owl hooted from the top of a dead maple. Somewhere on the mountain, a pheasant thumped a rapid drumbeat to its mate.

Luther removed his harmonica from his pocket and began to play. Juanita listened for a few moments and began to sing.

> "All things bright and beautiful,
> All creatures great and small,
> All things wise and wonderful,
> The Lord God made them all.
> Each little flower that opens,
> Each little bird that sings,
> He made their glowing colors,
> He made their tiny wings."

Juanita heard a noise behind her. She turned to look and saw Packy sitting less than ten feet away. Scarcely daring to breathe, she watched several other raccoons move into view. She recognized Mandy, Becky, Misty and Cindy. Fully grown now, their slick fur shined in the light from the fire. As she continued to sing, at least a dozen kits moved into view.

A strange, adult raccoon sat near Packy with four kits bunched close to her. Slowly, they all formed into families. Mandy and Cindy had three kits each, and Becky had two. Mandy had two new kits, and each had five rings on its tail. Her first family, also with five rings on their tails, and they sat in the background behind Mandy. Four other adult raccoons sat farther back.

As she and Luther continued to sing and play, the raccoons clustered close around them. Soon, Mandy sat in the crooks between Juanita's legs. Not to be outdone, Packy joined in. Emboldened by the older raccoons, the others moved even closer. Eventually, Juanita's voice became hoarse, and Luther was out of breath. They stopped and sat quietly. One by one, the raccoons moved away. Packy was the last to leave. At the edge of the light, he turned and churred, and then disappeared into the darkness.

The two humans sat quietly for a long time, not trusting themselves to speak. Finally, Juanita broke the silence.

"Can we come here often?"

"Sure babe, as often as you want."

"Not too often. About three or four times a year will do."

****

The next morning, Packy sat on a limb of a large oak tree, looking down on the happy couple. He watched as they broke camp and started out. He felt a heaviness in his chest he didn't understand. As they disappeared from sight, he churred loudly.

"Did you hear something?" Luther asked.

"Yes," Juanita answered quietly. "Packy said good-bye."

****

About the Author

Author, Roy Owenby, was born in Nantahala, NC. A Navy veteran, he graduated from Appalachian State University at age 40. After thirty years in various management positions, he is now retired.

Roy has traveled extensively throughout the United States, Canada, Mexico, Israel and Europe. A prolific storyteller, he is a featured writer for the Burningtown News, an online newspaper. He has written more than three hundred articles and short stories covering a variety of subjects.

He has also published, *"The Owl Knows,"* an Appalachian Trail Mystery and *"Blue Ridge Mountain Heritage, A Caricature of Southern Appalachian Mountain Life."* He has a fourth novel ready for publication and is working on a fifth. He is married to Nita Welch Owenby, also a writer.